Chekhov
for the Stage

The Sea Gull

Uncle Vanya

The Three Sisters

The Cherry Orchard

Anton Chekhov

Translated by Milton Ehre

Chekhov
for the Stage

Northwestern University Press

Evanston, Illinois

Northwestern University Press
Evanston, Illinois 60208-4210

Copyright © 1992 by Northwestern University Press. Published 1992. All
rights reserved.

Second paperback printing 1997

Printed in the United States of America

ISBN 1-8101-1048-2

Library of Congress Cataloging-in-Publication Data

Chekhov, Anton Pavlovich, 1860–1904.
   [Plays. English. Selections]
   Chekhov for the stage : The sea gull, Uncle Vanya, The three sisters ;
The cherry orchard / Anton Chekhov ; translated and with an introduc-
tion by Milton Ehre.
     p. cm.
   Translated from the Russian.
   Intended for use as performance texts.
   ISBN 0-8101-1023-7 (alk. paper). – ISBN 0-8101-1048-2
(pbk. : alk. paper)
   1. Chekhov, Anton Pavlovich, 1860-1904–Translations into English.
   I. Ehre, Milton, 1933– II. Title.
PG3456.A19E35 1992
891.72'3–dc20
                                              92-7634
                                                CIP

The paper used in this publication meets the minimum requirements of the
American National Standard for Information Sciences–Permanence of Paper
for Printed Library Materials, ANSI Z39.48-1984.

FOR MY STUDENTS

Contents

Russian Names and Words

Russian names are tripartite: given name, patronymic, and family name. Thus: Andrey Sergeyevich (son of Sergey) Prozorov, or Olga Sergeyevna (daughter of Sergey) Prozorova. The polite form of address is given name and patronymic—Andrey Sergeyevich (sometimes shortened, e.g., Sergeyich). Nicknames are frequent. I have, wherever feasible, simplified, preferring the given name in the form Chekhov most commonly uses.

Pronunciation of Russian names and words can be difficult for non-Russians. There are two helpful rules: (1) Russian words never have a secondary stress: compare English *òrganizátion* with Russian *organizátsiya*. Russian vowels, when not under stress, often do not receive full value—they are "reduced"—but the rules are fairly complicated (see Galina Stilman and William E. Harkins, *Introductory Russian Grammar*, or any other Russian grammar). However, if the actor remembers to come down hard on the stress and not to give a secondary stress, the result should be good enough. (Russian is a very musical language—sweep up to or down from the stress.) (2) There are no diphthongs in Russian. Vowels do not glide into other vowels or semivowels but remain "pure." Thus: **e** as in "met"; **a** as in "car"; **i** as in "see"; **o** as in "or"; **u** as in "ooze." A **y** before **e, a, o, u** indicates a sound like that in "yet," "yard," "yolk," "Yukon"; not preceding a vowel, it is like *i* in "sit."

The consonant represented by **kh** is close to Castilian Spanish *j*, as in "Juan," or German "ch," as in "Bach"; **zh** is like the *s* in "pleasure"; **ch** is like the same letters in "cheese"; **ts**, like the *ts* in "its."

The combination **shch** (Dani*shch*eese), if too difficult to pronounce, may be said as a long *sh* (Dani*sh*sheep).

Stresses are given in the "Casts of Characters." Below are stresses of Russian names and terms mentioned in the plays (in alphabetical order).

Aléko

Alexéy

Alexéyevich

Anastásy

Basmánnaya
Bátyushkov
Berdíchev
Bóbik
Bolshóy
Chádin
chekhartmá
cheremshá
Dáshenka
Derigánov
Dobrolyúbov
Elizavetográd
Fyódor
Gógol
Grigóry
Grísha
Grokhólsky
Ilích
Iván
Iványch
Izmáylov
Kardamónov
Khárkov
Kíev
Kirsánovsky
Kolotílin
Konstantín
Kosóy
Kozoyédov
Kózyrev
Lakedemónov
Lérmontov
Málitskoye
Matryóna
Mikhaíl
Molchánovka
Moskóvsky
Nemétskaya
Novo-Dévichy

Ostróvsky
Páshka
Pável
Petróvna
Petrúshka
Poltáva
Pólya
Potápych
Protopópov
Púshkin
Pýzhikov
Ragúlin
Rasplyúyev
Rozh(d)éstvennoye
Sadóvsky
Sarátov
Skvortsóv
Slavyánsky
Sófochka
Stanisláv
Súzdaltsev
Téstov
Timoféyevna
Tolstóy
Trofímovich
Tsitsihár
Túla
Turgénev
Véra
Yaroslávl
Yáshnevo
Yefím
Yefímyushka
Ygór
Yeléts
Yevstignéy
Zásyp
Znoykóv

Introduction

Anton Chekhov was born in the provincial town of Taganrog on the Sea of Azov in 1860. His father was a grocer; his grandfather had been a serf. A difficult childhood—poverty, an ambitious and tyrannical father, a long-suffering mother—left its scars: "In childhood I had no childhood." He was gregarious but had a streak of melancholy in his nature and fled from intimacy. "No one," his friend Ivan Bunin wrote, "not even those closest to him, knew what went on deep inside him. His self-control never deserted him." Neither did his good humor, his decency, his sense of personal dignity. In Chekhov's presence, Gorky remembered, "everyone involuntarily felt a desire to be simpler, more truthful, more oneself."

Chekhov reached maturity at the time when the Industrial Revolution finally hit Russia with full force. The social composition of Russian literature before the age of Chekhov can be summed up by the title of a Tolstoy story, "Master and Man"—or "Landowner and Serf." In Chekhov's works we find the full panoply of modern professions—lawyers, doctors, engineers, industrialists, traveling salesmen, factory workers. The new bourgeois ethos of "making it on your own" was beginning to influence people: Chekhov spoke of his lifelong battle to squeeze the slave out of himself drop by drop and become a free man. He worked his way through medical school by writing humorous sketches about the quirks of ordinary people and the absurdities of daily life for the new popular press. Medicine, he said, was his wife; literature, his mistress. As he became successful, he spent more time with his mistress than with his wife. His journalism trained him to an economy of expression and a dispassionate observation of human foibles.

Around 1886 he began to attract the attention of the serious reading public. His work took on increasing maturity and depth, although the humorous side of his talent never left him. He wore his fame lightly, with the "spiritual modesty" he accused Dostoevsky of lacking. One of the ambitions of this descendant of serfs was to acquire an estate of his own, and when he did, he took an active interest in its management and in local affairs, giving medical treatment to peasants without charge. Aligning himself with no political party or group, he was socially progressive, religiously agnostic, an advocate of science and enlightenment, firm in his belief that individual freedom is a precious thing: "I am neither liberal, nor conservative, nor gradualist, nor monk, nor indifferent. I should like to be a free artist and nothing else. . . . I hate lies and violence in all their forms. . . . I look upon tags and labels as prejudices. My holy of holies is the human body, health, intelligence, talent, inspiration, love, and the most absolute freedom imaginable, freedom from violence and lies."

In 1890 he made an arduous journey across Siberia to the convict colony on Sakhalin Island ("to pay off some of my debt to medicine"), and his book-length study of local conditions led to reforms in the Russian prison system. In 1901, three years before his death, he married Olga Knipper, a leading actress of the recently formed Moscow Art Theater. They lived mostly apart—Olga, in Moscow because of the demands of her career, Anton, in the south at Yalta because of his illness. In 1884 he had shown the first symptoms of tuberculosis, and in 1897 massive hemorrhaging from his lungs compelled him to acknowledge his fatal disease publicly. It is impossible to pinpoint the moment when Chekhov knew he was doomed—though a doctor, he long denied the facts—but at least the last three of the plays were written by a man who knew his days were numbered. He died in Germany on July 2, 1904. The train car that brought his remains back to Russia bore the sign FOR OYSTERS. He would have enjoyed the joke.

Chekhov's plays were an important part of the revolution in the theater taking place at the close of the nineteenth century. The century had not been a good one for theater. Fluffy farces and overblown melodramas were dominating the stage when Chekhov began to write plays. Like Ibsen, Strindberg, Hauptmann, Maeterlinck, and other innovators, he was trying to break out of the straitjacket of the formulaic "well-made plays" of Scribe and Sardou. He complained about the "avowals of love, infidelities of husbands and wives, the tears of widows and orphans" that were the shopworn furniture of the contemporary stage. "Plays should be written badly and insolently"—"the simpler the plot, the better." The action should be cumulative—"piled up, not polished and flattened out." Looser structures are necessary to capture common reality: "I would write of ordinary love and family life without angels or villains . . . , a life that is even, flat, ordinary, life as it really is."

Melodrama and farce are the fare of popular culture. Working for middle-brow weeklies, Chekhov cut his teeth on the very farces (usually in short-story form) that he was later to condemn. Although melodrama was less suited to his temperament, his first full-scale play, the juvenile *Platonov* (no later than 1879) is pure potboiler. His second effort, the more successful *Ivanov* (1889), shows psychological penetration but is still too talky and high-pitched—its subject, like that of *Platonov*, is a man who can find neither love nor an outlet for his talents—a "Russian Hamlet." While indulging in the melodramatic fashion, Chekhov parodied it. He continued to slap together farcical one-acters even after he had established a reputation as a serious writer, and some are still part of the repertoire.

Elements of farce and melodrama survive in his major plays, but they have become displaced from center stage or their conventions have been so deformed that they are barely recognizable. *The Sea Gull* turns on the stock formula of farce (and comedy)—A loves B who loves C who loves D; but instead of a resolution, in which the lovers find their proper partners, the young hero and heroine go their separate ways. *Uncle Vanya*, *The Three Sisters*, and *The Cherry Orchard* are all grounded on that recurrent plot of melodrama—the loss of property— which can be summed up by the old joke:

Villain: Pay the rent!
Heroine: I can't pay the rent!
Villain: Pay the rent!
Heroine: I can't pay the rent!
Hero: I'll pay the rent!
Heroine: My hero!

But in Chekhov's plays no hero turns up to save the day and the victims seem curiously indifferent to impending disaster. In *Uncle Vanya* the crisis over the sale of the estate does not appear until act 3, and the conflict between Professor Serebryakov and Vanya, though the most dramatically tense moment of the play, quickly turns ludicrous. The three sisters are aware that the vicious Natasha is taking over their home, but they remain strangely passive. Although the threat of the loss of the cherry orchard hangs like an ominous cloud over Madame Ranevskaya and her brother, Gayev, they talk about it only occasionally and never confront their dilemma head on.

It is as if Chekhov's characters willfully ignore the plot that destiny and art have woven for them. They chat about the weather, their lives and loves, their disappointments and miseries, the meaning of life. They "philosophize"—a recurring word in Chekhov's plays (though rendered in different ways in these translations)—and in the meantime they forget about the matter at hand. Their blithe obliviousness to what threatens their lives can be frustrating to audiences who expect a neat package where an action is confronted and resolved: Chekhov's first audiences did not know what to make of his plays, though in time they learned to love them.

But it would be a mistake to dismiss Chekhov's characters as spoiled weaklings or jaded gentry of a bygone era simply because they don't do what we want them to do. Many of them are weak, almost all of them suffer, but in their refusal to be governed by a controlling plot they assert their freedom. They see their lives as larger than a particular circumstance: sticking to daily habits, observing common courtesies, loving and being loved, asking why one is alive are the kinds of things we do even in moments of crisis. His people insist on being themselves even in the face of disaster.

> After all, in real life, people don't spend every moment in shooting one another, hanging themselves, or making declarations of love. They do not spend all their time saying clever things. They are more occupied with eating, drinking, flirting, and saying stupidities. These are the things which ought to be shown on the stage. A play should be written in which people arrive, depart, have dinner, talk about the weather, and play cards. Life must be exactly as it is and people as they are. . . . Let everything on the stage be just as complicated, and at the same time just as simple, as in life. People eat their dinner, just eat their dinner, and all the time their happiness is taking form, or their lives are being destroyed.

Zola and other naturalists were talking about the need for such plays, but Chekhov actually wrote them. Instead of untying the knot of a single action, he gives us many actions. His major plays take shape around arrival and departure. Visitors interrupt the humdrum routine of a landowner's estate (in *The Three Sisters*, a bourgeois home), bearing the baggage of a different way of life—Arkadina and Trigorin with their loose bohemian ways in *The Sea Gull*, the urbane professor and his dazzlingly beautiful and indolent wife in *Uncle Vanya*, Colonel Vershinin from Moscow, to which the three sisters long to escape, Madame Ranevskaya from Paris in *The Cherry Orchard*, with her mixture of grief and frivolity. Hopes, dreams, anxieties, and conflicts are stirred up, and then simply die down as the intruders depart. *The Sea Gull* is somewhat different in that Arkadina and Trigorin return to witness the climax. It is the last play of Chekhov to end, like the earlier melodramas, on a strong dramatic note; still, the suicide takes place offstage. In *Uncle Vanya* and *The Three Sisters* the visitors simply leave and life returns to the ordinary. In *The Cherry Orchard* all (except the servant Firs) go off to continue their lives. Although the plays have their share of pain and sadness, the view of life depicted in them is essentially comic—disaster is seldom final: Treplev is destroyed but Nina survives; the cherry trees are chopped down but life goes on.

Chekhov not only made the stage freer by loosening speech from the dictates of a controlling plot, he also made it more democratic. After *Platonov* and *Ivanov* no single hero dominates a Chekhov play. Our interest is spread over a wide range of characters—almost everyone is given a story to tell, a life to recount. Chekhov's plays have often been described as studies in the failure to communicate, and it is true that his people, like most of us, are better at talking than listening. They can also be extraordinarily open about their feelings. If they sometimes take each other for granted, it may be because they know each other so well. They live in extended Russian families, where relatives, neighbors, and friends are drawn into the domestic circle. Except perhaps for Tolstoy, no modern writer has been better at depicting the tensions, affections, and profound loyalties of familial life. In Chekhov's view, we are, for better or worse, social animals inextricably bound to each other.

Americans know Chekhov primarily through his plays; for Russians he is to this day a writer of short stories who digressed into the theater to produce a handful of masterpieces. He wrote hundreds of stories, many of them extraordinarily beautiful. Taken together, they comprise a Balzacian *comédie humaine* of Russian life at the turn of the century. His stories ferret out with a dispassionate eye every layer of Russian society—peasants, workers, professionals, emergent capitalists, the state bureaucracy. The plays have a narrower focus, concentrating on the declining gentry (and, in *The Three Sisters*, the upper middle class). The landowner's estate provided him a place where he could plausibly bring together a large cast of characters.

The Russian dramatic tradition had long emphasized character over plot. Gogol may have been the source of some of the slapstick that occurs in Chekhov's plays (especially *The Cherry Orchard*), though he had more than enough French farces, and their Russian imitations, to draw upon. Chekhov much admired Alexander Ostrovsky, Russia's first full-time playwright—most of the important plays of the nineteenth century, like Chekhov's, were also written by writers of prose fiction. Ostrovsky may have inspired his aim to show "life as it is," though Ostrovsky's plays, for all their marvelous fidelity to actual life and their extraordinary richness of language, are too high-keyed to have left a mark on Chekhov's softer music. Through Treplev of *The Sea Gull*, he showed his scorn for the second-rate followers of Ostrovsky, mere ethnographers who were content to show how people "eat, drink, love, walk about, wear their jackets." A more likely influence is Turgenev's masterpiece, *A Month in the Country*, which, like Chekhov's plays, concentrates its energies on psychological nuance. The action of Turgenev's play, however, is more carefully ordered, its speech more rationally constructed, than Chekhov's casual flow.

The glory of Russian literature after the age of Pushkin and until the end of the nineteenth century is, of course, the novel. The novel as a genre broke with classical views of character as fixed identity: in tragedy, to be revealed in a moment of crisis; in comedy, to be shown naked as the mask of pretension is ripped away. In the nineteenth century the disciplines of biology and history came into their own, and from Hegel through Marx and Darwin the emphasis was on development, growth, change, progress (even Darwin's natural selection was interpreted as a process of the gradual evolution of higher forms promising future perfection). Chekhov drew on his own short stories for his plays, often spoke of his plays as short stories or novellas (as did the critics), and, indeed, their structure is more novelistic than dramatic. There are no sudden revelations of "true" character ("Ah, so *that's* what X is like!"). He applies to drama the studied artlessness of the short story. His people reveal themselves slowly and incompletely, like neighbors or friends we get to know step by step but never know fully. There is always a shadow of mystery about his characters, some corner of their being we have not been able to dig into. We are touched by their sufferings, amused by their foolishness, and yet puzzled. Chekhov, in praising *Anna Karenina*, said that Tolstoy had done what an artist ought to do: he gave no answers, though he raised all the right questions. Chekhov wanted us to leave the theater mulling over the enigmas of human personality.

Chekhov wrote his major plays at a time when Russian poetry was enjoying a revival. Russian decadence and symbolism (the terms were used interchangeably) dominated the scene roughly from 1894 to 1910. Chekhov rejected the aestheticism of decadence and the mysticism of Russian symbolism. A physician by training, a journalist in his apprentice years, he always held to the naturalist's insistence on impartiality—"the writer must be as objective as a chemist." He also felt that art must serve some purpose. The great writers are "realists" but make us feel "life as it should be in addition to life as it is." In *The Sea Gull* he even parodied the decadent manner.

However, naturalism and symbolism, opposed to each other at the time, had something in common: they both turned their backs on realism's attempt to embrace all of life in the broad expanse of the novel. Life seemed too chaotic, too fragmented, to be caught whole. The naturalists turned to "a slice of life"; the symbolists, to a poem of mysterious allusion. By the 1880s the Russian realistic novel had passed from the scene. Short forms, like Chekhov's stories or symbolist lyrics, were the order of the day. Artists were trying to capture the fleeting moment, the impression of the surface, ripples in the stream of life that might suggest richer meanings. French impressionist painting had been introduced to Russia by *The World of Art* journal, one of the major organs of the new aestheticism. Despite Chekhov's professions of reportorial neutrality, there is a moving lyricism and suggestive symbolism in the best of his stories and plays. He was among the first to employ evocative silences on the stage. Chekhov did not remain untouched by the symbolist movement and may in turn have influenced it—indeed, the symbolists claimed him as one of their own. Theater critics, not knowing what to make of his peculiar mixture of comedy and pathos, often called his plays "plays of mood," "poems," or compared them to music.

His lyricism is sometimes nostalgic: his characters look back long-ingly to a time when life was better, or at least *seemed* better (the ironist in Chekhov is always lurking around the corner). Nature is often perceived poetically—the lake and the sea gull, the forest of *Uncle Vanya*, the birds Masha sees crossing the sky in *The Three Sisters*, the cherry orchard. Chekhov's lyrical apprehension of nature grew out of his sense that our human dramas are played out in a setting much larger than ourselves, that our lives are but ephemeral moments in the vast expanses of space and time, that if we fail and when we die, something will survive us.

Chekhov's Russia was acutely conscious of historical change. Urban-ization and industrialization brought the social dislocation and alien-ation that are still with us. Railroads fill the pages of Chekhov's stories and provide a metaphor for a world in flux—his art has been described as life seen from a moving railway car. A large city forms the backdrop of act 2 of *The Cherry Orchard*; Dr. Astrov of *Uncle Vanya* worries about the ravaged countryside. The gentry as a class was dying, and its death provoked the themes of loss and waste that are at the heart of Chekhov's plays. Rapid historical change is a cause of both anxiety and hope. Both were intensified in Russia by the widespread sense that the days of the prevailing political order were numbered; the regimes of Alexander III (1881–94) and Nicholas II (1894–1917) were reactionary, corrupt, and stupid. The yoke of the imperial state weighed heavily, the revolutionary movement was in temporary disarray, and the genera-tion of the 1880s felt itself lost. Liberal intellectuals contented them-selves with a program of "little deeds"—cultivating one's own garden, as Dr. Astrov cultivates his forest, so as to add a drop of improvement to the world's ocean of misery. In the 1890s revolutionary expectations revived, and we find premonitions of a radical transformation in Che-khov's last two plays, written on the eve of the upheaval of 1905. Baron Tuzenbach of *The Three Sisters* speaks of an "impending powerful, invigorating storm" that will blow away all the vices of the old order; Trofimov, in *The Cherry Orchard*, is confident that a "new life" is around the corner.

Change makes men and women aware of the passage of time—time is almost the hero of *The Three Sisters* and *The Cherry Orchard*. When Chekhov's people are not gazing nostalgically backward to the past, they look forward to the future with hope—which he continually undercuts. The character speaks confidently of how the world will be better, even perfect, in two or three hundred years, but we know him (the bombast belongs to the men) to be weak, passive, lazy. In Chekhov there is often no symmetry between word and action (or between the speech of one character and that of another), a discordance that is comic and ironic, and also quite "modern." This debunking of the rhetoric of progress has led some critics to interpret his message as saying that we must live only in the present. But Chekhov's letters express the same faith in progress that sounds so hollowly in the mouths of his heroes. He believed that "he who wants nothing, hopes for nothing, and fears nothing, cannot be an artist." A life lived for the present can only result in hedonistic despair. Perhaps the most poignant moment in all Chekhov's plays is the conclusion of *The Three Sisters,* when the sisters, in counterpoint to the nihilism of Dr. Chebutykin, insist upon continuing to hope when all the grounds of their hope have evaporated. As Dr. Astrov puts it, to give meaning to our lives, we have to have a sense of purpose, a destination, see "a light shining in the distance," even if it proves to be illusory. Characteristically, Astrov is drunk when he says this. Chekhov's men are caught in a web of abstraction. Even when they are mouthing their author's ideas, they are slightly comic. His women, fragile as they may be, seem closer to the pulse of life. Nina of *The Sea Gull* and Sonya of *Uncle Vanya,* like the three sisters, tell us that the important thing is "to endure."

In October of 1895, when Chekhov began work on *The Sea Gull,* he wrote to a friend, "I am sinning terribly against the conventions of the stage. It is a comedy with three female parts, six male, a landscape (a view of a lake), much talk of literature, little action and tons of love." He finished in November, though, as was his custom, he later made changes for production and publication. The play opened at the state-run Alexandrinsky Theater in St. Petersburg on October 17, 1896. It flopped badly. Despite Chekhov's anxious instructions, the actors insisted upon playing it tragically, in the nineteenth-century style of broad theatrical gestures, grand entrances and exits, heightened dramatic points. Audiences were bewildered by the commonplace characters, the absence of explicit motivation for their behavior, and the paucity of action—"Why do they play lotto and drink beer?" one viewer asked. (Complaints about the randomness of Chekhov's world dogged all of his plays.) The fashionable opening-night crowd booed after the first act, and though subsequent evenings were a bit better, the play closed after five performances.

In contrast, after December 17, 1898, the date of the first performance of *The Sea Gull* at the newly established Moscow Art Theater under the leadership of Konstantin Stanislavsky and Vladimir Nemirovich-Danchenko, Russians spoke of the dawn of a new era in the history of the theater. As the curtain descended on the last act, the theater was strangely silent. The actors, who this time had played it as Chekhov wanted, simply and without affectation, walked off the stage certain that they had failed; and then, after a long pause, the audience burst into resounding applause and shouts of praise. A creative collaboration of the greatest dramatist and greatest director of the age had begun. *Uncle Vanya* opened at the Moscow Art Theater on October 26, 1899 (though it had been shown earlier, in the provinces). *The Three Sisters* and *The Cherry Orchard* were written expressly for Stanislavsky's theater.

Relations between Chekhov and Stanislavsky were often strained. Chekhov complained about excessive stage effects—too much chirping of crickets, croaking of frogs, barking of dogs. Stanislavsky frankly admitted that he did not understand *The Sea Gull*; later they argued over *The Three Sisters* and *The Cherry Orchard*, Stanislavsky viewing them as a tragedies, Chekhov insisting they were comedies. Yet the two men complemented each other well. Stanislavsky's revulsion at the star system and introduction of ensemble acting, his insistence on naturalness of speech and gesture, his fervent, almost religious, dedication to the craft of acting, were all tailor-made for plays where almost everyone is a protagonist and psychological nuance conveys more than overt dramatic action. Without surrendering his naturalistic bias, Stanislavsky highlighted the lyrical dimension of Chekhov's plays. To achieve his goal of having actors live through a part, he wanted them to be in character before and after walking on and off stage, and Chekhov's plays do seem to commence in the midst of ongoing life that will continue after the curtain falls. They make extraordinary demands upon the actor—few things are as deadly as a Chekhov play played badly. The actor must be completely at ease and yet intensely alert to the subtle gradations of emotion in his own role and that of everyone else on stage. Stanislavsky's dedicated professionalism and Chekhov's lifelike plays made for a rare combination in the history of the stage. A sea gull was chosen as the logo for the Moscow Art Theater.

Chekhov was not entirely accurate when he implied that he had tossed overboard all the commonplaces of the stage in *The Sea Gull*. The conventional love triangles are there, even to surplus—almost everyone on stage is involved in one—and the play ends with the shock of a suicide. "Tons of love," is right, though the loves of *The Sea Gull* never find their true objects. To construct a play around unsatisfied longing was something new in the theater. So was the uncertainty of response the play seems to call for. "I'm in mourning for my life," Masha says as she opens act 1, and so is almost everyone else. The line is funny, but Masha is sad. Are we meant to be amused by her self-pity? Feel sorry for her? What the conventional theater considered important is given second place; what it considered trivial is brought to the forefront. Trigorin's love for Nina is played out with a coy reference to a line in one of his books (and then recounted retrospectively by Treplev, a theatrical device Chekhov dropped from his later plays). Arkadina changing the bandage of her son, Treplev, is given an entire scene. Of course, we learn much about Trigorin from the casual way in which he becomes enamored of the young and dreadfully naive Nina; the bandaging scene shows us the complex relations between mother and son. Chekhov's insight was that we reveal ourselves in the ordinary moments of our daily living.

The Sea Gull is a play about youth—hence its tons of love—and the deep divide between the generations. Mother and son, older successful writer and young aspiring writer, the aging star and the hopeful ingenue, find no common ground. But there are no victims, unless we see Treplev as his own victim. Chekhov wrote about *Ivanov* words that he might have used of all his major plays: "I wanted to be original—there is not a single villain or angel in my play (though I could not resist the temptation of putting in a few buffoons). I have not found anyone guilty, nor have I acquitted anyone." Yet we have more sympathy for Nina and Treplev than for Trigorin and Arkadina. The young are entitled to be foolish; those with experience ought to know better.

Uncle Vanya, on the other hand, is a play about middle age. It grew out of an earlier effort, *The Wood Demon*, which was first performed—and flopped—in 1889. Chekhov, stung by its failure, abandoned the theater for six years (until he wrote *The Sea Gull*) and reworked it, in 1896, into the masterpiece that is *Uncle Vanya*. *The Wood Demon* has too many characters to keep track of, they talk too much, everything ends cheerily as the assorted lovers are reconciled, and the character who was to become Vanya takes his own life and is quickly forgotten. To go from *The Wood Demon* to *Uncle Vanya* is to move from speechifying to conversation, from stereotypes to realized individuals, from argument to poetry.

The major characters of *Uncle Vanya,* like those of the other major plays, can be placed on a scale of age. Professor Serebryakov is old and whines. Sonya is young and hopes. Vanya and Astrov are middle-aged and worry that their lives have been failures. Vanya is angry and Astrov resigned. The "mermaid" Yelena (Russian for Helen) shows up, stoking a fire in these tired men, though she herself is cold. For Chekhov, as for Dostoevsky before him, beauty has a moral quality. In his story "The Beauties" (1888), the sight of beauty fills men with sadness, as it reminds them of their own imperfections, of what is missing from their lives. Perhaps what is wrong with Yelena is that her beauty is untouched by moral grace—she is indolent and as unhappy as the men.

There is something mysterious about the misery of Chekhov's people. Is Sonya really so ugly that Astrov could not be happy with her? Why can't Vanya feel at least some contentment about his very real achievement in holding the estate together? It is as if they are determined to make the wrong choices or are possessed of a will to suffer. The play turns in a circle, with the leavetaking of the ending repeating gestures and words of the opening—"nothing has changed," Vanya tells us. Then Sonya adds a memorable coda of hope as mysterious as the play's despair. Critics have been divided. Is it meant to be taken straight or is it ironic? Perhaps both. Chekhov certainly wanted us to feel the dignity of her refusal to surrender to despair, although he did not want us to abandon our critical detachment. His plays bring us too close to his characters for us to dismiss them, while a comic tone concurrently sets them at a distance. We watch them with what Shakespeare called a "parted eye": one part sees Vanya stumbling across the stage, revolver in hand, crying "Bang!" as he shoots at the hated professor, and we laugh; the other has not lost sight of his very real suffering.

The Three Sisters gave Chekhov a good deal of trouble—he worried about the difficulties of handling such a large cast of characters and three heroines. It was written from August through December of 1900 and opened at the Moscow Art Theater on January 31, 1901. During rehearsals Stanislavsky felt stuck, until it dawned on him that Chekhov's characters "don't at all wear their melancholy like a badge; to the contrary, they seek gaiety, laughter, cheerfulness; they want to live, not vegetate."

The Sea Gull describes a summer of love's infatuations and confusions, then, after a gap of two years, events are summarized and act 4 takes place in autumn—as do all the last acts of Chekhov's major plays. The others unfailingly show life in process. They are plays of loss: *Uncle Vanya* moves from summer to autumn, *The Cherry Orchard* from May to October. In *The Three Sisters* the process of loss takes place over a number of years, long enough for Natasha to bear two children. Again the movement is from spring to fall, with dark winters interspersed in acts 2 and 3, and another on its way at the end.

The Three Sisters opens with remembering, but it is really about forgetting. When they first meet, Vershinin cannot remember the sisters, nor they him. Chebutykin has forgotten medicine. Irina has forgotten Italian. Masha has forgotten her mother, how to play the piano, and eventually the lines of the Pushkin poem that obsess her throughout the play. By act 3 the party of act 1 has become a dim memory in Tuzenbach's mind; at the end, the sisters have apparently forgotten their dream of escape to Moscow. "People won't remember us too. We'll be forgotten," Masha laments. As time strips them of memory, Natasha dispossesses them of the space they inhabit. Acts 1 and 2 take place in a large living room with a ballroom in the background; act 3, in the bedroom Olga and Irina are sharing now that Natasha has taken over Olga's room. In act 4 they are out of the house altogether, and Natasha rules the roost. Life is remorseless, everything passes, almost nothing holds firm against the stream of time—"almost" because the sisters' deep affection for each other survives their losses.

The Three Sisters may be Chekhov's supreme achievement (some would vote for *The Cherry Orchard*). Here his art of suggesting the undercurrents of life is at its height. It is the only one of his four major plays to be subtitled "drama"—he called *The Sea Gull* and *The Cherry Orchard* "comedies," *Uncle Vanya* "scenes"—but its dramatic moments are mere eddies on the stream of time. Yet there is a drama submerged beneath time's inexorable course, one present in all of his plays but most powerfully felt in *The Three Sisters*—the struggle of men and women to extract meaning from a world beyond their control.

By 1901 the Russian public was moving away from the fashionable pessimism of the 1880s and demanding a more affirmative art. Critics, though they praised the "poetry" of *The Three Sisters*, objected to its dark view of life and accused Chekhov of repeating himself. Chekhov worried that his "manner was out of date." His next play, he promised, would be "definitely funny, very funny. . . ." At times he spoke of *The Cherry Orchard* as a "vaudeville." When he finished, he wrote his wife, "It is not a drama, but a comedy, in places even a farce." The writing was even tougher going than *The Three Sisters*. It is unclear just when he conceived the play; the traditional dating is the spring of 1901. It was completed in the fall of 1903 and opened at the Moscow Art Theater on January 17, 1904, in conjunction with a celebration of Chekhov's twenty-fifth year of literary activity; he died a mere five and a half months later.

The Cherry Orchard does have many elements of farce. Ranevskaya, the grande dame; Gayev, the effete nobleman; perpetually astonished Pishchik; clumsy and incoherent Yepikhodov; the Frenchified valet, Yasha; the love-struck soubrette Dunyasha, the odd-speaking "German" governess, Charlotta; Anya the ingenue; the faithful retainer, Firs (who has his counterpart in Ferapont of *The Three Sisters*) are stock figures of the kind of light comedy Russians called vaudeville. Yepikhodov takes his pratfalls; Varya swings a cue at him and almost hits her reluctant suitor; pompous Trofimov goes flying down a staircase. But again, too many of them are too fully realized as complex human beings to be entirely funny. If *The Three Sisters* is Chekhov's most moving play, *The Cherry Orchard* shows an extraordinary lightness of touch, an uncanny blend of comedy and pathos.

"It seems to me that in my play, no matter how boring it is, there is something new. In the entire play there is not one gun shot." Chekhov might have added that also new was the absence of an unfolding love affair. In the other plays the characters desire—Sorin of *The Sea Gull* would entitle the story of his life "The Man Who Wished," a title most of Chekhov's characters might accept for their life stories. Desire leads to some kind of action, however displaced from center stage, and results in the anguish of unfulfillment. In *The Cherry Orchard*

Lopakhin and Varya spend most of their energy avoiding each other; Trofimov, who sees himself as "above love," is more of Anya's chum than her lover; Ranevskaya agonizes over past affairs. The loss of the cherry orchard is always in the background, giving the play unity—at least we know what it's *about*. But it does not provide much action either, since its owners, no matter how much Lopakhin insists that they do something about it, do nothing. They would rather talk about themselves. More than in any other of Chekhov's plays, the spotlight is on the comedy of daily life.

In a passage Chekhov omitted in order to get the play through the censors, it is clear that Trofimov, the "eternal student," is a radical belonging to what Russians called the "intelligentsia"—a type Chekhov always mocked. He could never abide anyone who pretended to have the answers to the riddles of life. Yet Trofimov expresses many of Chekhov's own views—on the need to work, on social amelioration, on the necessity to envision a future. He may touch the heart of the play when he says, "To live in the present we first have to make up for our past, to have done with it once and for all." He is referring to the central ill of Russian history—its legacy of serfdom. But there are also personal histories the characters are struggling to come to terms with. Ranevskaya suffers painful guilt over the death of her child and her various love affairs, and the supporting cast echoes, even if in a comic mode, the theme of guilt for a misspent life—"They say I've eaten up my fortune in candy," Gayev quips. At the other end of the social scale, Lopakhin, the son of a serf, has not gotten over the loveless brutality of his peasant childhood. Perhaps Gayev and Ranevskaya cannot focus on the loss of their estate because, much as they love it, salvaging it will not solve their essential problem—to discover who they are. On the other hand, Lopakhin is obsessed by its acquisition because he is under the illusion that it will solve all his difficulties. *The Three Sisters* concluded with Olga's cry for self-knowledge—"if we only knew." In *The Cherry Orchard* Charlotta, in a voice half-pathetic, half comic, asks the question that nags all of us: who am I?

If *The Cherry Orchard* is vaudeville, it is so in the manner of *Waiting for Godot*—comic characters are adrift in a voiceless cosmos. "Suddenly a distant sound is heard, as if coming from the sky, the mournful dying sound of a breaking string" is the stage direction in the middle of lovely act 2. It is sunset, the characters are in a darkening meadow, the cherry orchard is nearby, and faraway on the horizon is the faint outline of a large city—symbols of the old ways and the new. Everyone onstage falls silent, in fear and awe. The stage has opened up upon the universe, upon some dark mystery at the heart of things. A tramp appears, and Ranevskaya gives him a gold coin, as if to propitiate the gods. As space opens to infinity, the characters contract, undergoing a diminution that lies at the heart of comedy. Gayev and Ranevskaya grieve over their loss; Lopakhin revels in his triumph, though he senses that his victory may be hollow. But their mourning and joy, their failure and success, are only things of a moment in the great scheme of things—if there is one. They pack their bags in yet another final scene of leavetaking. The pathos of tragedy has been robbed of its finality. Somewhere out there, the middle-aged Gayevs and Ranevskayas of the world are still grieving that their lives haven't turned out as they wished, the youthful Anyas are hoping that theirs will be different, old men like Firs are dying, and the human comedy rolls on.

This project began when I was asked to do performable versions of *The Sea Gull* and *Uncle Vanya* for theaters in Chicago. Thanks are due to Nicholas Rudall of the Court Theater for his helpful advice—among other things he told me to "make sure the actors can get their tongues around the words"—and to Lilia Guimaraes for her assistance with the final manuscript.

Milton Ehre

The University of Chicago
1991

The Sea Gull

A Comedy in Four Acts

Irína Nikoláyevna Arkádina Trépleva

by marriage, an actress

Konstantín Gavrílovich Tréplev (Kóstya)

her son, a young man

Pyotr Nikoláyevich Sórin (Petrúsha)

her brother

Nína Mikháylovna Zaréchnaya

a young woman, daughter of a rich landowner

Ilyá Afanásyevich Shamráyev

a retired lieutenant, the manager of Sorin's estate

Polína Andréyevna

his wife

Másha (Márya Ilínichna)

his daughter

Borís Alekséyevich Trigórin

a writer

Yevgény Sergéyevich Dorn

a doctor

Semyón Semyónovich Medvédenko

a teacher

Yákov

a workman

Cook

Maid

The action takes place on Sorin's estate. Two years pass between the third and fourth acts.

A C T I

The park on SORIN'S *estate. A wide lane leading away from the audience deep into the park and to a lake; the view of the lake is completely blocked by a stage hastily slapped together for family performances. To the left and right of the stage, bushes. Several chairs, a small table. The sun has just set.* YAKOV *and other* WORKMEN *are behind a lowered curtain of the stage set—coughs and hammering.* MASHA *and* MEDVEDENKO, *returning from a walk, enter from the left.*

MEDVEDENKO. Why do you always wear black?

MASHA. I'm in mourning for my life. I'm unhappy.

MEDVEDENKO. But why? (*Pondering*) I don't understand. . . . You're healthy, your father isn't rich, but he's comfortable. My life is much harder than yours. I earn only twenty-three rubles a month, not counting deductions for the pension fund. Yet I don't go around in mourning. (*They sit down.*)

MASHA. It's not a question of money. A beggar can be happy.

MEDVEDENKO. In theory. In practice there's me, my mother, two sisters, my younger brother, and a salary of only twenty-three rubles. We have to eat, don't we? We need our tea and sugar? And then there's tobacco. It's a tight squeeze.

MASHA (*looking at the stage*). The play will start soon.

MEDVEDENKO. Yes. Nina Zarechnaya will perform, the play is by Konstantin Gavrilovich. They're in love, and today they will be spiritually united in trying to present a single artistic impression. But there's no meeting of the minds for us. I love you, I'm too miserable to stay at home, every day I walk eight miles here and back only to meet with your indifference. It's only natural. I'm without means, I have a large family. . . . Who would want to marry a man as poor as a church mouse?

MASHA. Nonsense. (*Takes a pinch of snuff.*) Your love touches me, but I can't reciprocate, that's all there is to it. (*Offering him the snuff box.*) Have some.

MEDVEDENKO. I don't feel like it. (*Pause.*)

MASHA. It's sweltering. There's bound to be a storm tonight. You're always philosophizing or talking about money. You imagine there's no greater misfortune than poverty, but the way I see it, it's a thousand times easier to go in rags and beg than . . . but that's something you wouldn't understand. . . .

SORIN *and* TREPLEV *enter from the right.*

SORIN (*leaning on a cane*). I'm not myself in the country, my boy. Clear as day I'll never get used to it. Yesterday I went to bed at ten and woke up at nine feeling as if my brain were glued to my skull from sleeping too much. (*Laughs.*) And after dinner I dozed off again. Now I'm a complete wreck, my life's a nightmare, and so on and so forth. . . .

TREPLEV. Yes, Uncle, you ought to live in town. (*Seeing* MASHA *and* MEDVEDENKO.) My friends, when the play begins, we'll call you, but you can't stay here now. I'll have to ask you to leave.

SORIN (*to* MASHA). Masha, be a good girl and ask your father to have the dog let off its chain. Otherwise she'll howl. My sister didn't sleep a wink last night.

MASHA. Speak to my father yourself! I'm not about to, so please don't ask. (*To* MEDVEDENKO.) Let's go!

MEDVEDENKO (*to* TREPLEV). Be sure to tell us before it starts. (*Both go out.*)

SORIN. The damn dog will be barking all night. What a mess! I've never passed my time in the country the way I've wished. It used to be I'd take a month's vacation, come here to relax and that sort of thing, but they pestered me with so many trifles, after a day I was ready to fly off. (*Laughs.*) It was always a relief to get away from here. But now I'm retired, there's no place for me to go, and so on and so forth. Like it or not, you have to go on living. . . .

YAKOV (*to* TREPLEV). Konstantin Gavrilovich, we're going for a swim.

TREPLEV. Fine. Only be at your places in ten minutes. (*Looks at his watch.*) We start soon.

YAKOV. Yes, sir. (*Exits.*)

TREPLEV (*looking over the stage*). That's a theater for you. A curtain, two wings, and then—empty space. No scenery at all. The audience has an open view of the lake and the horizon. The curtain goes up at half past eight, with the rising of the moon.

SORIN. Splendid.

TREPLEV. Of course, if Nina is late, it will spoil the whole effect. She should be here by now. Her father and stepmother keep a sharp eye on her. Tearing herself away from her house is as tough as escaping from prison. (*Straightening his uncle's tie.*) Your hair and beard are unkempt. You could use a trim. . . .

SORIN (*combing his beard*). The tragedy of my life. Even when I was young I looked like a drunk. Women never loved me. (*Sits.*) Why is your mother in such a bad mood?

TREPLEV. She's bored. (*Sits next to him.*) And jealous. She has it in for me and my play because Nina may make a hit with her writer friend. She hasn't read a page, but already hates it.

SORIN (*laughing*). Come now, you're imagining things. . . .

TREPLEV. It annoys her that even here, on this measly little stage, it will be Nina's triumph, not hers. (*Checks his watch.*) My mother is a psychological curiosity. No question she's talented, clever. She can sob over a novel, reel off all of Nekrasov for you by heart, if you're sick she'll tend to you like an angel. But just try praising Duse when she's around. Oh-ho! You have to applaud her and no one else, write about her, rave, go into ecstasies over her extraordinary performance in *Camille* or *The Fumes of Life*. But since the country doesn't offer such stimulants, she's bored and irritable. And as for us—we're her enemies, we're all to blame. Besides, she's superstitious: three candles, the number thirteen, frighten her. And stingy. She has seventy thousand rubles in a bank in Odessa—I know that for a fact—but ask her for a loan and she'll burst into tears.

SORIN. You've got it into your head that your mother won't like your play and you're upset. Calm down. Your mother adores you.

TREPLEV (*tearing the petals from a flower*). Loves me, loves me not; loves me, loves me not; loves me, loves me not. (*Laughing.*) See, my mother doesn't love me. No wonder! She wants to live an exciting life, to fall in love, wear bright blouses. And I'm twenty-five, a constant reminder that she's no longer young. When I'm not around, she's only thirty-two; when I pop up—forty-three, and for that she hates me. Besides, she knows I don't respect our contemporary theater. She loves it, she imagines she's serving humanity, the cause of sacred art. But, as I see it, our theater is in a rut—it's so damn conventional. The curtain goes up on a room with three walls under artificial lighting, and these great talents, these high priests of sacred art, show me how people eat, drink, love, walk about, wear their jackets. And when they try to squeeze a moral from these commonplace scenes and phrases—a petty, easy moral fit for domestic consumption, when they feed me the same dish over and over and over again—then I run and keep on running as fast as Maupassant ran from the brain-crushing vulgarity of the Eiffel Tower.

SORIN. We can't manage without the theater.

TREPLEV. We need new forms. New forms. And if they're not to be found, then better nothing at all. (*Looks at his watch.*) I love my mother—I love her very much—but she smokes, drinks, lives openly with that writer of hers. The papers are always bandying her name about—and that depresses me. Sometimes normal human selfishness makes me regret that my mother is a famous actress. If she were an ordinary woman I think I would be the happier for it. Uncle, what could be more desperate and absurd than my position? Artists and writers used to visit our home, all of them celebrities, and I the only nobody in the lot. They put up with me merely because I'm her son. Who am I? What am I? I left the university in my third year, "under circumstances for which the editors are not responsible," as the saying goes. No talent, not a kopek to my name, a mere petty bourgeois from Kiev. My father, you see, was from the lower classes, though he was a well-known actor. So, when these assorted artists and writers were kind enough to take note of me, I imagined their glances were taking the measure of my insignificance—I guessed what they must be thinking . . . the humiliation was very painful. . . .

SORIN. By the way, what sort of a fellow is this writer of hers? There's no making him out. He never opens his mouth.

TREPLEV. He's intelligent, unpretentious, a bit melancholy, I'd say. Decent enough. He's well under forty, but he's already famous and content, stuffed to the gills with self-satisfaction. . . . Drinks only beer and loves only older women. As for his writing . . . what

g, talented . . . but . . . after Tolstoy and Zola
ead Trigorin.

SORIN. And I, my friend, am terribly fond of writers. I once very much wanted two things: to get married and to be a writer. Neither worked out. Yes, it's nice being even a small-time writer, and so on.

TREPLEV (*listening*). I hear her coming. . . . (*Embraces his uncle.*) I can't live without her. Even the sound of her footsteps is beautiful . . . I'm dizzy with happiness. (*Goes quickly to greet* NINA, *as she enters.*) My enchantress, my dream. . . .

NINA (*agitated*). I'm not late . . . surely I'm not late . . . ?

TREPLEV (*kissing her hands*). No, no, no. . . .

NINA. All day I was anxious, terrified! I was afraid father wouldn't let me. . . . But he drove off with my stepmother. The sky was a deep red, the moon was rising, I kept urging the horses on. (*Laughs.*) But now I'm happy. (*Warmly shakes* SORIN'S *hand.*)

SORIN (*laughs*). There are tears in your eyes. Ha, ha! That won't do!

NINA. Yes. . . . See how difficult it is for me to breathe. I'll leave in half an hour. I have to hurry. I can't stay, I just can't. For heaven's sake, don't detain me. My father has no idea I'm here.

TREPLEV. Actually it's time to start. We must call the others.

SORIN. I'll go. This minute. (*Goes to the right and sings.*) "In France two Grenadiers. . . ." (*Looks round.*) Once I sang like that and some assistant district attorney said to me, "You have a powerful voice, Your Excellency." . . . Then he added, "And a lousy one." (*Laughs and exits.*)

NINA. My father and his wife won't let me come here. They say it's very bohemian . . . they're afraid I'll become an actress. . . . But I'm drawn to this lake, as if I were a sea gull. . . . My heart is so full of you. (*Looks about.*)

TREPLEV. We're alone.

NINA. I think I hear someone. . . .

TREPLEV. There's no one. (*They kiss.*)

NINA. What is that tree?

TREPLEV. An elm.

NINA. Why is it so dark?

TREPLEV. It's evening, everything is turning dark. Don't leave early, please don't.

freedom

NINA. I have to.

TREPLEV. May I visit you, Nina? I'll stand in the garden all night gazing at your window.

NINA. You mustn't. The watchman will see you. Rex isn't used to you; he'll bark.

TREPLEV. I love you.

NINA. Shh . . .

TREPLEV (*hearing footsteps*). Who's there? Is that you, Yakov?

YAKOV (*behind the stage*). Yes, sir.

TREPLEV. Places! It's time. Is the moon up?

YAKOV. Yes, sir.

TREPLEV. Have you got the methylated spirits? The sulphur? When the red eyes appear, the scene must smell of sulphur. (*To* NINA.) Come, everything's ready. Are you nervous? . . .

NINA. Yes, very. Your mother doesn't bother me—I'm not afraid of her, but Trigorin . . . I'm embarrassed . . . really terrified to perform for him . . . a famous author like that. . . . Is he young?

TREPLEV. Yes.

NINA. What marvelous stories he's written!

TREPLEV (*coolly*). I can't say. I haven't read them.

NINA. It's difficult to act in your play. There are no living people.

TREPLEV. Living people! One must depict life not as it is, nor as it should be, but as it appears in dreams.

NINA. There's not much action, only speeches. As I see it, a play ought to have love . . . (*Both go behind the stage.*)

POLINA ANDREYEVNA *and* DORN *enter.*

POLINA ANDREYEVNA. It's damp. Go back in and put on your galoshes.

DORN. It's too hot.

POLINA ANDREYEVNA. You don't take care of yourself. Stubbornness, that's what it is. You're a doctor, you very well know damp air is bad for you, but you enjoy making me suffer. Yesterday you sat out on the porch all evening to spite me. . . .

DORN (*sings softly*). "Never say youth is wasted."

POLINA ANDREYEVNA. You got so carried away talking to Irina

Nikolayevna you didn't notice the cold. Admit it, you're attracted to her. . . .

DORN. I'm fifty-five.

POLINA ANDREYEVNA. Rubbish. For a man that's not old. You've kept your looks and women find you attractive.

DORN. Well, what would you have me do?

POLINA ANDREYEVNA. Before an actress you men are ready to fall to your knees. Every last one of you!

DORN (*sings*). "Before you once more I . . . " If people dote on artists and treat them differently from, let's say, storekeepers, that's just the way things are. You might call it idealism.

POLINA ANDREYEVNA. Women always fell in love with you, they hung on your neck. Do you call that idealism too?

DORN (*shrugging his shoulders*). What of it? There's much to be said for my relations with women. Mostly they loved me because I was a first-rate doctor. Ten, fifteen years ago, as you'll recall, I was the only decent obstetrician in our entire province. Besides I've always been honest.

POLINA ANDREYEVNA (*seizing his hand*). My darling!

DORN. Shh! They're coming.

Enter ARKADINA *arm in arm with* SORIN; *also* TRIGORIN, SHAMRAYEV, MEDVEDENKO, *and* MASHA.

SHAMRAYEV. Her performance in 1873 at the Poltava fair was amazing. A sheer delight! Wonderful acting! You wouldn't happen to know, madam, what the comic actor Chadin is doing these days? His Rasplyuyev was inimitable. Better than Sadovsky. You have my word for it, my esteemed lady. Where is he now?

ARKADINA. You keep asking about antediluvians. How on earth should I know! (*Sits.*)

SHAMRAYEV (*sighing*). Pashka Chadin! The likes of you are no longer with us. The stage has declined, Irina Nikolayevna! Once we saw mighty oaks, now nothing but stumps.

DORN. There are few brilliant talents nowadays, that's true, but the general level is much higher.

SHAMRAYEV. I can't agree with you there. But, of course, it's a matter of taste. *De gustibus aut bene, aut nihil.*

TREPLEV *appears from behind the stage.*

ARKADINA (*to her son*). My dear child, when does it begin?
TREPLEV. In a moment. Patience, please.
ARKADINA (*quotes* Hamlet).

> *O Hamlet, speak no more.*
> *Thou turn'st mine eyes into my very soul,*
> *And there I see such black and grainèd spots*
> *As will not leave their tinct.*

TREPLEV (*from* Hamlet).

> *Nay, but to live*
> *In the rank sweat of an enseamèd bed,*
> *Stewed in corruption, honeying and making love*
> *Over the nasty sty—*

A horn sounds from behind the stage.

TREPLEV. Ladies and gentlemen, curtain time! Attention, please!
(*Pause.*) I'll begin. (*Taps with a stick and speaks in loud voice.*) O
you venerable shades floating nightly over this lake, lull us to
sleep so we may dream of the world as it will be in two hundred
thousand years.
SORIN. In two hundred thousand years there'll be nothing.
TREPLEV. Then let them show us that nothing.
ARKADINA. Fine. We're asleep.

*The curtain rises, revealing the lake, the moon over the horizon, its
reflection in the water.* NINA ZARECHNAYA, *all in white, is sitting
on a large stone.*

NINA. Men, lions, eagles, partridges, deer with antlers, geese,
spiders, silent fish who dwell in the deep, starfish, and those the
eye cannot behold—all, all, all living things, have run their
sorrowful course and are now extinct. . . . For thousands of
centuries the earth has borne no living creature, and this poor
moon lights its lamp in vain. In the meadows cranes no longer
awaken with a cry, May beetles are silent in the lindens. Cold,

cold, cold. Empty, empty, empty. Dreadful, dreadful, dreadful. (*Pause.*) The bodies of living creatures have turned to dust, eternal matter has transformed them into stone, water, clouds, and all their souls have merged into one. I am that World Soul—I, I . . . In me resides the soul of Alexander the Great, of Caesar, Shakespeare, Napoleon, and of the lowliest leech. In me human consciousness has merged with animal instinct. I remember all, all, all, and I relive each and every life. (*Will-o'-the-wisps appear.*)

ARKADINA (*softly*). This smacks of decadence.

TREPLEV (*in an imploring and reproachful voice*). Mama!

NINA. I am alone. Once every hundred years I open my lips to speak, and my voice echoes mournfully in the void, and no one hears. . . . And you, pale fires, you do not hear me. . . . Toward morning the foul marsh begets you, you wander until dawn, bereft of thought, of will, of palpitating life. Fearful lest life should emerge in you, the father of eternal matter, the devil, at every moment shuffles the atoms in the waters and the stones and in you, pale fires, and you incessantly change. In the universe only spirit remains permanent and immutable. (*Pause.*) Like a prisoner hurled into a deep vacant well, I do not know where I am and what awaits me. Only one truth has been revealed to me—in cruel, persistent battle with the devil, the principle of material power, I am destined to triumph. Then matter and spirit will fuse in glorious harmony, and the kingdom of universal freedom will come to pass. But only step by step, through a long, long row of millennia. The moon, and radiant Sirius, and our earth will have turned to dust. . . . Till then, horror, horror. . . . (*Pause. Two red points appear over the lake.*) Behold, my mighty foe, the devil, draws near. I see his terrible crimson eyes. . . .

ARKADINA. It smells of sulphur. Is that part of it?

TREPLEV. Yes.

ARKADINA (*laughing*). Of course, it's a stage effect.

TREPLEV. Mama!

NINA. He languishes without man. . . .

POLINA ANDREYEVNA (*to* DORN). You've taken your hat off. Put it on or you'll catch cold.

ARKADINA. Our doctor has tipped his hat to the devil, the father of eternal matter.

TREPLEV (*flaring up, loudly*). The play is over! Enough! Curtain!

ARKADINA. Why are you angry?

TREPLEV. Enough! Curtain! Drop the curtain! (*Stamping.*) Curtain! (*The curtain falls.*) Excuse me. I lost sight of the fact that only the chosen few may write plays and act. I broke the monopoly! I, I . . . (*Wants to say more but waves his hand and goes off left.*)

ARKADINA. What's gotten into him?

SORIN. Irina dear, that's no way to treat a sensitive young man.

ARKADINA. But what did I say?

SORIN. You hurt his feelings.

ARKADINA. He told us his play was only a joke, so I regarded it as a joke.

SORIN. All the same. . . .

ARKADINA. Now it appears he's written a masterpiece! Come now! It's all too clear he got up this performance and suffocated us with sulphur not as a joke but to make a point. . . . He wanted to instruct us how to write and what to act. In a nutshell, it's getting tiresome. Say what you like, but these incessant attacks, these digs, would try anyone's patience! He's a conceited, egotistical brat.

SORIN. He wanted to please you.

ARKADINA. You think so? Then why didn't he choose some ordinary play instead of forcing us to listen to these decadent ravings. For the sake of a joke I'll listen even to ravings, but these pretensions to new forms, to a new era in art. . . . As I see it, this has nothing to do with new forms. He's just being nasty.

SORIN. Everyone writes what he likes as best he can.

ARKADINA. Let him write as he pleases, but leave me in peace.

DORN. Jupiter, thou art angry. . . .

ARKADINA. I'm not Jupiter, I'm a woman. (*Lights a cigarette.*) I'm not angry, only annoyed that a young man spends his time in such a tedious manner. I didn't mean to hurt his feelings.

MEDVEDENKO. Nobody has grounds for separating spirit from matter, since spirit itself may very well be an aggregate of atomic matter. (*To* TRIGORIN, *animatedly.*) You know, someone really ought to write a play showing how we schoolteachers live. We have a hard life, very hard!

ARKADINA. That's true, but let's not talk about plays or atoms.

What a glorious evening! Can you hear? They're singing. (*Listens.*) How splendid!

POLINA ANDREYEVNA. It's from the other shore. (*Pause.*)

ARKADINA (*to* TRIGORIN). Sit here beside me. Ten, fifteen years ago you would hear music and singing on the lake almost every night. There are six country houses along the shore. I can remember laughter, voices, shooting, and love affairs, endless love affairs. . . . The *jeune premier* and idol of those six houses was no other than our friend here—I give you Dr. Yevgeny Sergeyich Dorn (*nodding toward* DORN). He's charming now, then he was irresistible. But my conscience is starting to bother me. Why did I hurt my poor boy's feelings? I'm worried about him. (*Loudly.*) Kostya! Kostya! My son!

MASHA. I'll go look for him.

ARKADINA. Please do, my dear.

MASHA (*going to the left*). Yoo-hoo! Yoo-hoo! Konstantin! . . . Yoo-hoo! (*Goes out.*)

NINA (*coming out from behind the stage*). It seems we're not going to continue, so I may as well come out. Good evening! (*Kisses* ARKADINA *and* POLINA ANDREYEVNA.)

SORIN. Bravo! Bravo!

ARKADINA. Bravo! Bravo! We loved it. With your looks, that marvelous voice, it would be a terrible waste to remain in the country. No doubt you have talent. You simply must go on the stage!

NINA. Oh, that's my dream. (*Sighing.*) But it will never come true.

ARKADINA. Who can tell? But let me introduce a friend: Boris Alekseyevich Trigorin.

NINA. Oh, I'm so happy . . . (*Overcome with embarrassment.*) I'm always reading your . . .

ARKADINA (*seating her beside herself*). Don't be shy, my dear. He's famous, but good-natured. You see, he's shy too.

DORN. I suppose we may raise the curtain now. It's creepy.

SHAMRAYEV (*loudly*). Yakov, raise the curtain! (*The curtain is raised.*)

NINA (*to* TRIGORIN). It's a strange play. Don't you think so?

TRIGORIN. I didn't understand a word. But I enjoyed it. You played so sincerely. And the scenery was beautiful. (*Pause.*) There must be a lot of fish in this lake.

NINA. Yes.

TRIGORIN. I love fishing. There's nothing I enjoy so much as sitting on the bank of a river toward evening watching the bob on my line.

NINA. But I should have thought that for a man who has known the joy of creation, there can be no other pleasures.

ARKADINA (*laughing*). Don't talk like that. When people mouth pretty phrases to him, he goes to pieces.

SHAMRAYEV. I remember one evening in the Moscow opera house the great Silva took a low C. Now it so happened that the bass of our church choir was in the balcony, and suddenly—you can imagine our astonishment—we hear "Bravo, Silva!" booming from the balcony—a full octave lower . . . like this (*in a low bass*): "Bravo, Silva!" The audience was bowled over. (*Pause.*)

DORN. The angel of silence has flown by.

NINA. It's time. Goodbye.

ARKADINA. Where are you going? Why so early? We won't let you.

NINA. My father is expecting me.

ARKADINA. Who does he think he is, really. . . . (*They kiss.*) Well, there's no help for it. I'm so very sorry to let you go.

NINA. If you only knew how hard it is for me to leave!

ARKADINA. Someone ought to see you home, my pet.

NINA (*frightened*). Oh, no, no!

SORIN (*to her, beseeching*). Do stay!

NINA. I can't, Pyotr Nikolayevich.

SORIN. For an hour, that's all. Do. . . .

NINA (*thinking it over, tearfully*). I just can't. (*Shakes hands and hurriedly goes off.*)

ARKADINA. She's an unfortunate girl. They say her mother left her husband an enormous estate, everything down to the last kopek. He's already made a will leaving it all to his second wife, so now the poor girl has nothing. It's scandalous.

DORN. Yes, her father's pretty much of a swine, to give the man his due.

SORIN (*rubbing his cold hands*). Let's be off too, my friends, it's damp. My legs ache.

Sorin's legs

ARKADINA. It's as if they're made of wood. You can barely walk. Well, come along, my unlucky old man. (*Takes him by the arm.*)

SHAMRAYEV (*offering his arm to his wife*). Madam?

SORIN. That dog is howling again. (*To* SHAMRAYEV.) Please, Ilya Afanasevich, let him off his chain.

SHAMRAYEV. Impossible, Pyotr Nikolayevich. Thieves might break into the barn. I've got millet stored there. (*To* MEDVEDENKO *who is walking beside him.*) Yes, a full octave lower—"Bravo, Silva!" And he's not even a real singer, just a member of a church choir.

MEDVEDENKO. By the way, how much does the member of a church choir make? (*All go off, except* DORN.)

DORN (*alone*). Maybe I don't understand these things or I've lost my senses, but I liked that play. There's something to it. When that girl spoke about loneliness and then, when the devil's red eyes popped up, I was so excited my hands trembled. It's fresh, naive . . . I think I hear him coming. I'd like to say something encouraging.

TREPLEV (*entering*). No one's here.

DORN. I'm here.

TREPLEV. Masha has been trailing me all over the park. An insufferable creature.

DORN. I liked your play very much, Konstantin. It's a bit strange, I haven't heard the end, but all the same it made a powerful impression. You're a talented fellow, you ought to keep at it. (TREPLEV *presses his hand warmly and embraces him impulsively.*) Whew, what hysterics! Tears in your eyes. . . . What was it I wanted to say? You've taken your subject from the sphere of abstract ideas. And that's right, because a work of art ought to express a great idea. Only serious subjects can be truly beautiful. How pale you are!

TREPLEV. So you say I should keep at it?

DORN. Yes. . . . But write only about what is important and eternal. You know, in my life I've had all kinds of experiences. I've lived with style and enjoyed myself. But had it been my lot to know the ecstasy of the artist in the moment of creation, I think I would have despised my physical shell and everything that goes along with it and soared away into the heights.

TREPLEV. Excuse me, where is Nina?

DORN. One more thing. A work of art should have a clear and definite idea. You have to know why you're writing. If you take a route just for the scenery, without a specific destination, you'll get lost and your talent will destroy you.

TREPLEV (*impatiently*). Where is Nina?

DORN. She's gone home.

TREPLEV (*despairingly*). What am I to do? I want to see her . . . I must see her . . . I'm going. . . .

MASHA *enters.*

DORN (*to* TREPLEV). Calm down, my boy.

TREPLEV. Whatever you say, I'm going. I must go.

MASHA. Go into the house, Konstantin. Your mother wants you. She's upset.

TREPLEV. Tell her I left. And I ask all of you, leave me in peace! Leave me alone! Don't follow after me!

DORN. Come, come, my dear boy. . . . You can't go on like that. . . . It's not right.

TREPLEV (*tearfully*). Goodbye, doctor. Thanks for . . . (*Goes out.*)

DORN (*sighing*). Youth, youth!

MASHA. When people have nothing better to say, it's, "Youth, youth!" . . . (*Takes a pinch of snuff.*)

DORN (*takes the snuffbox from her and flings it into the bushes*). A vile habit! (*Pause.*) I think I hear music in the house. We'd better go in.

MASHA. Wait.

DORN. What is it?

MASHA. I wanted to tell you once again that . . . I long to talk. . . . (*Agitated.*) I don't care for my father . . . but I'm drawn to you. Somehow I feel I can trust you. . . . Help me. Help me or I'll do something stupid. I'll make a mockery of my life, ruin it . . . I just can't go on like this. . . .

DORN. What's wrong? How can I help?

MASHA. I'm suffering. No one, no one knows of my suffering! (*Laying her head on his chest, softly.*) I love Konstantin.

DORN. How hysterical they all are. How nervous! So much love. . . . O magical lake! (*Tenderly.*) But what can I do, my child? What? What?

Curtain

A C T I I

A croquet lawn. In the background, on the right, a house with a large veranda. On the left, the lake reflecting the sparkling sun. Flower beds. Midday. Hot. At the side of the croquet lawn in the shade of an old lime tree are ARKADINA, DORN, MASHA. *They are sitting on a bench.* DORN *has an open book on his knees.*

ARKADINA (*to* MASHA). Stand up. (*Both stand.*) Side by side. You're twenty-two, I'm almost twice your age. Yevgeny Sergeyich, which of us looks younger?

DORN. You, of course.

ARKADINA. There. . . . Now why is that so? Because I work, I express my emotions, I'm always on the go. And you stay put, you don't live. . . . I have a rule—don't look into the future. I never think about old age or death. What will be, will be.

MASHA. And I feel as if I was born long, long ago. I drag my life behind me like a gown with an endless train. . . . Often I have no desire to go on living. (*Sits.*) Of course, that's all nonsense. I ought to give myself a good shake, make a clean sweep.

DORN (*sings softly*). "Tell her my flowers . . ."

ARKADINA. I'm as correct as an Englishman. I keep myself fine tuned, as they say. I always dress and do my hair *comme il faut.* Would I leave the house in a dressing gown or with my hair uncombed? Never! That's why I've stayed young. I've never been a frump, never let myself go, like some women. . . . (*Strolls about the lawn, arms akimbo.*) There you are—graceful as a bird. I could play a girl of fifteen.

DORN. Hm, I might as well continue. (*Picks up the book.*) We left off at the flour dealer and the rats. . . .

ARKADINA. And the rats. Read on. (*Sits.*) But let me have it, I'll read. It's my turn. (*Takes the book and skims it.*) The rats. . . . Here we are. . . . (*Reads.*) "And it goes without saying that for society women to pamper novelists and lure them into their homes is as dangerous as a flour dealer breeding rats in his granaries. And yet they love them. When a woman has picked out a writer whom she wishes to capture, she lays siege with compliments, flattery, favors. . . ." Well, maybe the French, but we do nothing of the sort. We don't go by the book. In Russia, before she sets out to catch a writer, a woman is already head over heels in love with him. You don't have to look far, just take me and Trigorin. . . .

SORIN *enters, leaning on a cane,* NINA *at his side;* MEDVEDENKO, *behind them, pushing an empty wheelchair.*

SORIN (*in an affectionate tone one uses with children*). Yes? We're happy, aren't we? We're cheerful today, and so on and so forth? (*To his sister.*) We're happy! Papa and stepmother have gone off to Tver, and now we're free for three whole days.

NINA (*sits next to* ARKADINA *and embraces her*). I am happy! Now I'm all yours.

SORIN (*sits down in his wheelchair*). She's as pretty as a kitten today.

ARKADINA. Smartly dressed, intriguing. . . . That's very clever of you. (*Kisses* NINA.) But we mustn't praise you too much—it's bad luck. Where's Trigorin?

NINA. Down by the bathhouse, fishing.

ARKADINA. You'd think he'd be sick of it. (*About to continue reading.*)

NINA. What's that?

ARKADINA. Maupassant's "On the Water," my sweet. (*Reads a few lines to herself.*) Well, the rest is uninteresting and fake. (*Shuts the book.*) I'm worried. Tell me, what's wrong with my son? Why is he so moody and sullen? He spends entire days at the lake. I hardly ever see him.

MASHA. He's got something on his mind. (*To* NINA, *timidly.*) Please, read from his play!

NINA (*shrugging her shoulders*). You really want me to? It's so boring!

MASHA (*holding back her enthusiasm*). When Konstantin reads, his eyes blaze and his face turns pale. He has a beautiful, sad voice, and the bearing of a poet.

SORIN *snores.*

DORN. Sweet dreams!

ARKADINA. Petrusha!

SORIN. Huh?

ARKADINA. Are you asleep?

SORIN. Not at all. (*Pause.*)

ARKADINA. You're not taking any medicine, that's naughty of you, my dear.

SORIN. I'm willing, only our doctor here won't give me anything.

DORN. Medicine at the age of sixty!

SORIN. Even at sixty one wants to live.

DORN (*irritated*). Ugh! Well, take some valerian drops.

ARKADINA. I think it would do him good to go to some spa.

DORN. Well, he might go. And then again he might not.

ARKADINA. And what are we to make of that?

DORN. There's nothing to make of it. It's all quite clear. (*Pause.*)

MEDVEDENKO. Pyotr Nikolayevich should give up smoking.

SORIN. Ridiculous.

DORN. No, it isn't ridiculous. Tobacco and liquor rob you of your personality. After a cigar or a glass of vodka you're no longer Pyotr Nikolayevich, but Pyotr Nikolayevich plus somebody else. Your ego disintegrates and you see yourself as a third person— a "he."

SORIN (*laughing*). It's all very well for you to talk. You've lived your life, but what about me? I worked in the Department of Justice for twenty-eight years. But I haven't lived, haven't experienced anything, and so on and so forth. It's only natural, I very much want to live. You've had your fill and don't give a damn and that's why you have an itch for philosophy. But I want to live, so I drink sherry at dinner and smoke cigars. And that's all there is to it.

DORN. We ought to take life seriously. To go in for cures at the age of sixty and regret you didn't enjoy yourself enough when you were young—pardon me, but that's frivolous.

MASHA (*stands up*). It must be time for lunch. (*Walks indolently and listlessly.*) My leg's gone to sleep.. . . . (*Goes off.*)

DORN. She's off to down a couple of shots before lunch.

SORIN. She's unhappy in her personal life, the poor thing.

DORN. Empty words, Your Excellency.

SORIN. You reason like a man who's had too much of a good thing.

ARKADINA. Oh, what can be more boring than this sweet country boredom! It's hot, quiet, no one does anything, everyone chatters about ideas. . . . It's nice being with you, my friends, pleasant to listen to you, but . . . studying a part in a hotel room is a thousand times better!

NINA (*ecstatically*). Oh, yes! How well I understand you.

SORIN. Of course it's nicer in town. You sit in your study, your footman doesn't admit people unannounced, there's a telephone . . . cabs on the street and so on. . . .

DORN (*sings*). "Tell her my flowers . . ."

SHAMRAYEV *enters,* POLINA ANDREYEVNA *after him.*

SHAMRAYEV. Here they are. Good afternoon! (*Kisses* ARKADINA'S *hand, then* NINA'S.) Delighted to see you in good health. (*To* ARKADINA.) My wife tells me you intend to go to town with her today. Is that so?

ARKADINA. Yes, that's our intention.

SHAMRAYEV. Hm. . . . A first-rate idea, but how do you plan to get there, my esteemed lady? We're bringing in the rye today, all my men are busy. Which horses will you take, if I may ask?

ARKADINA. Horses? How in the world should I know!

SORIN. We have carriage horses.

SHAMRAYEV (*alarmed*). Carriage horses? And where am I to get collars for them? Tell me please, where am I to get the collars? Amazing! Incomprehensible! Most esteemed lady! Forgive me, I bend my knee before your talent, for you I'm prepared to sacrifice ten years of my life, but horses I can't give you!

ARKADINA. But if I must go? How queer!

SHAMRAYEV. Most esteemed lady! You have no idea what farming is all about!

ARKADINA (*flaring up*). The same old story! If that's how things stand I'm leaving for Moscow today. Have them hire horses for me in the village, or I'm going to the station by foot!

SHAMRAYEV (*flaring up*). In that case I quit! Find yourself another manager! (*Goes out.*)

ARKADINA. It's like this every summer. I come here every summer to be insulted! I'll never set foot here again! (*Goes out to the left, where the bathing house is situated; after a minute she passes into the house;* TRIGORIN, *with fishing rods and a pail, follows her.*)

SORIN (*angry*). This is impudence! This is the last straw! I'm sick and tired of it, and so on and so forth. Bring all the horses here immediately!

NINA (*to* POLINA ANDREYEVNA). To refuse Irina Arkadina, the famous actress! Isn't her every desire, her every whim, more important than all your farming? I just can't believe it.

POLINA ANDREYEVNA (*despairingly*). What can I do? Put yourself in my shoes—what can I do?

SORIN (*to* NINA). Let's go speak to my sister. . . . We'll beg her not to leave. Won't we now? (*Looking in the direction in which* SHAMRAYEV *left.*) Brute! Despot!

NINA (*preventing him from getting up*). Sit, sit. . . . We'll wheel you. . . . (*She and* MEDVEDENKO *wheel the chair.*) Oh, how awful!

SORIN. Yes, it's awful. . . . But he won't leave, I'll speak to him immediately.

They go off; only DORN *and* POLINA ANDREYEVNA *remain.*

DORN. People are tiresome. Actually someone should have chucked your husband out by the scruff of his neck. Now it'll all end with that old woman Pyotr Nikolayevich and his sister pleading for his forgiveness. Just wait and see!

POLINA ANDREYEVNA. He's even sent the carriage horses into the fields. Every day the same squabbles. If you only knew how it upsets me! It's making me sick—look, I'm trembling . . . I can't stand his coarseness. (*Imploring.*) Yevgeny, my dearest, my love, take me away. . . . Our time is passing, we're no longer young. If at least in the autumn of our lives we might stop dissembling and lying. . . . (*Pause.*)

DORN. I'm fifty-five years old, it's too late to change my ways.

POLINA ANDREYEVNA. I realize you're turning me down because there are other women you're intimate with. You can't very well live with all of them. I understand. Pardon me for boring you.

NINA *appears near the house, picking flowers.*

DORN. No, that's not so. . . .

POLINA ANDREYEVNA. Jealousy is making me miserable. Of course, you're a doctor. You can't avoid women. I understand. . . .

DORN (*to* NINA, *who approaches them*). How are they?

NINA. Irina Nikolayevna is crying and Pyotr Nikolayevich is having an attack of asthma.

DORN (*stands*). I'd better give both of them valerian drops. . . .

NINA (*gives him the flowers*). Please, these are for you!

DORN. *Merci bien.* (*Goes to the house.*)

POLINA ANDREYEVNA (*following him*). What pretty flowers! (*Near the house, in a muffled voice.*) Give me those flowers! Give me those flowers! (*Receiving them, she tears them to shreds and hurls them away. Both go into the house.*)

NINA (*alone*). How strange. A famous actress crying, and over such a trifle! And a celebrated writer, the darling of the public—they write about him in the newspapers, his photograph's for sale, he's been translated into foreign languages. Yet he spends his days fishing and goes into raptures when he catches two chubs. I always imagined that famous people were proud, unapproachable, contemptuous of the vulgar crowd. It was as if their fame and brilliance were their revenge on the world for putting rank and wealth above art. But here they are—crying, fishing, playing cards, laughing, and losing their tempers like everybody else. . . .

TREPLEV (*enters without a hat, carrying a gun and a dead sea gull*). You're alone?

NINA. Yes.

TREPLEV *lays the sea gull at her feet.*

NINA. What's this all about?

TREPLEV. I was so vile as to kill this sea gull today. I lay it at your feet.

NINA. What's the matter with you? (*She lifts the sea gull and gazes at it.*)

TREPLEV (*after a pause*). Soon I'll kill myself in the same way.

NINA. I no longer know you.

TREPLEV. Yes, since I stopped knowing you. Your feelings for me have changed, your eyes are cold. I'm in the way.

NINA. Lately you've become irritable, I can't make you out, you speak in symbols. I suppose this sea gull is also a symbol, but excuse me, I don't understand. . . . (*Lays the sea gull on the bench.*) I'm just too ordinary to understand you.

TREPLEV. It all began that evening my play flopped so stupidly. Women never forgive failure. I burned it, every last scrap. If you only knew how unhappy I am! Your coldness is terrifying, puzzling. It's as if I wakened to find that the lake had suddenly dried up or sunk into the earth. You just said you're too ordinary to understand me. What's there to understand? You didn't care for my play, you hold my inspiration in contempt, consider me a mediocrity, a nobody, like most people. . . . (*Stamping his foot.*) How well I understand, how well! It's as if a spike had been driven into my brain! And damn my vanity! Vanity which sucks my blood like a viper. . . . (*Sees* TRIGORIN, *who walks in reading a book.*) Here comes the real genius. He parades around like Hamlet, and with a book to boot. (*Mimicking.*) "Words, words, words. . . ." The star has not yet approached you and you're all smiles, your eyes have brightened in his rays. I won't get in your way. (*Goes out quickly.*)

TRIGORIN (*taking notes in a notebook*). Takes snuff and drinks vodka. . . . Always in black. The teacher is in love with her. . . .

NINA. Hello, Boris Alekseyevich!

TRIGORIN. Hello. Things have taken an unexpected turn. It seems we're leaving today. It's unlikely we'll ever see each other again. A pity. I don't often get the chance to meet young girls, young and interesting. I've already forgotten how it feels to be eighteen or nineteen, I can't picture it clearly. That's why in my stories the girls are usually artificial. I'd like to be in your shoes for an hour, to find out what makes you tick, and, in general, what sort of animal you are.

NINA. And I'd like to be in your shoes.

TRIGORIN. What for?

NINA. To find out how it feels to be a famous, talented writer. What is fame like? How does it affect you?

TRIGORIN. How does it affect me? I'd say, not at all. I've never given it any thought. (*Reflecting.*) There are two possibilities: either you're exaggerating my fame or it's not something one feels.

NINA. But when you read about yourself in the newspapers?

TRIGORIN. When they praise me, it's nice. And when they abuse me, I'm in a rotten mood for a day or two.

NINA. What a marvelous world you move in! How I envy you! People have such different destinies. Some just drag out their dull existence, unnoticed, all of them alike, all of them unhappy. Others, you for example—you're one in a million—you've been blessed with an interesting life, a dazzling and meaningful life. . . . You're a happy man. . . .

TRIGORIN. Me? (*Shrugging his shoulders.*) Hm. . . . You speak of fame, happiness, an interesting and splendid life, but for me all these pretty words are like so much marmalade, which I never eat. You're very young and very kind.

NINA. Your life is beautiful!

TRIGORIN. What's so especially beautiful about it? (*Looks at his watch.*) I ought to be working now. Excuse me, I have no time to . . . (*Laughs.*) You've touched my sore spot and here I go, getting flustered and a bit annoyed. All right, we'll talk. We'll talk about my beautiful, dazzling life. . . . Well, where do we start? (*Ponders briefly.*) There are fixed ideas—day and night some fellow thinks only about—well, let's say, the moon. I'm stuck with such a moon of my own. Day in and day out I'm haunted by a single thought and I can't shake it off—write, write, write. . . . I barely finish a story, and I have to write a second, then a third, then a fourth. . . . I write without letup, on the run, and I can't manage otherwise. What's so beautiful and splendid about that? Oh, what an absurd life! Here I am, together with you, I'm excited, and yet I can't forget for a moment that an unfinished story is hanging over my head. I glance at that cloud, it looks like a piano. I think to myself—mention in some story that a cloud floated by looking like a piano. There's a scent of heliotrope. I rush to make a mental note: cloying smell, widow's flower, use in describing a summer's evening. I catch my every sentence, every word—yours too—and rush to lock them up in my literary storehouse—maybe they'll come in handy! When I'm done working, I run off to the theater or go fishing. If I could only relax, forget myself, but nothing doing! A cannonball starts rolling around in my head—a new subject! It drives me to my desk—hurry, write, keep on writing. And it's always like that. I can't escape myself. I feel like a parasite feeding on my own life. For the sake of the honey I give someone out there, I'm stripping the pollen from my finest flowers, ripping them out of the ground, trampling their roots. Do I seem crazy to you? Do my friends and relatives treat me as if I were sane? "What are you writing? What are you going to give us next?"—the same old tune, over and over. My friends' interest in me, their praise and admiration, seem to me a hoax. They're leading me on as they would an invalid. I'm afraid any moment they'll steal up on me and cart me off to a madhouse, like the poor fellow in Gogol's story. And in my best years, when I was young and just starting out, writing was absolute torture. A beginning writer, especially when he has no luck, thinks he's clumsy, awkward, an odd man out. His nerves are on edge, at the point of snapping. He can't help tagging after the literary crowd, but nobody pays him any mind. Like a gambler gone broke, he's afraid to look people in the eye. My readers were strangers to me, but for some reason I imagined them as unfriendly and suspicious. I was afraid of the public, it terrified me. Every time it came to putting on a new play I thought the brunettes in the audience were hostile and the blondes cold and indifferent. How awful! And how painful!

NINA. But inspiration and the creative process must give you moments of great happiness?

TRIGORIN. Yes. While I'm writing, I enjoy it. I even enjoy reading proofs, but as soon as a work's in print I can't stomach it. I realize it's all wrong, a mistake, that I shouldn't have written it. I'm irritated, I feel rotten. . . . (*Laughing.*) And people read it and say: "Yes, charming, clever. . . . Charming, but a far cry from Tolstoy." Or: "A fine piece, but Turgenev's *Fathers and Sons* is better." And so on to my dying day—clever and charming, clever and charming—nothing more. And when I die my friends will pass my grave and say: "Here lies Trigorin. Not a bad writer, but Turgenev was better."

NINA. Excuse me, but I refuse to go along with you. You've merely been spoiled by success.

TRIGORIN. Success? What success? I've never liked myself. I don't like myself as a writer. The worst part is that I live in a sort of dream. Often I have no idea what it is that I'm writing. . . . I love this lake, the trees, the sky. I have a feel for nature, it fires me with inspiration I can't resist. But I'm not merely a painter of landscapes. I'm also a citizen. I love my country, my people. If I'm a writer, then it's my obligation to speak of the people, their sufferings, their future. I ought to write about science, about the rights of man and so on. And so I write about everything. I'm in a rush, driven from all sides, berated by everyone. I dash about like a fox tracked down by a pack of hounds. I see life and science moving farther and farther ahead, while I fall more and more behind, like a peasant late for his train. When all is said and done, I feel that all I'm able to do is landscapes, and as for the rest, I'm a fraud, a fraud to the marrow of my bones.

NINA. You're overworked. You don't have the time and you're not in a mood to appreciate how important you really are. So you're dissatisfied with yourself. But for others you're great and wonderful! If I were a writer of your stature, I'd gladly give my life to the people, but I would recognize that their only happiness is to rise to my level. They would harness themselves to my chariot.

TRIGORIN. A chariot. . . . Who am I—Agamemnon? (*Both smile.*)

NINA. For the happiness of a writer's or artist's life, I'd endure poverty, disillusionment, the hostility of those close to me. I'd live in a garret, eat nothing but black bread, suffer from dissatisfaction with myself, from consciousness of my imperfections, but in return I'd demand fame . . . genuine, sensational fame . . . (*Covers her face with her hands.*) My head's spinning. . . . Oh! . . .

ARKADINA (*calling from the house*). Boris!

TRIGORIN. They're calling me. I suppose it's to pack. But I don't feel like leaving. (*Gazes over the lake.*) Look—paradise! . . . How glorious!

NINA. Can you see the house and garden on the other shore?

TRIGORIN. Yes.

NINA. That was my mother's house. I was born there. I've spent all my life on this lake. I know every island.

TRIGORIN. It's lovely here! (*Seeing the sea gull.*) And what's this?

NINA. A sea gull. Konstantin killed it.

TRIGORIN. A beautiful bird. I really don't feel like leaving. Try and talk Irina into staying. (*Writes in his notebook.*)

NINA. What are you writing?

TRIGORIN. Oh, just taking notes. . . . A subject flashed through my head. . . . (*Puts the notebook away.*) A subject for a short story: A young girl lives all her life on the shore of a lake. She loves the lake, and is happy and free, like a sea gull. By chance a man comes, sees her, and having nothing better to do, destroys her. Here, like this sea gull. (*Pause.*)

ARKADINA (*appearing in a window*). Boris, where are you?

TRIGORIN. Coming! (*Goes, looking back at* NINA.) Well?

ARKADINA. We're staying. (TRIGORIN *enters the house.*)

NINA (*approaches the edge of the stage; after a moment of thought*). A dream!

Curtain

ACT III

The dining room of SORIN'S *house. Doors on the left and right. A sideboard. A cupboard for medicines. A table in the middle of the room. A trunk and cartons; signs of preparation for departure.* TRIGORIN *is having lunch;* MASHA *stands at the table.*

MASHA. I'm telling you this because you're a writer. You can make use of it. I'm being honest—had he seriously injured himself, I wouldn't have gone on living another minute. But I'm not a coward. I decided on the spot, I'm going to tear this love out of my heart, tear it out by the roots.

TRIGORIN. How are you going to do that?

MASHA. I'm getting married. To Medvedenko.

TRIGORIN. The schoolteacher?

MASHA. Yes.

TRIGORIN. I don't see the need for that.

MASHA. To love without hope, to spend years waiting. . . . But when I'm married there won't be time for love, new cares will deaden old feelings. Anyhow, it'll be a change. Shall we have another?

TRIGORIN. Won't that be one too much?

MASHA. Oh, come on! (*Fills his glass.*) Don't look at me like that. Women drink more often than you think. A few drink openly, like me, most on the sly. That's so. And it's always vodka or cognac. (*Clinks glasses.*) Cheers! You're a good man, I'm sorry our paths are parting. (*They drink.*)

TRIGORIN. I don't feel like leaving.

MASHA. Ask her to stay on.

TRIGORIN. No, she won't stay. Her son is behaving very tactlessly. First he shoots himself, and now they say he's going to challenge me to a duel. And what for? He sulks, sneers, preaches new forms. . . . But there's room for everybody, for the new as well as the old—why shove and push?

MASHA. Jealousy. But that's none of my business. (*Pause.* YAKOV *crosses from the right to the left with a trunk;* NINA *enters and stands by the window.*) My schoolteacher isn't very bright, but he's kind and he's poor, and he's crazy about me. I'm sorry for him. And I'm sorry for his mother. Well, let me wish you the best of everything. And don't think badly of me. (*Shakes his hand firmly.*) I'm very grateful for the interest you've taken in me. Send me your books, and be sure to add an inscription. Only don't write "Dear friend." Just "To Masha, who doesn't remember where she came from or why she's alive." Goodbye! (*Goes off.*)

NINA (*stretching out her hand to* TRIGORIN, *her fist clenched*). Odds or evens.

TRIGORIN. Evens.

NINA (*sighs*). Wrong. See, there's only one pea in my hand. I was trying my fortune—do I go into the theater or not? If only someone would advise me.

TRIGORIN. One can't give advice about these things. (*Pause.*)

NINA. We're parting and . . . perhaps we'll never meet again. Please, take this medallion to remember me by. I had your initials engraved . . . and on the other side, the title of your book. See— *Days and Nights.*

TRIGORIN. How thoughtful! (*Kisses the medallion.*) A charming present!

NINA. Think of me now and then.

TRIGORIN. I will. I will think of you on that sunny day— remember?—a week ago . . . you were wearing a white dress . . . we spoke . . . there was a white sea gull on the bench.

NINA (*pensively*). Yes, a sea gull. . . . (*Pause.*) We can't talk now, someone's coming. . . . Let me have two minutes of your time before you leave, please. . . . (*Goes off to the left.*)

As she leaves ARKADINA, SORIN *in a frock coat with a decoration (a star) pinned on it, and then* YAKOV, *busy with the luggage, enter from the right.*

ARKADINA. Stay at home, old man. Traipsing about with your rheumatism! (*To* TRIGORIN.) Who was that? Nina?

TRIGORIN. Yes.

ARKADINA. *Pardon*, we interrupted you. . . . (*Sits.*) I believe we're all packed. I'm worn to the bone.

TRIGORIN (*reads the inscription on the medallion*). *Days and Nights,* page 121, lines 11 and 12.

YAKOV (*clearing the table*). Pack your fishing rods, sir?

TRIGORIN. Yes, I'll be needing them. You can give the books away.

YAKOV. Yes, sir.

TRIGORIN (*to himself*). Page 121, lines 11 and 12. What on earth is in those lines? (*To* ARKADINA.) Do we have any copies of my books in the house?

ARKADINA. In my brother's study, the bookcase in the corner.

TRIGORIN. Page 121. . . . (*Goes off.*)

ARKADINA. Really, Petrusha, you ought to remain at home. . . .

SORIN. You're leaving, it'll be dreary without you.

ARKADINA. And what's doing in town?

SORIN. Nothing special, but still. . . . (*Laughs.*) There'll be the cornerstone ceremony for the town hall and that sort of thing. . . . I want to escape life in this fish-tank, if only for an hour or two. As it is I've been on the shelf too long, like some chewed-up cigarette holder. I've ordered horses for one o'clock. We'll set off together.

ARKADINA (*after a pause*). Stay here. Don't be bored and don't catch cold. Look after my son. Take care of him. Give him advice. (*Pause.*) Now that I'm leaving I'll never find out why he shot himself. I imagine the chief reason was jealousy. The sooner I take Trigorin away from here, the better.

SORIN. How should I put this? There were other reasons as well. It's only natural—an intelligent young man stuck in the country, in the . . . middle of nowhere, without money, without a position, no future to speak of. There's nothing for him to do. He's ashamed of his idleness and afraid of it. I love him dearly, he's attached to me, yet he feels he doesn't really belong here, that he's a sponger and parasite. It's only natural, his self-respect. . . .

ARKADINA. Oh, what a burden he is! (*Pondering.*) Maybe he should go into the civil service. . . .

SORIN (*whistles, then hesitantly*). I think, it would be best, if you . . . if you gave him some money. To start with, he ought to dress like a human being and so on. Just look at him—for the last three years he's been dragging himself around in the same miserable jacket. . . . (*Laughs.*) And it wouldn't hurt the boy to kick up his heels and have some fun. . . . Maybe travel abroad. . . . It wouldn't cost much.

ARKADINA. Well . . . I could buy him a suit, but as for going abroad. . . . No, right now I can't even manage a suit. (*Decisively.*) I have no money! (SORIN *laughs.*) No, I say!

SORIN (*whistles*). Quite so. . . . Forgive me, my dear sister, don't be angry. I believe you. . . . You're a generous woman.

ARKADINA (*tearfully*). I have no money!

SORIN. If I had some cash, of course I'd help him out, but I don't have anything, not a kopek. (*Laughs.*) My manager snatches up my pension and spends it on the farm, the cattle, the bees. Money down the drain. The bees die, the cows die, they never let me have horses. . . .

ARKADINA. Well, I do have something, but I'm an artist. My dresses alone are enough to ruin me.

SORIN. You're kind, a good person . . . I respect you . . . Yes. . . . There it goes again. (*Staggers.*) I'm dizzy. (*Grabs at the table.*) I feel sick and so on.

ARKADINA (*alarmed*). Petrusha! (*Trying to support him.*) Petrusha, my darling. . . . (*Cries out.*) Help! Help!

TREPLEV, *with a bandage on his head, and* MEDVEDENKO *enter.*

ARKADINA. He's fainted.

SORIN. I'm all right, it's nothing. . . . (*Smiles and drinks some water.*) It's passed . . . and so on. . . .

TREPLEV (*to his mother*). Don't be alarmed, mama, it's not serious. Uncle often has these fits now. (*To his uncle.*) You should lie down, uncle.

SORIN. For a minute or two, yes. . . . But I'm still going to town. . . . I'll rest a while and then go . . . it's only natural. . . . (*Goes out, leaning on his cane.*)

MEDVEDENKO (*taking him by the arm*). Here's a riddle for you: morning on all fours, noon on two legs, evening on three. . . .

SORIN (*laughs*). You said it! And at night flat on his back. Thank you, I can manage on my own. . . .

MEDVEDENKO. Now why stand on ceremony! . . . (*He and* SORIN *go out.*)

ARKADINA. The scare he put into me!

TREPLEV. Living in the country is bad for him. He gets depressed. Now, mama, if for once you showed a bit of generosity and loaned him a thousand or two, he could spend a year in town.

ARKADINA. I have no money. I'm an actress, not a banker. (*Pause.*)

TREPLEV. Mama, change my bandage for me. You do it so well.

ARKADINA (*takes some iodoform out of the medicine cabinet and a box of bandages*). The doctor's late.

TREPLEV. He said he'd be here by ten and it's already noon.

ARKADINA. Sit down. (*Removes the bandage from his head.*) It looks like a turban. Yesterday somebody in the kitchen asked about your nationality. It's almost all healed. Only a scratch left. (*Kisses him on the head.*) And you won't do bang-bang again when your mother is away?

TREPLEV. No, mama. That was a moment of terrible desperation, I couldn't control myself. It won't happen again. (*Kisses her hand.*) You have such capable hands. I remember, a very long time ago, you were still acting in the Imperial Theater—I was a child then—there was a brawl in our yard, a laundress from our building was badly beaten. Remember? They found her unconscious . . . you looked after her, brought her medicine, washed her children in a tub. You must remember?

ARKADINA. No. (*Puts on a new bandage.*)

TREPLEV. Two ballerinas lived in our building then. . . . They would drop in for coffee. . . .

ARKADINA. That I remember.

TREPLEV. They were very religious. (*Pause.*) Lately . . . these last few days, I find that my love for you is as tender and generous as when I was a child. Besides you I have no one. Only why . . . why has this man come between us?

ARKADINA. You don't understand him, Konstantin. He's an honorable man. . . .

TREPLEV. And yet when I was prepared to challenge him to a duel, his sense of honor didn't prevent him from playing the coward. He's skipping out. It's disgraceful, the way he's running!

ARKADINA. That's silly! I'm the one who's taking him away. Of course, our intimacy can't be pleasant for you. But you're sensible and intelligent. I have the right to demand that you respect my freedom.

TREPLEV. I do respect your freedom. But allow me my freedom to regard him my way. An honorable man! Here you and I are near to quarreling over him, and at this very moment he's somewhere in the living room or the garden laughing at us, feeding Nina with culture, trying his best to convince her he's a genius.

ARKADINA. You enjoy saying disagreeable things to me. I respect this man and ask you to refrain from speaking ill of him in my presence.

TREPLEV. And I don't respect him. You want me to think of him as a genius too, but, excuse me, I can't lie. His books make me sick.

ARKADINA. You're jealous. People with pretensions instead of talent can only denigrate real talent. Small comfort in that!

TREPLEV (*ironically*). Real talent! (*Furiously.*) If it comes to that, I'm more talented than the lot of you lumped together! (*Tears the bandage from his head.*) You hacks with your shopworn conventions have seized the upper hand in the arts. You imagine only what you do is legitimate and genuine. Everything else you stifle and crush! I refuse to acknowledge you! Not you or him!

ARKADINA. Decadent! . . .

TREPLEV. Go back to your precious little theater and perform in those trivial, vapid plays!

ARKADINA. I've never acted in such plays. Leave me alone! You're incapable of writing even a second-rate vaudeville sketch. All you are is a petty bourgeois from Kiev! Parasite!

TREPLEV. Miser!

ARKADINA. Brat! (TREPLEV *sits down and silently weeps.*) Nonentity! (*Walking up and down in agitation.*) Don't cry. You mustn't cry. . . . (*She cries.*) Don't . . . (*Kisses him on his forehead, his cheeks, his head.*) My dear child, forgive me . . . forgive your sinful mother. Forgive a poor, unhappy woman.

TREPLEV (*embraces her*). If you only knew! I've lost everything. She doesn't love me, I can't write any more . . . all my hopes have gone up in smoke. . . .

ARKADINA. Don't despair. . . . Everything will work out. I'll take him away, she'll love you again. (*Wipes away his tears.*) Enough now. There, we've already made up.

TREPLEV (*kissing her hand*). Yes, mama.

ARKADINA (*tenderly*). Make it up with him too. There's no need for a duel . . . that's so, isn't it?

TREPLEV. All right. . . . Only don't make me spend time with him, mama. It's painful for me . . . more than I can take. (TRIGORIN *enters.*) Here he is . . . I'm going. (*Hastily puts away the medicines in the medicine chest.*) The doctor will bandage me.

TRIGORIN (*perusing a book*). Page 121 . . . lines 11 and 12. . . . Here we are. . . . (*Reads.*) "If you ever have need of my life, come and take it."

TREPLEV *picks up the bandage from the floor and goes out.*

ARKADINA (*looking at her watch*). The horses will be here soon.

TRIGORIN (*to himself*). "If you ever have need of my life, come and take it."

ARKADINA. I trust you're all packed?

TRIGORIN (*impatiently*). Yes, yes. . . . (*Musing.*) Why do I feel sadness in this appeal of an innocent heart? It wrings my heart. . . . "If you ever have need of my life, come and take it." (*To* ARKADINA.) Let's stay another day! (ARKADINA *shakes her head to indicate* "no.") We're staying!

ARKADINA. My dear, I know what's keeping you here. But show some self-control. You're a bit intoxicated, sober up!

TRIGORIN. And you be sober too, be sensible and reasonable. I'm asking you to look upon all this as a true friend. . . . (*Presses her hand.*) You're capable of sacrifice. . . . Be a friend, give me my freedom. . . .

ARKADINA (*in extreme agitation*). Are you so infatuated?

TRIGORIN. I'm drawn to her! Maybe it's just what I need.

ARKADINA. The love of a provincial girl? How little you know yourself!

TRIGORIN. Sometimes people sleep on their feet. Here, I'm speaking to you and it's as if I'm asleep and dreaming of her. . . . Sweet, wonderful dreams have cast a spell over me. . . . Set me free.

ARKADINA (*trembling*). No, I won't. . . . I'm an ordinary woman, you can't talk to me like this. . . . Don't torture me, Boris. . . . It frightens me. . . .

TRIGORIN. If you wished you could be more than ordinary. Young love, charming, poetical, sweeping one away into a world of dreams—that alone can give happiness on this earth of ours! I've never known a love like that. . . . When I was young I didn't have the time, what with knocking on the doors of editors, struggling against poverty. . . . And here it is, love, it's come at last. I find it fascinating. . . . What's the sense in running from it?

ARKADINA (*furious*). You're out of your mind!

TRIGORIN. So be it.

ARKADINA. You've all conspired to torment me today! (*Weeps.*)

TRIGORIN (*clutching his head*). You don't understand! You don't want to understand!

ARKADINA. Am I really so old and ugly that you can speak to me of other women without embarrassment? (*Embraces and kisses him.*) Oh, you've lost your senses! My beautiful, wonderful man. . . . You're the last page in my life! (*Falls to her knees.*) My joy, my pride, my happiness. . . . (*Embraces his knees.*) If you abandon me, even for an hour, I won't get over it, I'll go mad. My splendid, marvelous man, my master. . . .

TRIGORIN. Someone may come in. (*Helps her to get up.*)

ARKADINA. Let them. I'm not ashamed of my love for you. (*Kisses his hand.*) My treasure, my daredevil, you want to let yourself go, but I won't have it, I won't set you free. . . . (*Laughs.*) You're mine . . . mine. . . . This forehead is mine, these eyes are mine, your beautiful hair, as soft as silk, is mine. . . . You're all mine. You're so talented, intelligent, the best of our contemporary writers, Russia's only hope. . . . Sincerity, simplicity, freshness, good-natured humor—that's you! With a stroke of the pen you can convey the essence of a person or landscape, your characters are so alive. Oh, reading you is ecstasy! Do you think I'm laying it on thick? That this is mere flattery? Then look me in the eyes . . . look. . . . Are these the eyes of a liar? I'm the only one who can appreciate you, who tells you the truth, my precious, my wonderful lover. . . . Are you going with me? You won't abandon me, will you? . . .

TRIGORIN. I have no will of my own. . . . Never have. . . . Flabby, feeble, always submissive—can that really appeal to a woman? Take me, sweep me away from here, only don't let me out of your sight. . . .

ARKADINA (*to herself*). Now he's mine. (*Free and easy as if nothing had happened*). But if you feel like it, you can stay. I'll go by myself, and you can come in a week. After all, what's the rush?

TRIGORIN. No, we'd better go together.

ARKADINA. Suit yourself. Together then. . . . (*Pause.* TRIGORIN *jots something down in his notebook.*) What are you doing?

TRIGORIN. I heard a nice phrase this morning: "Forest of the Maids." It may come in handy. (*Stretches.*) So we're off? Back on the road—railroad cars, stations, snack bars, meat loaf, endless chatter. . . .

SHAMRAYEV (*entering*). I have the sad honor to announce that the horses are ready. Esteemed lady, it's time to start for the station. The train is due at five minutes past two. Be so kind, Irina Nikolayevna, don't forget to make some inquiries—what is the actor Suzdaltsev doing these days? Is he alive and well? We used to have a drink or two together. . . . He was incomparable in *The Mail Robbery.* . . . As I recall, the tragedian Izmaylov worked with him in Elizavetograd, also a remarkable personality. . . . No need to hurry, esteemed lady, we have five minutes. Once they were playing conspirators in a melodrama. When they were caught redhanded, they were supposed to say, "We've fallen into a trap," and Izmaylov says, "We've fallen into the crap." . . . (*Roars with laughter.*) "Into the crap."

While he is speaking YAKOV *busies himself with the luggage, a* MAID *brings* ARKADINA *her hat, cloak, umbrella, and gloves; they all help* ARKADINA *put on her things. The* COOK *looks in from the door on the left and after a while enters hesitantly.* POLINA ANDREYEVNA *enters; then* SORIN *and* MEDVEDENKO.

POLINA ANDREYEVNA (*carrying a basket*). Some plums for the road. . . . They're very sweet. You may want a snack. . . .

ARKADINA. You're very kind, Polina.

POLINA ANDREYEVNA. Goodbye, my dear! If anything wasn't as you wished, I'm truly sorry. (*Weeps.*)

ARKADINA (*embraces her*). Everything was fine, just fine. Only you mustn't cry.

POLINA ANDREYEVNA. Our time is passing!

ARKADINA. What can we do?

SORIN (*in a greatcoat with a cape, a hat, and cane, enters from the door on the left and walks across the room*). Sister, it's time, we don't want to be late, and so on. I'm getting into the carriage. (*Goes off.*)

MEDVEDENKO. And I'll walk over to the station . . . to see you off. I'll be there in a jiffy. . . . (*Goes off.*)

ARKADINA. Goodbye, my darlings. . . . If we're alive and well, we'll see each other again next summer. . . . (*The* MAID, COOK, *and* YAKOV *kiss her hand.*) Don't forget me. (*Handing the* COOK *a ruble.*) Here's a ruble for the three of you.

COOK. Thank you kindly, ma'am. A good trip to you! We appreciate your generosity!

YAKOV. God bless you!

SHAMRAYEV. A letter would cheer us up! Goodbye, Boris Alekseyevich!

ARKADINA. Where is Konstantin? Tell him I'm on my way. I must say goodbye. So, think well of me. (*To* YAKOV.) I gave a ruble to the cook. It's for the three of you.

All go out on the right. The stage is empty. Behind the scene sounds of leavetaking. The MAID *comes back to take the basket of plums from the table and goes out again.*

TRIGORIN (*returning*). I forgot my cane. It must be on the terrace. (*Goes, and at the door on the left runs into* NINA *entering.*) Ah, it's you! We're leaving. . . .

NINA. I had a feeling we'd meet once more. (*Excited.*) Boris Alekseyevich, I've come to a final decision, the die is cast. I'm going on the stage. Tomorrow I won't be here. I'm leaving my father, turning my back on everything, and starting a new life. . . . I'm also going . . . to Moscow. We'll run into each other there.

TRIGORIN (*looking round*). Stay at the Slavyansky Bazaar. . . . Let me know the moment you arrive. . . . Molchanovka Street, at Grokholsky's. . . . I have to hurry. . . . (*Pause.*)

NINA. Just one moment more. . . .

TRIGORIN (*in a whisper*). You're so lovely. . . . Oh, what happiness! To think we'll meet soon! (*She lays her head on his chest.*) Once more I'll see these lovely eyes, your tender smile, beautiful beyond words . . . this gentle face, its look of angelic purity. . . . My darling. . . . (*A prolonged kiss.*)

Curtain

ACT IV

Between Act III *and* Act IV *two years have passed. One of the living rooms in* SORIN'S *house, converted into a study for* KONSTANTIN TREPLEV. *On the right and left, doors leading to other rooms. In the center, a glass door to the terrace. Besides the usual living-room furniture, a desk in the right corner, a Turkish sofa near the left-hand door, a bookcase, books on the windowsills, on chairs. Evening. A single shaded lamp is lit. Half dark. Rustling of trees and the wind howling in the chimneys. A* WATCHMAN *taps.* MEDVEDENKO *and* MASHA *enter.*

MASHA (*calling*). Konstantin! Konstantin! (*Looking round.*) No one's here. The old man keeps asking, "Where's Kostya, where's Kostya?" . . . He can't live without him. . . .

MEDVEDENKO. He's afraid of being alone. (*Listening.*) Terrible weather. Two days of it now.

MASHA (*turns up the lamp*). There are waves on the lake. Gigantic waves.

MEDVEDENKO. It's pitch-dark in the garden. We ought to tell them to tear down that stage. It looms there, naked and ugly as a skeleton. The curtain flaps in the wind. When I passed by last night, I thought I heard someone crying.

MASHA. You're at it again! . . . (*Pause.*)

MEDVEDENKO. Let's go home, Masha!

MASHA (*shakes her head*). I'm staying overnight.

MEDVEDENKO (*imploring*). Masha, please come home! The baby must be hungry.

MASHA. Nonsense. Matryona will feed him. (*Pause.*)

MEDVEDENKO. I'm sorry for the child. It's the third night without his mother.

MASHA. You're a bore. Before you at least spouted ideas. Now it's "baby, home, baby, home"—that's all I hear from you.

MEDVEDENKO. Let's go, Masha!

MASHA. Go yourself!

MEDVEDENKO. Your father won't give me horses.

MASHA. He will. Just ask.

MEDVEDENKO. All right, I'll ask. You'll come home tomorrow?

MASHA *(taking snuff)*. Fine, tomorrow. What a pest you are. . . .

TREPLEV *and* POLINA ANDREYEVNA *enter.* TREPLEV *is carrying cushions and a blanket,* POLINA ANDREYEVNA *sheets and pillow cases. They put them on the sofa, and then* TREPLEV *goes to his desk and sits down.*

MASHA. What is this for, mama?

POLINA ANDREYEVNA. Pyotr Nikolayevich asked to have his bed made near Konstantin.

MASHA. Let me . . . *(Makes up the bed.)*

POLINA ANDREYEVNA *(sighing)*. Old people are like children. . . . *(Goes to the desk and, leaning on her elbow, looks at a manuscript. Pause.)*

MEDVEDENKO. Well, I'll be on my way. Goodbye, Masha. *(Kisses his wife's hand.)* Good night, mother. *(Attempts to kiss his mother-in-law's hand.)*

POLINA ANDREYEVNA *(irritated)*. What now? If you're going, go.

MEDVEDENKO. Good night, Konstantin Gavrilovich.

TREPLEV *extends his hand without speaking;* MEDVEDENKO *leaves.*

POLINA ANDREYEVNA *(looking at the manuscript)*. No one would have guessed that you would turn out to be a real writer, Kostya. And now the magazines have started sending you money—we can thank God for that. *(Runs her hand through his hair.)* And you've become handsome. . . . Sweet Kostya, good Kostya, show some affection to my Masha! . . .

MASHA *(making up the bed)*. Leave him alone, mama.

POLINA ANDREYEVNA *(to TREPLEV)*. She's a nice girl. *(Pause.)* Kostya, a woman doesn't ask for much, just a kind look. I know from my own experience.

TREPLEV *gets up from the desk and leaves without speaking.*

MASHA. Now you've made him angry. You just had to keep after him!

POLINA ANDREYEVNA. I feel so sorry for you, Masha.

MASHA. That's all I need!

POLINA ANDREYEVNA. My heart aches for you. I see what's going on, I understand.

MASHA. It's all idiotic. Unrequited love—you find that only in novels. A lot of hogwash! You can't let yourself go to pieces standing by the seashore waiting for the weather to turn. . . . Once love has planted itself in your heart, you have to pluck it out. They've promised to transfer my husband to another district. When we move there, I'll forget . . . I'll rip love out of my heart by the roots.

A melancholy waltz plays from another room.

POLINA ANDREYEVNA. Kostya is playing. He must be depressed.

MASHA (*noiselessly dances a few waltz steps*). The trick is not to have to see him, mama. If they only would give my Semyon his transfer. Believe me, I'll forget him in a month. Anyhow it's all nonsense.

The door on the left opens; DORN *and* MEDVEDENKO *wheel in* SORIN *in his wheelchair.*

MEDVEDENKO. I have six little ones at home now. And flour is up to four kopeks a kilogram.

DORN. Yes, it's a tight squeeze.

MEDVEDENKO. You can afford to laugh. You're rolling in money.

DORN. Money? Thirty years of a busy medical practice, my friend, I was at it night and day—my life wasn't my own. In all that time I managed to stash away some two thousand rubles. And not too long ago I went through that on a holiday abroad. I have nothing.

MASHA (*to her husband*). You're still here?

MEDVEDENKO (*guiltily*). What am I to do if they won't give me horses?

MASHA (*with bitter annoyance, in a low voice*). I can't bear the sight of you!

The wheelchair stops in the left side of the room; POLINA

ANDREYEVNA, MASHA, *and* DORN *sit beside it;* MEDVEDENKO *sadly walks off to the side.*

DORN. But how many changes you've made! You've turned the living room into a study.

MASHA. Konstantin finds it convenient to work here. When he feels like it he can go out into the garden and be alone with his thoughts. (*The* WATCHMAN *taps.*)

SORIN. Where's my sister?

DORN. Off to meet Trigorin at the station. She'll be back soon.

SORIN. Since you thought it necessary to send for my sister, I must be seriously ill. (*Falls silent.*) It's a queer thing, I'm seriously ill and they don't give me any medicine.

DORN. What would you like? Valerian drops? Quinine? Mineral water?

SORIN. Here we go, philosophy again! Oh, what a nuisance! (*Nodding toward the sofa.*) Is that made up for me?

POLINA ANDREYEVNA. Yes, Pyotr Nikolayevich.

SORIN. Thank you.

DORN (*sings*). "The moon floats in the evening sky. . . ."

SORIN. I'd like to give Kostya a subject for a short story. Call it, "The Man Who Wished," "*L'homme qui a voulu.*" In my youth I wished to become a writer—and I didn't. I wished to speak well— and I spoke abominably. (*Mimicking himself:*) "And so on and so forth, and maybe yes and maybe no" . . . I'd try to make sense of it, wrap it all up into a neat package, until I broke into a sweat. I wished to get married—and I never married. I wished to live in the city—and here I am, ending my life in the country, and so on and so forth.

DORN. He wished to reach the rank of state councillor—and he made it.

SORIN (*laughing*). That I never had an itch for. It happened on its own.

DORN. To be dissatisfied with life at the age of sixty-two is not very gracious.

SORIN. You're as stubborn as a mule! Don't you understand, I want to live!

DORN. That's frivolous. According to the laws of nature every life must come to an end.

SORIN. You talk like a man whose belly is full. You're satisfied with yourself and that's why you're indifferent to life, nothing matters to you. But when it comes to dying, you too will be terrified.

DORN. The fear of death is an animal fear. . . . One must overcome it. It's reasonable only for believers in an eternal life in terror of their sins. But in the first place, you're a nonbeliever, and in the second—what kind of sins do you have to worry about? You were a drudge in the Department of Justice for twenty-five years— that's the long and short of it.

SORIN (*laughs*). Twenty-eight. . . .

TREPLEV *enters and sits on a stool at* SORIN'S *feet.* MASHA *never takes her eyes off him.*

DORN. We're keeping Konstantin from his work.

TREPLEV. No, it's all right. (*Pause.*)

MEDVEDENKO. Allow me to ask, doctor, what is your favorite foreign city?

DORN. Genoa.

TREPLEV. Why Genoa?

DORN. The wonderful crowds in the streets. Leave your hotel in the evening and the street is jammed with people. You wander aimlessly, zigzagging through the crowd, living its life, mentally merging with it, until you start believing there might really be a single world soul. Like the thing Nina Zarechnaya performed in your play. By the way, where is she now? How is she getting along?

TREPLEV. Fine, I suppose.

DORN. I hear she's been leading a somewhat unusual life. What's that all about?

TREPLEV. It's a long story, doctor.

DORN. Then make it short. (*Pause.*)

TREPLEV. She ran away from home and took up with Trigorin. You know about that?

DORN. Yes.

TREPLEV. She had a child. The child died. Trigorin cooled toward her and went back to his old attachment, as might have been expected. Not that he ever really gave up his former tie. In his spineless way he contrived to have his cake and eat it too. As far as I can make out, Nina's personal life is a complete disaster.

DORN. And the stage?

TREPLEV. Even worse, it seems. She made her debut in a summer theater near Moscow, and then went off to the provinces. All that time I never lost sight of her, wherever she went I trailed after. She always took the lead roles, but she acted crudely, without taste, wailing, gesturing violently. There were moments when she gave out a talented shriek or died with talent, but they were only moments.

DORN. Then she does have talent?

TREPLEV. Hard to tell. I suppose she does. I saw her but she didn't want to see me. The maid at the hotel wouldn't let me in. I appreciated the mood she was in and didn't insist. (*Pause.*) What else? Later, after I returned home, letters came—warm, intelligent, interesting letters. She didn't complain, but I felt that she was profoundly unhappy. Every line spoke of sick, strained nerves. And her mind was a bit unhinged. She signed her letters "Sea gull." In Pushkin's "The Mermaid" the miller says he's a raven, and she kept insisting she's a sea gull. Now she's here.

DORN. What do you mean, here?

TREPLEV. In town, at the inn. She's been there for five days now. I went over, Masha went too, but she won't see anyone. Medvedenko believes he saw her in the fields yesterday afternoon, about a mile from here.

MEDVEDENKO. Yes, I saw her. She was walking toward town. I bowed to her and asked why she doesn't visit us. She said she would.

TREPLEV. She won't. (*Pause.*) Her father and stepmother won't have anything to do with her. They've set watchmen everywhere to keep her from coming near the house. (*Walks with the doctor to the desk.*) How easy it is to be a philosopher on paper, doctor, and how hard in life!

SORIN. She was a charming girl.

DORN. What's that?

SORIN. A charming girl. For a while even State Councillor Sorin was in love with her.

DORN. Our old Lovelace. (SHAMRAYEV'S *laugh is heard from offstage.*)

POLINA ANDREYEVNA. They must be back from the station. . . .

TREPLEV. Yes, I hear mother.

ARKADINA, TRIGORIN, *after them* SHAMRAYEV, *enter.*

SHAMRAYEV (*entering*). We're all getting old, we're weather-beaten from exposure to the forces of nature, but you, my esteemed lady, are forever young . . . you're wearing a bright blouse, you're lively . . . graceful. . . .

ARKADINA. You only want to bring me bad luck with your flattery, you tedious man!

TRIGORIN (*to* SORIN). How are you, Pyotr Nikolayevich? Still ailing? That's no way to behave! (*Noticing* MASHA, *warmly.*) Masha!

MASHA. You remember me? (*Shakes his hand.*)

TRIGORIN. Married?

MASHA. For a long time now.

TRIGORIN. Happy? (*Bows to* DORN *and* MEDVEDENKO, *then hesitantly approaches* TREPLEV.) Your mother says you've forgotten the past and are no longer angry. (TREPLEV *holds out his hand.*)

ARKADINA (*to her son*). Boris has brought the magazine with your new story.

TREPLEV (*taking the magazine, to* TRIGORIN). Thank you. That's very good of you. (*They sit.*)

TRIGORIN. Your admirers send their best wishes. . . . They're very interested in you in Moscow and Petersburg, always asking about you: what's he like, how old is he, does he have blond or brown hair? For some reason everyone takes you for an older man. And no one knows your real name since you publish under a pseudonym. You're as mysterious as the Iron Mask.

TREPLEV. Will you be staying long?

TRIGORIN. No, I think I'm going to Moscow tomorrow. Have to. I'm in a rush to finish a story and I promised something for an anthology. In a word—the same old business!

While they are talking, ARKADINA *and* POLINA ANDREYEVNA *place a card table in the middle of the room and open it.* SHAMRAYEV *lights candles and arranges chairs. A lotto game is brought from the bookcase.*

TRIGORIN. This weather hasn't given me a friendly welcome. A cruel wind out there. Tomorrow morning, if it dies down, I'll go to the lake for some fishing. By the way, I ought to see the garden and that spot where your play was performed. Remember? I've got an idea for a story. It's taken shape, and I only have to refresh my memory of the setting.

MASHA (*to her father*). Papa, please let my husband have a horse! He has to go home.

SHAMRAYEV (*mimicking her*). A horse . . . has to go home. . . . (*Sternly.*) You can see for yourself—they've just been to the station. We can't be driving them out again.

MASHA. But there are other horses. . . . (*Seeing that her father does not respond, waves her hand in resignation.*) Try and talk to you. . . .

MEDVEDENKO. I can walk, Masha. Really. . . .

POLINA ANDREYEVNA (*sighing*). Walk, in such weather. . . . (*Sits down at the card table.*) Come, ladies and gentlemen. . . .

MEDVEDENKO. Really, it's only four miles. . . . Good night! . . . (*Kisses his wife's hand.*) Good night, mama. (*His mother-in-law reluctantly holds out her hand for him to kiss.*) I wouldn't have bothered anyone if not for the child. . . . (*Bows to all.*) Good night. . . . (*Goes out with a guilty step.*)

SHAMRAYEV. He can go by foot. He's no general.

POLINA ANDREYEVNA (*taps on the table*). Please. There's no time to waste, they'll soon be calling us for supper. (SHAMRAYEV, MASHA, *and* DORN *sit at the card table.*)

ARKADINA (*to* TRIGORIN). When the long autumn evenings come, they play lotto here. Look, it's our old lotto set, mother played with us when we were children. Won't you try a game before supper? (*She and* TRIGORIN *sit at the table.*) It's dull but not so bad once you're used to it. (*Hands out three cards to everyone.*)

TREPLEV (*turning the pages of the magazine*). He's read his own story and hasn't even cut the pages of mine. (*Puts the magazine on the desk and makes for the door on the left; passing his mother, kisses her on the head.*)

ARKADINA. And what about you, Kostya?

TREPLEV. Sorry, I don't feel like it . . . I'm going. (*Goes out.*)

ARKADINA. The stake is ten kopeks. Put it down for me, doctor.

DORN. All right.

MASHA. Has everyone placed their bets? I'll begin. . . . Twenty-two!

ARKADINA. I have it.

MASHA. Three!

DORN. Yes.

MASHA. Do you have three? Eight! Eighty-one! Ten!

SHAMRAYEV. Not so fast.

ARKADINA. The reception I had in Kharkov! Good Lord, my head is still spinning!

MASHA. Thirty-four!

A melancholy waltz is played offstage.

ARKADINA. The students gave me an ovation . . . three baskets of flowers, two wreaths and this. . . . (*Unfastens a brooch from her chest and tosses it on the table.*)

SHAMRAYEV. Yes, that's really something. . . .

MASHA. Fifty!

DORN. Fifty on the dot?

ARKADINA. I wore a marvelous outfit. . . . Say what you will, but I know how to dress.

POLINA ANDREYEVNA. Kostya is playing the piano. The poor boy's depressed.

SHAMRAYEV. The papers have been raking him over the coals.

MASHA. Seventy-seven!

ARKADINA. As if that were worth noticing.

TRIGORIN. He has no luck. He just can't hit upon a style of his own. There's something strange and vague about his work, at times it's almost like delirium. Not a single living character.

MASHA. Eleven!

ARKADINA (*looking round at* SORIN). Petrusha, are you bored? (*Pause.*) He's asleep.

DORN. The state councillor sleeps.

MASHA. Seven! Ninety!

TRIGORIN. If I lived on an estate like this, by a lake, do you think I'd write? I'd fight down that obsession of mine and do nothing but fish.

MASHA. Twenty-eight!

TRIGORIN. To land a perch or a bass—what bliss!

DORN. Well, I believe in Konstantin. There's something to him! Yes, there's something to him. He thinks imaginatively, his stories are colorful, vivid. They move me deeply. Only it's a shame he has no definite purpose. He creates an impression, that's all, and impressions won't take you far. Irina, are you pleased that your son is a writer?

ARKADINA. Can you believe it? I haven't read a line of his yet. There's never any time.

MASHA. Twenty-six.

TREPLEV *enters quietly and goes over to his desk.*

SHAMRAYEV (*to* TRIGORIN). Boris Alexeyevich, we still have that thing of yours.

TRIGORIN. What thing?

SHAMRAYEV. Konstantin Gavrilovich once shot a sea gull, and you told me to have it stuffed.

TRIGORIN. I don't remember. (*Reflecting.*) I don't remember!

MASHA. Sixty-six! One!

TREPLEV (*flings open the window and listens*). How dark it is! I don't know why I feel so uneasy.

ARKADINA. Kostya, shut the window, you'll let in a draft. (TREPLEV *closes the window.*)

MASHA. Eighty-eight!

TRIGORIN. Ladies and gentlemen, the game is mine!

ARKADINA (*cheerfully*). Bravo! Bravo!

SHAMRAYEV. Bravo!

ARKADINA. That man has luck in everything. (*Stands.*) And now let's have a bite. Our great man hasn't eaten today. After supper we'll continue. (*To her son.*) Kostya, leave your manuscripts, come to supper.

TREPLEV. I don't feel like it, mama. I'm not hungry.

ARKADINA. As you like. (*Wakes* SORIN.) Petrusha, supper time! (*Takes* SHAMRAYEV *by the arm.*) Let me tell you about my reception in Kharkov. . . .

POLINA ANDREYEVNA *puts out the candles on the table, then she and* DORN *wheel out* SORIN'S *chair. All leave by the door on the left.* TREPLEV *remains at his desk, alone onstage.*

TREPLEV (*settling down to write, runs through what he has already written*). I spoke so much about new forms, and now I feel myself slipping into a rut. (*Reads.*) "The placard on the wall proclaimed. . . ." "A pale face in its frame of dark hair. . . ." Proclaimed, frame of dark hair . . . that's feeble. (*Crosses out.*) I'll pick it up where the sound of rain wakens the hero and throw the rest out. The description of the moonlit night is long and artificial. Trigorin has worked out his tricks, it's easy as pie for him. . . . He has the neck of a broken bottle glittering on a dam and a mill wheel casting a black shadow—and there's your moonlit night. And I have "tremulous light, the gentle flickering of the stars, the distant strains of a piano dying away in the silent aromatic air. . . ." Painful. . . . (*Pause.*) Yes, I'm becoming more and more convinced it isn't a question of old and new forms. We have to write not thinking about forms at all, write because it springs freely from our inner being. (*A tapping at the window closest to the desk.*) What's that? (*Looks out the window.*) I can't make anything out. . . . (*Opens the glass door and looks out into the garden.*) Someone ran down the steps. (*Calls out.*) Who's out there? (*Goes out. Can be heard walking quickly along the terrace; after a half-minute returns with* NINA ZARECHNAYA.) Nina! Nina! It's you! . . . you . . . I knew you'd come. All day my heart ached for you so. (*Takes her hat and cape.*) Oh, my sweet, my precious, you've come! We mustn't cry, no crying now.

NINA. There's someone here.

TREPLEV. There's no one.

NINA. Lock the doors, or they'll barge in.

TREPLEV. They won't.

NINA. I know Irina Nikolayevna is here. Lock the doors. . . .

TREPLEV (*locks the door on the right and goes to the door on the left*). There's no lock on this one. I'll put a chair up against it. (*Places an armchair against the door.*) Don't worry, no one will come in.

NINA (*gazing intently into his face*). Let me look at you. (*Looking round.*) It's warm, cozy. . . . This used to be the living room. Have I changed much?

TREPLEV. Yes. . . . You've grown thin, your eyes are larger. Nina, it's strange seeing you. Why didn't you let me visit you? Why haven't you come till now? I know you've been here for almost a week. . . . I went over several times a day, stood under your window like a beggar.

NINA. I was afraid you'd hate me. Every night I dream you look at me but don't recognize me. If you only knew! From the moment I arrived, I've been walking . . . by the lake. Often I passed near your house but couldn't bring myself to go in. Let's sit down. (*They sit.*) We'll sit and talk. It's nice here, warm and cozy. . . . Do you hear the wind? There's a line in Turgenev: "Happy the man who on nights like these has a roof over his head and a warm nook." I'm a sea gull. . . . No, that's not it. (*Rubs her forehead.*) What was I saying? Oh, yes . . . Turgenev. . . . "And God help all homeless wanderers." . . . I'm all right. (*Sobs.*)

TREPLEV. Nina, you're crying again . . . Nina!

NINA. I'm all right, it does me good . . . I haven't cried for two years. Late last night I went to the garden to see if our theater was there. It's still standing. I cried for the first time in two years. I breathed more easily and my heart was calm. See, I'm not crying any more. (*Takes his hand.*) So, you've become a writer. . . . You're a writer, I'm an actress. . . . We've entered the whirlpool. . . . Once I lived joyously, like a child—I would wake up in the morning singing. I loved you, I dreamed of fame, and now? Early tomorrow I'm going to Yelets third-class . . . in a car with peasants. And in Yelets our cultured businessmen will pester me with their proposals. . . . A shabby life!

TREPLEV. Why Yelets?

NINA. I've taken an engagement for the winter. . . . It's time I was on my way.

TREPLEV. Nina, I cursed you, hated you, tore up your letters and photographs, but every moment I knew my soul was bound to yours forever. I can't stop loving you, Nina. Ever since I lost you, just when my work first saw print, my life has been unbearable—I'm suffering. . . . My youth was suddenly swept from under my feet. I feel as if I've been living for ninety years. I call out to you, I kiss the ground you walk on, your face appears to me everywhere, that tender smile which brightened the best years of my life. . . .

NINA (*distractedly*). Why do you talk like that, why?

TREPLEV. I'm alone, warmed by no one's affection, cold, as if buried in a cellar. Whatever I write is dry, stale, gloomy. Nina, I beg you, remain here, or let me go with you! (NINA *hastily puts on her hat and cape.*) Nina, why? For God's sake, Nina. . . . (*Watches as she puts on her things. Pause.*)

NINA. My carriage is at the gate. Don't see me out, I'll go alone. . . . (*Tearfully.*) Let me have some water. . . .

TREPLEV (*gives her water*). Where are you heading now?

NINA. To town. (*Pause.*) Is Irina Nikolayevna here?

TREPLEV. Yes. . . . Uncle took a turn for the worse on Thursday. We telegraphed for her.

NINA. Why do you say you kiss the ground I walked on? I deserve to be killed. (*Leans on the table.*) I'm so tired. If I could only rest . . . rest! (*Raises her head.*) I'm a sea gull! . . . No, that's not right. I'm an actress. Yes! (*Hearing* ARKADINA *and* TRIGORIN *laughing, she pauses to listen, then runs to the door on the left and looks through the keyhole.*) And he's here too. . . . (*Turning back to* TREPLEV.) Yes. . . . it doesn't matter. . . . Yes. . . . He didn't believe in the theater, he laughed at my dreams, and gradually I stopped believing too, I lost heart. . . . And then the worries that go along with a love affair, jealousy, constant anxiety for my child. . . . I grew petty, small, my acting had no point to it. . . . I didn't know what to do with my hands, how to stand on the stage, I couldn't control my voice. You can't imagine what it's like when you know your acting is awful. I'm a sea gull. No, that's not right. . . . Remember—you shot a sea gull? By chance a man came, saw a sea gull, and having nothing better to do, destroyed it. . . . A subject for a short story. . . . No, that's not right. . . . (*Wipes her forehead.*) What was I saying? I was talking about the stage. I've changed . . . I've become a real actress. I enjoy it, I act with enthusiasm. I forget myself on the stage and feel I'm beautiful.

And now, while living here, I go walking. I walk and think, and I can feel my spiritual powers growing with every passing day. . . . I understand now, Kostya, that in our work—acting or writing, it makes no difference—what matters isn't fame or glory, it isn't all the things I dreamed about, but the capacity to endure. To bear your cross and have faith. I have faith and it doesn't hurt so much now. When I think of my vocation, I don't fear life.

TREPLEV (*sadly*). You've found your way, you know where you're going, and I'm still floating in a chaos of dreams and images. I don't believe in anything and I don't know my vocation.

NINA (*listening*). Shh. . . . I'm going. Goodbye. When I become a great actress, come and see me. Promise? But now. . . . (*Presses his hand.*) It's late. I can barely stand on my feet . . . I'm exhausted and hungry. . . .

TREPLEV. Stay, I'll bring you supper. . . .

NINA. No, no. . . . Don't see me off, I'll manage. . . . My carriage is nearby. . . . So, she brought him along. Well, it doesn't matter. When you see Trigorin, don't say anything to him. . . . I love him. I love him even more than before. . . . A subject for a short story. . . . I love him, I love him passionately, desperately. Kostya, how good our life was! Do you remember? How serene, warm, joyous, and pure! And our feelings—they were like tender, delicate flowers. . . . Do you remember? "Men, lions, eagles, partridges, deer with antlers, geese, spiders, silent fish who dwell in the deep, starfish, and those the eye cannot behold—all, all, all living things, have run their sorrowful course and are now extinct. For thousands of centuries the earth has borne no living creature, and this poor moon lights its lamp in vain. In the meadows cranes no longer awaken with a cry, May beetles are silent in the lindens. . . ." (*Embraces* TREPLEV *impulsively and runs out through the glass door.*)

TREPLEV (*after a pause*). It would be unfortunate if someone ran into her in the garden and told mama. That might upset mama. . . .

For about two minutes he silently tears up all his manuscripts and hurls them under the desk, then unlocks the door on the right and goes out.

DORN (*trying to open the door on the right*). That's odd. The door seems to be locked. . . . (*Enters and puts the armchair back in its place.*) A regular obstacle course.

ARKADINA *and* POLINA ANDREYEVNA *enter, after them* YAKOV *carrying bottles and* MASHA, *then* SHAMRAYEV *and* TRIGORIN.

ARKADINA. Set the red wine and the beer for Boris Alekseyevich here on the table. We'll play and drink. Let's take our seats, friends.

POLINA ANDREYEVNA (*to* YAKOV). Bring tea too. (*Lights the candles, sits at the card table.*)

SHAMRAYEV (*leading* TRIGORIN *to the bookcase*). Here's the item I was telling you about. . . . (*Takes the stuffed sea gull from the bookcase.*) Just as you ordered.

TRIGORIN (*gazing at the sea gull*). I don't remember! (*Musing.*) I don't remember!

The sound of a shot from offstage right, everyone starts.

ARKADINA (*frightened*). What was that?

DORN. Nothing. Something in my medicine bag must have exploded. No need to be alarmed. (*Goes out the door on the right, returns after a half minute.*) That was it. A bottle of ether burst. (*Hums.*) "I stand before you once more, enchanted. . . ."

ARKADINA (*sitting down at the table*). Oh, the scare it gave me! I was reminded of how . . . (*Covers her face with her hands.*) Everything went black. . . .

DORN (*leafing through a magazine, to* TRIGORIN). About two months ago an article appeared . . . a letter from America. Among other things, I wanted to ask you . . . (*Puts his arm around* TRIGORIN'S *waist and leads him to the edge of the stage.*) . . . as I'm very much interested in this question. . . . (*Lowering his voice.*) Get Irina Nikolayevna away from here. The fact is, Konstantin Gavrilovich has shot himself. . . .

Curtain

Uncle Vanya

Scenes from Provincial Life in Four Acts

CAST OF CHARACTERS

Serebryakóv, Alexander Vladímirovich
a retired professor
Yeléna Andréyevna
his wife
Sófya Alexándrovna (Sonya)
his daughter from an earlier marriage
Voynítskaya, Maria Vasílyevna
widow of a Privy Councillor, mother of the professor's first wife
Voynítsky, Iván Petróvich (Ványa)
her son
Ástrov, Mikhaíl Lvóvich
a doctor
Telégin, Ilyá Ilích
an impoverished landowner
Marína
an old nanny
Workman
Watchman

The action takes place on Serebryakov's estate.

A C T   I

The garden. The house with its terrace is partly visible. A table set for tea on a lane under an old poplar. Chairs, benches, a guitar on one of them. Porch swing not far from the table. Mid-afternoon. Overcast. MARINA, *a plump, slow-moving old woman, sits by the samovar knitting a stocking while* ASTROV *paces nearby.*

MARINA (*pouring tea*). Have some tea, my dear.

ASTROV (*reluctantly taking the glass*). Somehow I don't feel like it.

MARINA. A drop of vodka then?

ASTROV. No. I don't drink vodka every day. Besides it's sweltering. (*Pause.*) Nanny, how many years have we known each other?

MARINA (*reflecting*). How many years? Lord, let me think. . . . You came . . . when was it now? Sonya's mother was still alive. You dropped by for two winters. . . . Well, that would make it eleven years. (*Pondering.*) Maybe more. . . .

ASTROV. Have I changed much?

MARINA. Yes. You were young then. Handsome. And now you've aged. You're not so handsome. What's more, you drink.

ASTROV. That's true. In ten years I've become a different man. And why is that? Work has worn me to the bone. From morning to evening I'm on my feet, not a moment's peace, and at night I lie under my blanket afraid they'll haul me off to another patient. In all the time I've known you I haven't had a free day. Who wouldn't age? Life is boring, stupid, nasty. . . . This life of ours drags us down. Cranks all around us, as thick as flies. Spend two, three years among them and bit by bit, without noticing it, you turn into a crank yourself. Our inevitable lot. (*Twirling his long mustache.*) Ugh, what an enormous mustache I've grown . . . a silly mustache. Yes, Nanny, I've become a crank. . . . It's not that I'm stupid. Thank God, my brains are still in place. But my feelings seem dead. I desire nothing, need nothing, love no one. . . . Perhaps I love only you. (*Kisses her on the head.*) As a child I had a nanny like you.

MARINA. Maybe something to eat?

ASTROV. No. In the third week of Lent I drove over to Malitskoye.

... A typhus epidemic. . . . The huts were crammed, people lying in rows. . . . Filth, smoke, the stench. Calves on the floor side by side with the patients. . . . Pigs too. . . . I was on the run all day, not a scrap of food touched my mouth. When I got home, they still gave me no rest. A switchman from the railroad was brought in. I laid him on the table to operate, gave him chloroform, and he up and dies on me. And just when I had no use for them, my feelings returned. I felt twinges of conscience, as if I had intentionally killed him. . . . I sat down, covered my eyes—here, like this—and thought to myself: the men and women who will live a hundred or two hundred years after us, for whom we are beating out a path, will they remember us with a kind word? No nanny, they won't remember!

MARINA. People won't remember, but God remembers.

ASTROV. Thank you, Nanny. Well said.

VOYNITSKY *enters. He has come out of the house. After lunch he had a good nap and has a rumpled appearance. Sits on a bench and straightens out his foppish tie.*

VOYNITSKY. Yes. . . . (*Pause.*) Yes. . . .

ASTROV. Sleep well?

VOYNITSKY. Yes. . . . Very. (*Yawns.*) Since the professor and his wife moved in, my life has gone off the rails. . . . I sleep at odd hours, stuff myself on rich sauces, guzzle wine . . . bad for the health! It used to be I didn't have a free minute. Sonya and I worked—you should have seen the way we worked! Now only Sonya does anything, and I sleep, eat, drink. . . . Bad! Bad!

MARINA (*shaking her head*). Topsy-turvy! The professor gets up at noon, and the samovar's been boiling away since morning. Before we had dinner by one, like decent folks. Now it's not until six. Nights the professor stays up reading and writing. It'll be near two in the morning, out of the blue the bell will ring. . . . "What is it, sir?" Tea! Go wake the servants, put up the samovar. . . . Yes, topsy-turvy!

ASTROV. Will they be staying on much longer?

VOYNITSKY (*whistles*). A hundred years. The professor has decided to make his home here.

what is this?
stew?

MARINA. Now, too. The samovar's been on the table for two hours, and they're traipsing about.

VOYNITSKY. They're coming, they're coming. . . . Don't get into a stew. *{ samovar → a pun ?*

Voices. From the far end of the garden, SEREBRYAKOV, YELENA ANDREYEVNA, SONYA, *and* TELEGIN *approach, returning from their stroll.*

SEREBRYAKOV. Splendid, splendid. . . . Enchanting views.

TELEGIN. Remarkable, Your Excellency.

SONYA. Tomorrow we're driving to the forest preserve, Papa. Would you like to join us?

VOYNITSKY. Ladies and gentlemen, teatime!

SEREBRYAKOV. My friends, be so good as to have my tea sent to my study. I still have some business to attend to today.

SONYA. You're certain to enjoy the forest. . . .

YELENA ANDREYEVNA, SEREBRYAKOV, *and* SONYA *go into the house.* TELEGIN *sits at the table next to* MARINA.

VOYNITSKY. It's broiling and our great scholar wears a coat, galoshes, gloves, and carries an umbrella.

ASTROV. You can see he takes care of himself.

VOYNITSKY. How lovely she is! How lovely! I've never seen a woman more beautiful.

TELEGIN. If I ride through the fields, Marina Timofeyevna, or stroll in the shady garden, or simply gaze at this table, I experience inexpressible bliss! The weather is charming, birds tweet, we live in peace and harmony. Who could ask for anything more? (*Taking a glass.*) I thank you from the depths of my heart!

VOYNITSKY (*dreamily*). Her eyes! . . . a marvelous woman!

ASTROV. Say something, Vanya.

VOYNITSKY (*listlessly*). What's there to say?

ASTROV. Anything new?

VOYNITSKY. Nothing. . . . It's the same old story. I'm the man I've always been, maybe worse. Lazy, idle. An old fogy who can only grumble. My venerable magpie of a mother is still prattling about woman's emancipation. She has one eye fixed on the grave, while the other scours her highbrow pamphlets for the dawn of a new era.

ASTROV. And the professor?

VOYNITSKY. As usual he's in his study from morning to the dead of night. Writing. "With wrinkled brow we write and write, No word of praise our odes requite." I feel sorry for the paper. He'd do better to slap together his autobiography. A perfect topic! A retired professor, a doddering, dried-up stick, an educated crab. . . . Gout, rheumatism, migraines. His liver swollen from envy and jealousy. . . . And this crab lives on the estate of his first wife, resentful that he can't afford the city. Complains constantly about his unhappiness, though in reality he's extraordinarily happy. (*Nervously.*) Just think of his good fortune! The son of a common church sexton, a mere seminary student, yet he managed to lay his hands on a degree, a chair at the university. He's "Your Excellency," son-in-law to a senator, etcetera, etcetera. But all that's small change. Here's something to chew on. A man spends twenty-five years of his life reading and writing about art without understanding a damn thing about it. Twenty-five years of rehashing other people's ideas of realism, naturalism, and other nonsense. Twenty-five years of reading and writing what intelligent people know only too well and fools couldn't care less about. That adds up to twenty-five years of pouring water through a sieve. And the egotism of the man! The pretension! He's retired, not a living soul has heard of him, he's a nobody. For twenty-five years he's been an imposter. But look at him—strutting about like some demigod!

ASTROV. You seem to be jealous.

VOYNITSKY. Yes, I'm jealous! The luck he has with women! No Don Juan ever had such success! His first wife, my sister, a lovely gentle creature, as pure as that blue sky, gracious, generous. . . . She had more admirers than he had students. And she loved him the way angels love those as pure and beautiful as themselves. My mother adores him, to this day she's in awe of him. His second wife, a beautiful woman, intelligent—you just saw her—she married him when he was already an old man, gave him her youth, her freedom, her dazzling beauty. For what? Why?

ASTROV. Is she faithful to the professor?

VOYNITSKY. Unfortunately, yes.

ASTROV. Why "unfortunately"?

VOYNITSKY. Because her faithfulness is fake from start to finish. It's rhetoric, not logic. Deceive an old husband whom you can't stand and it's immoral. Smother your poor youth and every vital feeling—and that's not immoral!

TELEGIN (*in a whining tone*). Vanya, I don't care for that sort of talk. Why . . . whoever deceives a husband or wife is disloyal. Such a person might even betray the fatherland!

VOYNITSKY (*annoyed*). Pipe down, Waffles!

TELEGIN. Let me speak, Vanya. The day after my wedding my wife ran off with her lover. On account of my unprepossessing appearance. Despite that I haven't neglected my duty. I still love her and am true to her. I help out any way I can. My property has gone for the education of the children she's had by her lover. Happiness has been denied me, but I've been left my pride. And what about her? Youth has fled, her beauty has faded under the impact of the laws of nature, her lover is dead. . . . What has been left her?

SONYA *and* YELENA ANDREYEVNA *enter; a bit later* MARIA VASILYEVNA, *book in hand; she sits and reads, is served tea and drinks without looking up.*

SONYA (*hurriedly, to the* NANNY). The peasants have come, Nanny. Go speak to them. I'll take care of the tea. . . . (*Pours. The* NANNY *goes out.* YELENA ANDREYEVNA, *sitting on the porch swing, takes her cup and drinks.*)

ASTROV (*to* YELENA ANDREYEVNA). I'm here because of your husband. You wrote that he's very ill, rheumatism and so on, and it turns out he's as fit as a fiddle.

YELENA ANDREYEVNA. Last night he was out of sorts. He complained of pains in his legs. But today he's all right. . . .

ASTROV. And I galloped at full speed for twenty miles. Well, it's not the first time. I'll stay till morning. At least I'll get some sleep.

SONYA. How nice. It's a rare treat to have you stay the night. You haven't eaten, have you?

ASTROV. No, I haven't.

SONYA. Then you're just in time for dinner. We now dine after six. (*Drinks.*) The tea is cold.

TELEGIN. The temperature in the samovar has significantly decreased.

YELENA ANDREYEVNA. It doesn't matter, Ivan Ivanych. We'll drink it cold.

TELEGIN. Sorry, madam. Not Ivan Ivanych, but Ilya Ilich . . . Ilya Ilich Telegin. Or as some call me—Waffles. On account of my pockmarked face. I stood godfather to Sonya, and His Excellency, your husband that is, knows me well. I live with you now, madam, on this estate. . . . You may have noticed, every day we have dinner together.

SONYA. Ilya Ilich is a great help, our right hand. (*Tenderly.*) Pass your cup, Godfather. I'll fill it for you.

MARIA VASILYEVNA. Oh!

SONYA. What is it, Grandmother?

MARIA VASILYEVNA. I forgot to tell Alexander . . . my memory is going . . . I received a letter today from Pavel Alexeyevich in Kharkov. . . . He sent his latest pamphlet. . . .

ASTROV. Interesting?

MARIA VASILYEVNA. Yes, but somehow odd. He refutes the position he defended seven years ago. That's dreadful!

VOYNITSKY. There's nothing the least bit dreadful about it. Drink your tea, *Maman.*

MARIA VASILYEVNA. But I prefer to speak!

VOYNITSKY. For fifty years we've been blabbering and reading pamphlets. It's high time to put an end to it.

MARIA VASILYEVNA. For some reason you find it disagreeable when I speak. Forgive me, Jean, but over the last year you've changed so that I hardly recognize you. . . . You were once a man of definite convictions, an enlightened individual. . . . (*Pause.*)

VOYNITSKY. Oh, certainly! An enlightened individual from whom no one had any light. . . . (*Pause.*) An enlightened individual. . . . What a nasty joke! I'm forty-seven years old. Until last year I deliberately tried to cloud my eyes with these theories of yours. Anything so as not to see real life. And I thought I was doing the right thing. But now . . . if you only knew! I lie awake nights, furious that I've so stupidly let time slip by when I might have had everything that old age now denies me!

SONYA. Boring, Uncle Vanya!

MARIA VASILYEVNA (*to her son*). You seem to lay the blame on your former convictions. . . . But they're not at fault—you are. You have forgotten that convictions are in themselves nothing, a dead letter. . . . One must act.

VOYNITSKY. Act? Not everyone is capable of being a writing machine like your Herr Professor.

MARIA VASILYEVNA. What do you mean by that?

SONYA (*imploringly*). Grandmother! Uncle Vanya! Please!

VOYNITSKY. I'm quiet. I'm quiet and I beg your pardon. (*Pause.*)

YELENA ANDREYEVNA. Nice weather we're having today. . . . Not too hot. . . . (*Pause.*)

VOYNITSKY. Nice weather to hang yourself. . . .

TELEGIN *tunes his guitar.* MARINA *walks by the house, calling to the chickens.*

MARINA. Cheep, cheep, cheep. . . .

SONYA. Nanny, what did the peasants want? . . .

MARINA. The same old thing . . . that plot of empty land. Cheep, cheep cheep. . . .

SONYA. Whom are you calling?

MARINA. Speckles. . . . She's gone off with her chicks. . . . The crows'll snatch them. . . . (*Goes out.*)

TELEGIN *plays a polka. All listen in silence. A* WORKMAN *enters.*

WORKMAN. Is the doctor here? (*To* ASTROV.) Excuse me, Doctor, you're needed.

ASTROV. Where?

WORKMAN. At the factory.

ASTROV (*annoyed*). Thanks a million. No use, I have to go. . . . (*Looks around for his cap.*) Damn nuisance. . . .

SONYA. How disagreeable. . . . When you're through at the factory, come dine with us.

ASTROV. No, it'll be late. Now where could . . . ? (*To the* WORKMAN.)

Be a good fellow and bring me a glass of vodka. (*The* WORKMAN *goes out.*) Where could . . . ? (*Locates the cap.*) In some play by Ostrovsky there's a character with a large mustache and little talent. . . . That's me all over. Well, ladies and gentlemen, my respects. . . . (*To* YELENA ANDREYEVNA.) Should you drop by my place one of these days—with Sonya that is—I would be genuinely pleased. I have a small estate, eighty acres in all, but there's an excellent garden and a nursery that might interest you. You won't find the likes of it for seven hundred miles. A state forest is nearby. . . . The forester is an old man, so I actually run it.

YELENA ANDREYEVNA. I've been told that you very much love the forests. Of course, that can be quite useful, but doesn't it interfere with your true calling? After all, you are a doctor.

ASTROV. Only God knows our true calling.

YELENA ANDREYEVNA. Do you find it interesting?

ASTROV. Yes.

VOYNITSKY (*ironically*). Very!

YELENA ANDREYEVNA (*to* ASTROV). You're still a young man. By your looks . . . well, I'd guess thirty-six or thirty-seven. . . . No, it can't be as interesting as you say. Nothing but forests. Monotonous, I would imagine.

SONYA. Not at all. It's extraordinarily interesting. Every year Mikhail Lvovich plants new forests. They've already given him a bronze medal and a citation. He takes pains to preserve the older forests from destruction. If you only heard him speak, you would agree completely. He says that the forests adorn the earth, that they teach people to understand beauty and inspire lofty feelings. Forests soften a harsh climate. In countries where the climate is mild, less energy is wasted on the struggle with nature. Men are also more tender and gentle. People are handsome, supple, easily inspired. Speech is elegant, movements graceful. Science and art flourish. Their philosophy isn't gloomy, their relations with women are refined and noble. . . .

VOYNITSKY (*laughing*). Bravo, bravo! That's all very sweet, but unconvincing. (*To* ASTROV.) With your kind permission, my friend, I'll just keep on burning firewood in my stove and building my barns with lumber.

ASTROV. You can burn peat and build with stone. Well, I'll grant we have to cut down some trees, but why destroy entire forests? Our Russian forests crack under the ax, millions of trees perish, birds and animals desert their nests, rivers grow shallow, marvelous landscapes vanish never to return—and all because lazy men lack the good sense to bend over and pick up their fuel from the ground. (*To* YELENA ANDREYEVNA.) That's true, isn't it? You have to be an unthinking barbarian to incinerate beauty, to destroy what we can't create. Man has the gift of reason and creative power. He ought to increase what he's been given, but so far he hasn't created, only destroyed. The forests thin out, rivers run dry, wild life becomes extinct, the climate is ruined. With every passing day this earth of ours is more impoverished and ugly. (*To* VOYNITSKY.) You're looking at me ironically, everything I say seems unserious to you and . . . Well, maybe it is crankiness, but going past forests I've saved from the peasant's ax or hearing the rustle of saplings planted by my own hands, I'm aware that the climate is to some extent in my power. If in a thousand years men are happy, a small share of the credit will be mine. When I see a young birch I've planted turn green and sway in the breeze, my heart fills with pride, and I . . . (*Notices the* WORKMAN *bringing a glass of vodka on a tray.*) But . . . (*drinks*) I must be going. Perhaps it's only crankiness after all. It's been a pleasure! (*Bows and goes to the house.*)

SONYA (*taking him by the arm and accompanying him*). When will you be visiting us?

ASTROV. I don't know. . . .

SONYA. Again in a month? . . .

ASTROV *and* SONYA *go into the house.* MARIA VASILYEVNA *and* TELEGIN *remain by the table.* YELENA ANDREYEVNA *and* VOYNITSKY *walk to the terrace.*

YELENA ANDREYEVNA. You were impossible, Vanya. Did you have to provoke your mother with that crack about the writing machine! And at breakfast you again argued with Alexander. How petty!

VOYNITSKY. But if I can't stand him!

YELENA ANDREYEVNA. There's no point in hating Alexander. He's like everybody else. No worse than you.

VOYNITSKY. If you could only see yourself, your face, the way you move. . . . How indolent you are, too indolent to live!

YELENA ANDREYEVNA. Yes, indolent and bored! Everybody rails at my husband, they regard me with pity: "The unfortunate woman, she has an old man for a husband." How well I understand their concern! Astrov said it just now—you recklessly destroy the forests and soon the earth will be empty. In the same way you recklessly destroy human beings, and soon, thanks to you, the earth will be empty of loyalty, purity, and the capacity for self-sacrifice. Why can't you look at a woman who doesn't belong to you with detachment? That doctor is right—there's a demon of destruction in all of you. You have no pity for the forests, or the birds, or for women, or for one another. . . .

VOYNITSKY. This speech making is not to my taste! (*Pause.*)

YELENA ANDREYEVNA. That doctor has a tired, tense face. An interesting face. Sonya is obviously taken with him, she's fallen in love. I understand her. During my stay he's visited three times, but I'm reserved—I haven't spoken to him once properly, or shown him any kindness. He must take me for a shrew. You and I, Vanya, are probably such good friends because we're both tiresome, dull people! Tiresome! Don't look at me like that. I don't care for it.

VOYNITSKY. Can I look at you differently when I love you? You are my happiness, my youth, life itself! I realize that my chances are slim, equal to zero, but I require nothing. Only let me gaze at you, listen to your voice. . . .

YELENA ANDREYEVNA. Shh! They can hear! (*They go to the house.*)

VOYNITSKY (*following her*). Let me speak of my love, don't drive me away—that alone would be the height of happiness. . . .

YELENA ANDREYEVNA. This is agony. . . . (*They go into the house.*)

TELEGIN *strikes the strings of his guitar and plays a polka.* MARIA VASILYEVNA *makes some notes in the margins of a pamphlet.*

Curtain

ACT II

The dining room of SEREBRYAKOV'S *home. Night. In the garden the* WATCHMAN *is tapping on his board.* SEREBRYAKOV *is in an armchair near an open window, dozing;* YELENA ANDREYEVNA *beside him, also dozing.*

SEREBRYAKOV (*waking up*). Who is it? Is that you, Sonya?

YELENA ANDREYEVNA. It's me.

SEREBRYAKOV. You, Yelena. . . . The pain is unbearable.

YELENA ANDREYEVNA. Your blanket has dropped to the floor. (*She wraps up his legs.*) I'll close the window.

SEREBRYAKOV. No, I'm suffocating. . . . I dozed off and dreamed my left leg wasn't mine. An excruciating pain woke me. No, it's not gout, more likely rheumatism. What time is it?

YELENA ANDREYEVNA. Twenty minutes past twelve. (*Pause.*)

SEREBRYAKOV. In the morning, search the library for a volume of Batyushkov. I believe we have him.

YELENA ANDREYEVNA. What?

SEREBRYAKOV. Look for Batyushkov in the morning. As I recall, we had him. Why am I having such difficulty breathing?

YELENA ANDREYEVNA. You're tired. You haven't slept for two nights.

SEREBRYAKOV. They say that Turgenev began with gout and ended with angina. I'm afraid I might have it. Damned loathsome old age! Since turning old, I find myself repulsive. No doubt all of you find me repulsive.

YELENA ANDREYEVNA. You talk about your old age as if we're to blame.

SEREBRYAKOV. Most of all I'm repulsive to you. (YELENA ANDREYEVNA *moves away and sits at a distance.*) I'm not stupid; I know what's going on. You're young, healthy, beautiful. You want a full life, and I'm an old man, practically a corpse. Do you think I don't understand? It's certainly stupid of me to remain alive. But wait a while, I'll soon release the lot of you. I won't be dragging this carcass around for long.

YELENA ANDREYEVNA. For heaven's sake, be still . . . I'm worn out.

SEREBRYAKOV. Thanks to me everyone is worn out, bored, wasting their youth, while I alone enjoy life and am content. Yes, of course.

YELENA ANDREYEVNA. Stop it! You've exhausted me.

SEREBRYAKOV. I've exhausted everyone. Of course.

YELENA ANDREYEVNA (*in tears*). I can't stand it! What is it you want from me?

SEREBRYAKOV. Nothing.

YELENA ANDREYEVNA. In that case, keep quiet. I beg you.

SEREBRYAKOV. How queer. If Ivan Petrovich opens his mouth, or the senile idiot he calls his mother—that's fine, everybody listens. But if I so much as say a word, you're all miserable. Even my voice is repulsive. Well, suppose I am repulsive, an egoist, a despot—don't I have a right to some egoism in my old age? Haven't I earned it? Haven't I a right to a peaceful old age, to some consideration?

YELENA ANDREYEVNA. No one is disputing your rights. (*The window bangs from the wind.*) A wind is blowing up. I'll shut the window. (*Shuts it.*) It'll rain soon. No one is disputing your rights. (*Pause. In the garden the* WATCHMAN *taps his board and sings.*)

SEREBRYAKOV. A man serves science all his life, feels at home in his study, in the lecture hall. He becomes accustomed to the company of distinguished colleagues—and suddenly, for no rhyme or reason, he finds himself in this tomb. Day in and day out the same stupid faces, the same meaningless conversations. . . . I want to live, I love success, fame, activity, and it's as if I'm in exile. Constantly brooding over the past, keeping an eye on the accomplishments of others, fearing death. . . . I just can't! It's too much for me! And to add insult to injury they won't forgive me my old age!

YELENA ANDREYEVNA. Have patience—in five or six years I'll be old too.

SONYA (*enters*). Papa, you had us send for Doctor Astrov, and now that he's here, you refuse to receive him. That's inconsiderate. We've bothered the man for nothing. . . .

SEREBRYAKOV. What do I need your Astrov for? He knows as much about medicine as I do about astronomy.

SONYA. We can't very well summon the entire medical faculty for your gout.

SEREBRYAKOV. I won't even talk to that quack.

SONYA. Suit yourself. (*Sits.*) It's all the same to me.

SEREBRYAKOV. What time is it now?

YELENA ANDREYEVNA. One.

SEREBRYAKOV. I'm suffocating . . . Sonya, hand me my drops from the table!

SONYA. Here you are. (*Hands them over.*)

SEREBRYAKOV (*annoyed*). Not these! I can't even make a simple request!

SONYA. Please, don't play games. Some people may find it appealing, but be so kind as to spare me. I don't care for it. Besides I haven't the time. We're mowing tomorrow morning and I have to get up early.

VOYNITSKY (*enters in a robe, carrying a candle*). A storm is brewing. (*Lightning.*) There you are! Hélène and Sonya, go to bed. I've come to relieve you.

SEREBRYAKOV (*frightened*). No, no! Don't leave me alone with him! No. The way he talks, it'll be the death of me.

VOYNITSKY. But you have to give them some rest! They haven't slept for two nights.

SEREBRYAKOV. They may go to bed, but you leave also. Please, I implore you. In the name of our former friendship, don't refuse. We'll chat later.

VOYNITSKY (*with a smile*). Our former friendship. . . . Former . . .

SONYA. Be still, Uncle Vanya.

SEREBRYAKOV (*to his wife*). My dearest, don't leave me alone with him! His talk will be the death of me.

VOYNITSKY. This is getting ridiculous.

MARINA *enters with a candle.*

SONYA. You should be in bed, Nanny. It's quite late.

MARINA. The samovar hasn't been put away. Not likely I'll be sleeping soon.

SEREBRYAKOV. Everybody's awake, tired. I alone am blissfully happy.

MARINA (*steps over to* SEREBRYAKOV, *tenderly*). What is it, my dear? Does it hurt? My legs, too, they just throb and throb. (*Straightens *out his blanket.*) That's an old trouble of yours. Vera Petrovna, Sonya's mother, may she rest in peace, she would be up nights, worrying herself sick. . . . She loved you very much. . . . (*Pause.*) Old folks are like children. They want someone to feel sorry for them, but no one feels sorry for you when you're old. (*Kisses* SEREBRYAKOV *on the shoulder.*) Come to bed, my pet. . . . Come, my angel. . . . I'll pour some lime tea for you, and warm your legs. . . . I'll pray for you.

SEREBRYAKOV (*touched*). Yes, Marina.

MARINA. My legs just throb and throb. (*Sees him out along with* SONYA.) Vera Petrovna would worry all the time, she'd cry and cry. . . . You were little then, Sonya, a silly thing. . . . Come, come, my pet. . . . (SEREBRYAKOV, SONYA, *and* MARINA *go out.*)

YELENA ANDREYEVNA. He's drained me. I can barely stand on my feet.

VOYNITSKY. He's a burden to you; I, to myself. I haven't slept for three nights.

YELENA ANDREYEVNA. Life has gone sour in this house. Your mother detests everything and everyone, except her pamphlets and the professor. The professor is irritable—he doesn't trust me and is afraid of you. Sonya is angry at her father and annoyed at me. She hasn't spoken to me for two weeks. You hate my husband and flaunt your contempt for your mother. I'm edgy—twenty times today I was on the verge of tears. . . . There's something terribly wrong in this house.

VOYNITSKY. Let's drop the philosophy!

YELENA ANDREYEVNA. You're an educated and clever man, Vanya. You ought to understand that the world isn't dying because of robbers or arsonists but from hatred, enmity, from all these petty squabbles. It's your responsibility to stop sulking and reconcile us.

VOYNITSKY. First reconcile me to myself! My darling. . . . (*Bends to her hand.*)

YELENA ANDREYEVNA. Leave me be! (*Pulls her hand away.*) Go away!

VOYNITSKY. In a moment the rain will pass. All nature will be refreshed and come alive. I alone won't be revived by the storm. Day and night the thought that my life is irrevocably lost chokes me like some phantom at my throat. I have no past—it's been stupidly squandered on trivia, and the present is terrible in its absurdity. Here, I give you my life and my love—where shall I put them, what am I to do with them? My feelings are perishing uselessly, like a ray of sunlight falling into a black hole. I'm dying.

YELENA ANDREYEVNA. When you speak to me of your love, for some reason I grow numb and don't know how to respond. Forgive me, but I have nothing to say to you. (*Wants to go.*) Good night.

VOYNITSKY (*blocking her path*). If you only knew how I suffer from the thought that near me, in this very house, another life is perishing—yours! What are you waiting for? What damned morality is holding you back? Understand, you must understand. . . .

YELENA ANDREYEVNA (*looks intently at him*). Vanya, you're drunk!

VOYNITSKY. Maybe, maybe. . . .

YELENA ANDREYEVNA. Where is the doctor?

VOYNITSKY. There, in my room . . . he's staying the night. Maybe, maybe. . . . Anything may be, anything!

YELENA ANDREYEVNA. You've been drinking again? Why?

VOYNITSKY. At least it feels like life. . . . Don't interfere, Hélène!

YELENA ANDREYEVNA. You never used to drink. And you never talked so much. . . . Go to bed! You're boring me.

VOYNITSKY (*falling to her hand*). My darling . . . my enchantress!

YELENA ANDREYEVNA (*annoyed*). Let go of me. This is all so repugnant. (*Goes out.*)

VOYNITSKY (*alone*). She's gone. . . . (*Pause.*) We met ten years ago at my sister's. She was seventeen, I was only thirty-seven. Why didn't I fall in love and propose to her then? It was so possible! Today she would be my wife. . . . Yes. . . . The storm would waken us—she'd be frightened of the thunder, I'd hold her in my arms and whisper, "Don't be afraid, I'm here." Oh, a wonderful dream. So glorious—I'm even laughing. . . . But, dear God, the way my thoughts get tangled in my head. . . . Why have I grown old? Why can't she understand me? Her rhetoric, that lazy morality of hers, silly, lazy ideas about the death of the world—it's all so hateful to me. (*Pause.*) How I've been cheated! I worshiped that professor, that pitiful gout-ridden stick of a man. I slaved for him like an ox! Sonya and I squeezed the last drop out of this estate. We peddled vegetable oil, peas, cottage cheese—as if we were peasants. Grudged ourselves scraps of food, hoarded our kopeks so that we might send him rubles by the thousands. I took pride in his scholarship, I lived and breathed through him! His every word seemed a stroke of genius. . . . My God! And now? Now he's retired and the sum total of his life is in. Not a single page of his work will last. He's a complete zero, a nobody! The life of a soap bubble! I've been cheated. . . . I see it now—taken for a fool. . . .

ASTROV *enters in a frock coat, without vest and tie. He's a bit tight.* TELEGIN *comes in after him, carrying a guitar.*

ASTROV. Play!

TELEGIN. But they're sleeping!

ASTROV. Play! (TELEGIN *strums softly.* ASTROV *to* VOYNITSKY.) You're alone? No ladies? (*Arms akimbo, he sings softly.*)

> *My hut is down, gone is my bed,*
> *No place for the master to lay his head . . .*

The storm woke me. Quite a rain. What time is it?

VOYNITSKY. Who the hell knows.

ASTROV. I thought I heard Yelena Andreyevna's voice.

VOYNITSKY. She just left.

ASTROV. A gorgeous woman. (*Examines the phials on the table.*) Medicines. What a collection! Kharkov, Moscow, Tula. . . . He's bored the whole country with his gout. Is he sick or is he faking it?

VOYNITSKY. He's sick. (*Pause.*)

ASTROV. Why are you so down in the dumps today? Feeling sorry for the professor?

VOYNITSKY. Leave me alone.

ASTROV. Or have you fallen for the professor's wife?

VOYNITSKY. We're friends.

ASTROV. Already?

VOYNITSKY. What do you mean, "already"?

ASTROV. A woman can be a man's friend only in the following sequence: first an acquaintance, then his mistress, finally his friend.

VOYNITSKY. A vulgar view.

ASTROV. What's that? Well . . . I have to confess, I am becoming vulgar. As you see, I'm even drunk. I make it a rule to get tight once a month. Under the influence I'm extremely arrogant and audacious. Nothing fazes me! I'll tackle the most difficult operations and pull them off beautifully. My imagination draws sweeping plans for the future. At such moments I don't see myself as an eccentric. I'm confident that I'll make enormous contributions to humanity . . . enormous! When I'm drunk I have my own philosophical system, and you, my good fellows, seem to me so many tiny insects . . . microbes. (*To* TELEGIN.) Play, Waffles!

TELEGIN. For you, my dear friend, gladly, with all my heart, but you must realize, people are sleeping!

ASTROV. Play! (TELEGIN *strums softly.*) I could use a drink. Let's go to our room, I think there's some cognac left. And at daybreak we can drive over to my place. Righto? I have an assistant who never says "right," only "righto." An out-and-out son-of-a-bitch. Righto? (*Sees* SONYA *entering.*) Excuse me, I'm not wearing a tie. (*Goes off quickly,* TELEGIN *after him.*)

SONYA. Uncle Vanya, you've been drinking with the doctor again. A fine pair you make. That's the way he is, but why must you . . . ? At your age it doesn't become you.

VOYNITSKY. Age has nothing to do with it. When real life goes, you live on mirages. Better than nothing.

SONYA. We've already mown the hay, for days on end it's been raining, everything's turning to rot, and you busy yourself with mirages. You've completely neglected the estate. . . . I work alone. I haven't an ounce of strength left. (*Frightened.*) Uncle, you have tears in your eyes!

VOYNITSKY. Tears? No, it's nothing . . . nonsense. . . . The way you looked at me now, it reminded me of your mother. My darling. . . . (*Greedily kisses her hands and face.*) My sister . . . my dear, sweet sister. . . . Where is she now? If she only knew! If she only knew!

SONYA. Knew what, uncle? Knew what?

VOYNITSKY. Painful, bad. . . . Nothing. . . . Later. . . . Nothing. . . . I must go. . . . (*Goes out.*)

SONYA (*knocking at the door*). Mikhail Lvovich! You're not asleep, are you? Give me just a minute!

ASTROV (*from behind the door*). I'll be right out! (*Enters a moment later. He has put on a vest and tie.*) What can I do for you?

SONYA. Drink, if you don't find it disgusting, but I ask you not to encourage my uncle. It's bad for him.

ASTROV. Fine. We won't drink anymore. (*Pause.*) I'm going home immediately. Signed, sealed, and delivered! By the time they harness the horses, it will be dawn.

SONYA. It's raining. Wait till morning.

ASTROV. The storm is passing to the side, only the edge will catch us. No, I'm going. And please, don't call me for your father any more. I tell him "gout"—he says "rheumatism." I ask him to lie down—he sits. And today he wouldn't speak to me at all.

SONYA. He's spoiled. (*Searches the sideboard.*) Would you care for a bite to eat?

ASTROV. Why not? Yes.

SONYA. I love snacking at night. There seems to be something left in the sideboard. They say he's had great success with women, and they've spoiled him. Here, have some cheese. (*They eat, standing at the sideboard.*)

ASTROV. I haven't eaten today, only drunk. Your father is a difficult man. (*Takes a bottle from the sideboard.*) May I? (*Drinks up a glass.*) No one's here, we can speak frankly. You know, I don't think I would last a month in your home. I'd choke in this atmosphere. . . . Your father, who has buried himself in his gout and his books, Uncle Vanya with his melancholy, your grandmother, and finally, your stepmother. . . .

SONYA. My stepmother?

ASTROV. Everything about a human being ought to be beautiful— her face and clothes, her thoughts, even her soul. She is beautiful, no doubt about it, but . . . all she does is sleep, eat, go for walks, and enchant us with her beauty. She has no responsibilities, others work for her. . . . Isn't that so? An idle life can't be pure. (*Pause.*) But perhaps I'm too severe. Like your Uncle Vanya, I'm dissatisfied with life. We're both turning into grouches.

SONYA. You're dissatisfied with life?

ASTROV. I love life in general. It's our life that I can't stand. Narrow

Russian provincialism—I despise it to the marrow of my bones. As for my personal life, God knows there's nothing especially worthwhile about it. You know, when a man walks through a forest in the dead of night and sees a light shining in the distance, he doesn't notice his weariness, or the darkness, or the branches with thorns lashing his face. . . . I work—you're aware of that—no one in the county works as hard. Tough luck hits me without letup, at times I can't bear my sufferings. But there's no light for me in the distance. I no longer expect anything, I don't like people. . . . For some time now I've loved no one.

SONYA. No one?

ASTROV. No one. I do feel a certain tenderness for your nanny—for old times' sake. The peasants are all alike—backward, living in filth. Our educated people are difficult to get along with. They tire you out. All our good friends think petty thoughts, have petty feelings, and don't see farther than their noses. To put it bluntly—they're stupid. And the more prominent and brainy ones are hysterics—analysis and introspection are eating at their guts. . . . They whine, they're spiteful, their slander is morbid. They'll edge up to a man, give him a sidelong glance, and decide on the spot: "This one's a neurotic!" "That one's a windbag!" And when they have no idea what label to stick on my forehead, it's "Oh, he's a strange one!" I love the forests—that's strange. I don't eat meat—that's also strange. We no longer have a pure, free, and spontaneous relation to nature and man. . . . No, a thousand times no! (*Attempts to drink.*)

SONYA (*preventing him*). Please, don't drink any more.

ASTROV. Why not?

SONYA. It's not you! You're refined, your voice is so tender. . . . More than that, you're unlike anyone I know . . . you're beautiful. Why do you want to be ordinary, and drink and play cards? Oh, don't, please don't! You're always saying men destroy their God-given talents instead of creating. Then why are you destroying yourself? You mustn't, you mustn't, I beg you.

ASTROV (*extending his hand to her*). I won't drink any more.

SONYA. Promise.

ASTROV. Word of honor.

SONYA (*squeezing his hand firmly*). I'm so grateful!

ASTROV. *Basta!* I've sobered up. See, I'm completely sober and I'll stay that way to the end of my days. (*Looks at his watch.*) Well, let's continue. As I was saying, my time has passed, it's too late for me now. . . . I'm old, played out, mediocre. My feelings are dulled. I don't believe I could form an attachment to another human being. I love no one and . . . I'm not about to. Only beauty still fascinates me. I'm not indifferent to it. Now if Yelena Andreyevna wished, she could turn my head in a day. But that's not love, not an attachment. . . . (*Covers his eyes and trembles.*)

SONYA. What's the matter?

ASTROV. It's nothing. . . . During Lent a patient of mine died under chloroform.

SONYA. It's time you forgot about that. (*Pause.*) May I ask something, Mikhail Lvovich? . . . If I had a girl friend, or a younger sister, and you found out that she . . . well, suppose she fell in love with you. How would you respond?

ASTROV (*shrugging his shoulders*). I don't really know. Probably not at all. I would have her understand that I can't reciprocate . . . that my mind is on other things. But if I'm to go, it's high time. Otherwise we'll be at it till morning. Goodbye, my pet. (*Presses her hand.*) If it's all right with you, I'll leave by way of the living room. I'm afraid your uncle might detain me. (*Goes out.*)

SONYA (*alone*). He said nothing. . . . His heart is still a mystery to me. Why, then, do I feel so happy? (*Laughs from happiness.*) I told him: you're refined, honest, you have such a tender voice. . . . Was that inappropriate? His voice is vibrant, caressing . . . I can still feel it trembling in the air. When I brought up a younger sister, he didn't take the hint. . . . (*Wringing her hands.*) Oh, how terrible that I'm not pretty! I'm homely, I know it, I just know it. After church last Sunday I overheard the women gossiping about me: "She's kind and generous, only it's a pity she's so homely." . . . Homely. . . .

YELENA ANDREYEVNA (*enters; opens the windows*). The storm has passed. How fresh the air is! (*Pause.*) Where is the doctor?

SONYA. He left.

YELENA ANDREYEVNA. Sonya!

SONYA. What?

YELENA ANDREYEVNA. How long will you stay cross with me? We haven't done each other any harm. Why should we be enemies? Let's put an end to it. . . .

SONYA. I was also meaning to . . . (*Embraces her.*) We've quarreled enough.

YELENA ANDREYEVNA. Splendid. (*They are both emotional.*)

SONYA. Has papa gone to bed?

YELENA ANDREYEVNA. No, he's in the living room. . . . We haven't spoken for weeks, God knows why. . . . (*Noting that the sideboard is open.*) What's this?

SONYA. Mikhail Lvovich had some supper.

YELENA ANDREYEVNA. There's wine. . . . Let's drink to friendship.

SONYA. Let's.

YELENA ANDREYEVNA. From the same glass. . . . (*Pours.*) It's nicer this way. Well, friends?

SONYA. Friends. (*They drink and kiss.*) For some time now I've wanted to make up, but I felt embarrassed. . . . (*Weeps.*)

YELENA ANDREYEVNA. But why are you crying?

SONYA. For no reason.

YELENA ANDREYEVNA. There, there. . . . (*Weeps.*) Silly thing that I am, now you have me crying too. . . . (*Pause.*) You're angry at me because you imagine I married your father for money. . . . If you trust oaths, then I'll swear, it was love. He was a scholar, he was famous, and that intrigued me. My love was not genuine—it was make-believe—but then it seemed genuine enough. I'm not to blame. And from the day of our wedding you haven't stopped punishing me with those clever, suspicious eyes of yours.

SONYA. Come, let's make peace. Bygones be bygones.

YELENA ANDREYEVNA. You shouldn't look at me the way you do—it doesn't suit you. We must trust people. Otherwise life is impossible. (*Pause.*)

SONYA. Tell me honestly, like a friend. . . . Are you happy?

YELENA ANDREYEVNA. No.

SONYA. I knew it. Just one more question. Be frank—would you have preferred a young husband?

YELENA ANDREYEVNA. What a child you are. Of course! (*Laughs.*) Now ask me something else, anything. . . .

SONYA. Do you find the doctor attractive?

YELENA ANDREYEVNA. Yes, very much so.

SONYA (*laughing*). I look silly, don't I? He's gone and yet I hear his voice and footsteps. If I glance at that window, his face appears in the darkness. Let me say what's in my heart. . . . But I can't speak so openly, I'm embarrassed. Come to my room, we'll chat there. You must think me silly? Admit it. . . . Tell me about him.

YELENA ANDREYEVNA. What, for instance?

SONYA. He's clever . . . capable, he can do anything, heal the sick, plant forests. . . .

YELENA ANDREYEVNA. It's not a question of forests and medicines. . . . My sweet child, you must understand, it's talent! And do you know what talent means? Daring, mental freedom, breadth of vision. . . . He will plant a sapling and see the consequences of his act in a thousand years, he has a dream of human happiness. Men like that are rare, one must love them. . . . He drinks, he can be coarse—but what of it? In Russia a man of talent can't remain without faults. Judge for yourself, what is this doctor's life like? Roads thick with mud, frosts, blizzards, immense distances, a rough and savage people. Poverty and disease everywhere you turn. In such circumstances a man who works, who struggles day in and day out, finds it difficult to keep himself sober and spotless. . . . (*Kisses her.*) With all my heart I wish you happiness, you deserve it. . . . (*Stands.*) As for me, I'm a tedious woman, one might say an incidental character. . . . In my music, in my husband's home, through all my romances, I've been only an incidental character. Come to think of it, Sonya, I'm a very unhappy woman! (*Paces the stage in agitation.*) The world holds no happiness for me. None! Why are you laughing?

SONYA (*laughs, covering her face*). I'm so happy . . . so happy!

YELENA ANDREYEVNA. I have the urge to play something. . . .

SONYA. Do! (*Embracing her.*) I'm not sleepy. . . . Do play!

YELENA ANDREYEVNA. In a moment. Your father is awake. When he's ailing, music irritates him. Go ask him. If he has no objections, I'll play. Go ahead.

SONYA. I'll be right back. (*Goes out.*)

The WATCHMAN *taps in the garden.*

YELENA ANDREYEVNA. It's been so long. I'll play and cry, cry like a fool. (*Calls through the window.*) Is that you, Yefim?

WATCHMAN (*from offstage*). It's me.

YELENA ANDREYEVNA. Don't tap. The master isn't feeling well.

WATCHMAN (*from offstage*). I'm on my way! (*Whistles.*) Hey you, Blackie. Good boy! Hey, Blackie! (*Pause.*)

SONYA (*returning*). We can't play.

Curtain

ACT III

The living room. Three doors: right, left, and center. Day. VOYNITSKY *and* SONYA *(seated) and* YELENA ANDREYEVNA *(pacing and ruminating).*

VOYNITSKY. The Herr Professor has deigned to request our company in the living room at one. (*Looks at his watch.*) It's a quarter to. He wishes to reveal something to the world.

YELENA ANDREYEVNA. Probably a business matter.

VOYNITSKY. He has no business. What he does is write rubbish, grumble, and envy others.

SONYA (*reprovingly*). Uncle!

VOYNITSKY. All right, all right, I'm sorry. (*Points to* YELENA ANDREYEVNA.) Feast your eyes—the way she walks, swaying so lazily. Nice, very nice!

YELENA ANDREYEVNA. Buzz, buzz—that's how you spend the day. How tiresome! (*Pained.*) I'm dying of boredom, I don't know what to do with myself.

SONYA (*shrugging her shoulders*). Isn't there plenty to do? If you only wanted to.

YELENA ANDREYEVNA. For example.

SONYA. Help with running the estate, teach, care for the sick. Isn't that enough? Why, before you and Papa came, Uncle Vanya and I personally traveled to the market and sold off our flour.

YELENA ANDREYEVNA. I don't know how. Besides it's dull. Only in novels where they're trying to make some point do people teach and tend to peasants. For no reason am I suddenly to run off giving lessons and caring for strangers?

SONYA. And I don't understand how one can fail to do so. In time you'll get used to it. (*Embraces her.*) Don't be melancholy, my precious. (*Laughing.*) You're bored, you can't find a place for yourself. Boredom and idleness are contagious. Look at Uncle Vanya—he does nothing except trail after you like your shadow. I dropped my work and came running to chat with you. I've grown lazy and can't help myself! Doctor Astrov used to visit only now and then, maybe once a month, it was all we could do to prevail upon him. Now he's here every day. He's neglected his forests and his medical practice. You must be an enchantress.

VOYNITSKY. Why waste away? (*With animation.*) Come, my darling, my gorgeous creature, use your brains! The blood of mermaids flows in your veins—so be a mermaid! For once in your life let yourself go, fall head over heels for some water sprite. Plunge into the whirlpool. Let the Herr Professor and the rest of us stand gaping on the shore!

YELENA ANDREYEVNA (*furiously*). Leave me in peace! How cruel you are! (*Starts to leave.*)

VOYNITSKY (*preventing her*). Now, now, my darling, my joy. Forgive me. . . . I'm sorry. (*Kisses her hand.*) Peace.

YELENA ANDREYEVNA. You would try the patience of an angel.

VOYNITSKY. As a token of peace and harmony I'll bring you a bouquet of roses. I picked them for you this morning. . . . Autumn roses—lovely and sad. . . . (*Goes out.*)

SONYA. Autumn roses—lovely and sad. . . . (*Both look out the window.*)

YELENA ANDREYEVNA. September already. How shall we get through the winter! (*Pause.*) Where's the doctor?

SONYA. In Uncle Vanya's room. He's writing. I'm glad Uncle left. I must have a talk with you.

YELENA ANDREYEVNA. About what?

SONYA. About what? (*Lays her head on* YELENA ANDREYEVNA'S *breast.*)

YELENA ANDREYEVNA. There, there. . . . (*Smoothing* SONYA'S *hair.*) That's enough now.

SONYA. I'm ugly.

YELENA ANDREYEVNA. You have beautiful hair.

SONYA. No! No! (*Turns to look at herself in a mirror.*) When a woman is plain, they tell her: "Your eyes are beautiful, you have beautiful hair." . . . I've loved him for six years now, he's more dear to me than my mother. Not a minute passes that I don't hear his voice, feel the touch of his hand. I watch the door, waiting, imagining that he's about to come in. I drop in on you only to speak about him. Now he's here every day, but he doesn't look at me, doesn't see me. . . . It's such agony! I have no hope, none, none! (*Despairingly.*) Oh, God, give me strength. . . . All night I prayed. . . . Often I'll draw near him, open a conversation, gaze into his eyes . . . I have no pride left, no self-control. . . . Yesterday

I couldn't restrain myself and told Uncle Vanya. . . . Even the servants know I'm in love with him. Everybody knows.

YELENA ANDREYEVNA. Does he?

SONYA. He doesn't know I exist.

YELENA ANDREYEVNA (*reflecting*). He's a strange man. . . . You know what? Let me speak to him. . . . I'll be circumspect and merely hint. . . . (*Pause.*) Really, how long can you remain uncertain. . . . Do I have your permission? (SONYA *nods assent.*) Splendid! Either he loves you or he doesn't—that shouldn't be difficult to ascertain. Now don't be embarrassed, my pet, don't be uneasy—I'll question him tactfully, he won't notice a thing. We merely have to find out, is it yes or no? (*Pause.*) If no, then have him stop coming here. Agreed? (SONYA *nods in agreement.*) It'll be easier not seeing him. We won't put it off but sound him out immediately. He wanted to show me some sketches. . . . Go tell him that I wish to see him.

SONYA (*extremely agitated*). You'll let me know the whole truth?

YELENA ANDREYEVNA. Of course. It seems to me that the truth, no matter what, is not as terrible as uncertainty. Trust me, my sweet.

SONYA. Yes, yes. . . . I'll tell him that you want to see his sketches. . . . (*On her way out stops at the door.*) No, uncertainty is better. . . . At least there's hope. . . .

YELENA ANDREYEVNA. What's that?

SONYA. Never mind. (*Goes out.*)

YELENA ANDREYEVNA (*alone*). Nothing is worse than knowing another's secret and not being able to help. (*Reflecting.*) He's not in love with her—that's clear. But why shouldn't he marry her? She's not pretty but she would make an excellent match for a country doctor getting on in years. She's intelligent, kind, pure. . . . No, that's not it. . . . (*Pause.*) How well I understand that poor girl. In the midst of desperate boredom, when gray shadows instead of human beings drift by and you hear nothing but banal chatter. All people do is eat, drink, and sleep . . . then he appears. He's not like the others, he's handsome, attractive, fascinating, a bright moon ascending in the darkness. . . . To submit to the charm of a man like that, to forget yourself. . . . It seems even I'm a bit drawn to him. I'm bored when he's away, just thinking about him makes me smile. . . . Uncle Vanya says that the blood of mermaids flows in my veins. "Let yourself go for once in your life." . . . Why not? Perhaps I should. . . . To fly free as a bird, far from the lot of you, from your drowsy faces, your idle talk, to forget you exist. . . . But I'm shy, a coward. . . . My conscience would torment me. . . . He's here every day, I can guess why. I already feel so guilty. I could fall to my knees before Sonya, ask her forgiveness, weep. . . .

ASTROV (*enters, carrying a cartogram*). Good afternoon! (*Shakes her hand.*) You wanted to see my sketches?

YELENA ANDREYEVNA. Yesterday you promised to show me your work. . . . Are you free?

ASTROV. Oh, certainly. (*Spreads the cartogram on a card table and tacks it down with thumb tacks.*) Where were you born?

YELENA ANDREYEVNA (*assisting him*). St. Petersburg.

ASTROV. And educated?

YELENA ANDREYEVNA. In the Conservatory.

ASTROV. This must bore you.

YELENA ANDREYEVNA. Why? It's true I don't know the countryside, but I've read a good deal.

ASTROV. I have my own desk here . . . in Vanya's room. When I'm dog-tired, numb with fatigue, I drop everything and run over to amuse myself with my toy for an hour or two. . . . Vanya and Sonya work at the abacus, I'm nearby at my desk, dabbling away. It's cozy, peaceful, you can hear the crickets chirping. But I don't allow myself such pleasures often, about once a month. . . . (*Pointing to the cartogram.*) Now let's have a look. This is a map of our region as it was fifty years ago. The dark and bright green represent the forest, they cover half the area. Where the red grid crosses the green, goats and wild elk thrived. . . . Here I indicate the flora and fauna. On this lake there were swans, geese, ducks—as the old-timers say, a slew of birds, more than the eye can make out—clouds of them rushing across the sky. Besides the villages, you can see scattered settlements, farmsteads, Old Believer monasteries, water mills. . . . Cattle and horses were plentiful. They're shown in blue. Here, in this district, the blue is quite thick—entire herds once roamed there, three horses for every household. (*Pause.*) Now look farther down. The way things were twenty-five years ago. Only a third of the area is forest. The goats are gone, though you can still find elk. The green and blue have become paler. Now the third section—the region as it is today. There's some green here and there, but only in patches. The elk, swans, and grouse have vanished. . . . Not a trace of the old settlements, farms, monasteries, and water mills. All in all, a picture of ongoing decay—no doubt about it. In some ten or fifteen years it may be complete. You'll tell me about the impact of culture, that the old must inevitably give way to the new. Well, I could understand if highways and railroads ran through these devastated forests, if there were industries, factories, schools—our people would be healthier, more prosperous, better educated—but there's nothing of the sort! The swamps and mosquitoes are still with us, the same bad roads, poverty, typhus, diphtheria, outbreaks of fire. . . . Here's the situation we're faced with— things have slipped so badly because the struggle for survival is too much for people, because they're backward, ignorant, and totally lacking self-knowledge. To salvage what remains of their lives, to protect their children, cold, hungry, and sick men instinctively clutch at anything that might slake their hunger or keep them warm. They ravage the countryside without a thought for the future. . . . By now almost everything has been destroyed and nothing created to take its place. (*Coldly.*) I see by your expression that this doesn't interest you.

YELENA ANDREYEVNA. But I understand so little of it. . . .

ASTROV. There's nothing to understand. It's just uninteresting.

YELENA ANDREYEVNA. To be frank, my thoughts were elsewhere. Forgive me. I have to ask you a few small questions and I'm embarrassed. I don't know where to start.

ASTROV. Questions?

YELENA ANDREYEVNA. Yes, but . . . they're quite innocent. Let's sit down! (*They sit.*) It concerns a certain young person. We'll speak candidly, as friends, without beating about the bush. We'll have our little talk and forget about it. Do you agree?

ASTROV. All right.

YELENA ANDREYEVNA. It concerns my stepdaughter, Sonya. Do you like her?

ASTROV. Yes, I respect her.

YELENA ANDREYEVNA. Are you attracted to her as a woman?

ASTROV (*hesitating*). No.

YELENA ANDREYEVNA. A few more words and that will be the end of it. You've noticed nothing?

ASTROV. Nothing.

YELENA ANDREYEVNA (*taking his hand*). No, you don't love her, I can see it in your eyes. . . . She suffers so. . . . You must understand and . . . stop coming here.

ASTROV (*rises*). My sun has set. . . . Besides I haven't the time. . . . (*Shrugging his shoulders.*) When should I . . . ? (*He's embarrassed.*)

YELENA ANDREYEVNA. Ugh, this is such a disagreeable conversation! I'm so agitated, as if I had an enormous weight on my shoulders. Well, thank heavens, it's over and done with. Let's put it out of mind, pretend we never spoke . . . and you really must go away. You're a sensible man, you realize . . . (*Pause.*) I'm even blushing.

ASTROV. Had you told me a month or two ago, I might have considered it, but now . . . (*Shrugs his shoulders.*) Though if she's suffering, then of course . . . Only there's one thing I don't understand—why did you find these "small questions" necessary? (*Looks into her eyes, wagging his finger.*) Ah, you're a sly one!

YELENA ANDREYEVNA. What do you mean by that?

ASTROV (*laughing*). Sly! Let's assume Sonya is suffering, I'll readily allow that, but what's the point of this interrogation? (*Preventing her from speaking; animatedly.*) Please, don't look so surprised, you know very well why I come here every day. . . . Why and for whom. You charming bird of prey, don't stare at me like that. I'm a wise old owl. . . .

YELENA ANDREYEVNA (*puzzled*). Bird of prey? What are you talking about?

ASTROV. My beautiful fluffy polecat. . . . You must have your victims! For an entire month now I haven't done a stitch of work. I've let everything slide, all I do is greedily seek you out—and that delights you immensely, immensely. . . . Well, why not? I'm yours, you knew that even without your "questions." (*Folding his hands and bowing his head.*) I surrender. Here I am. Devour me!

YELENA ANDREYEVNA. You're mad!

ASTROV (*laughing ironically*). You're only shy. . . .

YELENA ANDREYEVNA. Oh, I'm better than you think! I assure you.
. . . (*Starts to leave.*)

ASTROV (*blocking her way*). I'm leaving today, I won't visit again,
but . . . (*takes her hand, looking about*). Where do we meet? Tell
me quickly—where? Someone may come in. Quick. . . .
(*Passionately.*) How marvelous you are, how lovely. . . . One kiss.
. . . Just let me kiss your fragrant hair. . . .

YELENA ANDREYEVNA. I swear to you. . . .

ASTROV (*preventing her from speaking*). Why swear? No need for
that. No unnecessary words. . . . Oh, how beautiful! Your lovely
hands. (*Kisses her hands.*)

YELENA ANDREYEVNA. Enough now. . . . Please, go. . . . (*Pulls her
hands away.*) You've forgotten yourself.

ASTROV. Tell me, I insist, where shall we meet tomorrow? (*Takes
her by the waist.*) It's inevitable. We have to meet. (*Kisses her
just as* VOYNITSKY *enters with a bouquet of roses and stops at
the door.*)

YELENA ANDREYEVNA (*not noticing* VOYNITSKY). Pity me . . . let me
go. . . . (*Lays her head against* ASTROV'S *chest.*) No! (*Tries to go.*)

ASTROV (*restraining her at the waist*). The forestry tomorrow . . .
two o'clock. . . . Will you come? Will you?

YELENA ANDREYEVNA (*seeing* VOYNITSKY). Let me go! (*Walks to the
window, extremely agitated.*) Horrible.

VOYNITSKY (*places the bouquet on a chair; upset, he wipes his
face and neck with a handkerchief*). It's nothing. . . . No. . . .
Nothing. . . .

ASTROV (*sullenly*). The weather today, my esteemed Ivan Petrovich,
isn't half bad. It looked like rain this morning, but now it's sunny.
As a matter of fact, it's turned out to be a beautiful autumn. . . .
The winter crops are in good shape. (*Rolls up his cartogram.*)
Only the days are getting shorter. . . . (*Goes out.*)

YELENA ANDREYEVNA (*rushing up to* VOYNITSKY). See to it that my
husband and I leave this place today! Use your influence. Do you
hear me? Today!

VOYNITSKY (*wiping his face*). What? Oh, yes . . . fine . . . Hélène, I
saw everything, everything. . . .

YELENA ANDREYEVNA (*nervously*). Do you hear me? I must leave
today!

SEREBRYAKOV, SONYA, TELEGIN, *and* MARINA *enter.*

TELEGIN. I'm not too well, either, Your Excellency. For two days now I've been ailing. Something in my head. . . .

SEREBRYAKOV. Where are the others? I don't like this house. A veritable labyrinth. Twenty-six enormous rooms, people wander off, and I can never find anyone. (*Rings.*) Tell Maria Vasilyevna and Yelena Andreyevna I want them here at once!

YELENA ANDREYEVNA. I am here.

SEREBRYAKOV. Ladies and gentlemen, be seated.

SONYA (*drawing close to* YELENA ANDREYEVNA, *anxiously*). What did he say?

YELENA ANDREYEVNA. Later.

SONYA. You're trembling? You're agitated? (*Searches her face inquiringly.*) I understand. . . . He said he won't be coming here any more. . . . Isn't that so? (*Pause.*) Tell me, that's so, isn't it? (YELENA ANDREYEVNA *nods in assent.*)

SEREBRYAKOV (*to* TELEGIN). One can become reconciled to ill health, as bad as it gets, but what I can't stomach are the routines of country life. I feel as though I've dropped onto some alien planet. Ladies and gentleman, be seated, please. Sonya! (SONYA *isn't listening. She stands with her head lowered sadly.*) She doesn't hear me. (*To* MARINA.) Nanny, you sit too. (*The* NANNY *sits down and knits a stocking.*) Ladies and gentlemen. Rivet your ears, so to speak, to the post of attention. (*Laughs.*)

VOYNITSKY (*agitated*). Perhaps I'm not needed here? May I be excused?

SEREBRYAKOV. No. Your presence is the most indispensable of all.

VOYNITSKY. What do you want from me?

SEREBRYAKOV. From you . . . ? But why are you angry? (*Pause.*) If I've offended you in any way, please excuse me.

VOYNITSKY. Drop that tone. Let's get down to business. . . . What do you want?

MARIA VASILYEVNA *enters.*

SEREBRYAKOV. And here's *Maman.* My good friends, now I may begin. (*Pause.*) I've summoned you, ladies and gentlemen, to announce that an Inspector General is on his way. But joking aside. This is a serious matter. My friends, I've assembled you to ask your assistance and advice. Cognizant of your habitual kindness, I may hope to be its beneficiary. I am a scholar, a man of letters. I have always been a stranger to practical life. To manage without the guidance of experienced people is beyond my powers, and I ask you, Ivan Petrovich, and you, Ilya Ilich, and you, *Maman.* . . . The fact is that *manet omnes una nox*—in other words, we are all God's creatures. I'm an old man, I'm not well, and hence find it timely to put my affairs in order as far as they concern my family. My life is over. I'm not thinking of myself, but I have a young wife, an unmarried daughter. (*Pause.*) To go on living in the country is impossible. We were not made for rural life. To live in town on the income we receive from this estate is out of the question. Suppose we were to sell some woodland—that is an extraordinary measure to which we cannot resort annually. We must seek out arrangements that might guarantee a regular and fixed income. I have devised such an arrangement and respectfully offer it for your consideration. Passing over the details, I'll set forth its general outline. Our estate averages a profit of no more than two percent. I propose to sell. If we invest our earnings in securities, we shall receive from four to five percent. According to my calculations, there will even be a surplus of several thousand, which would permit us to purchase a small cottage in Finland.

VOYNITSKY. Hold it. . . . My hearing must be bad. Repeat what you just said.

SEREBRYAKOV. Invest in securities and employ what remains to purchase a cottage in Finland.

VOYNITSKY. Not the Finland business. . . . You said something else.

SEREBRYAKOV. I propose to sell the estate.

VOYNITSKY. That's it. You're selling the estate—that's rich, first-rate. . . . And what's to become of me, and my mother, and Sonya here?

SEREBRYAKOV. We'll discuss that in due time. Not everything at once.

VOYNITSKY. Hold on. It's obvious that until now I haven't been blessed with a drop of good sense. Until now I was stupid enough to think that this estate belongs to Sonya, since my father bought it as a dowry for my sister. Until now I've been naive. I understood our laws, not as some Turk might, but imagined that the estate passed from my sister to Sonya.

SEREBRYAKOV. Yes, the estate belongs to Sonya. Who is disputing that? I wouldn't think of selling it without Sonya's permission. Besides, it's for her benefit.

VOYNITSKY. Unbelievable, unbelievable! Either I'm out of my mind or . . . or . . .

MARIA VASILYEVNA. Jean, don't contradict Alexander. Trust me, he knows best.

VOYNITSKY. Water, let me have some water. (*Drinks.*) Go ahead, say what you want, whatever you want!

SEREBRYAKOV. I cannot understand why you're upset. I'm not saying my plan is perfect. If all of you find it unsuitable, I won't insist. (*Pause.*)

TELEGIN (*embarrassed*). Your Excellency, not only do I cherish a feeling of veneration for scholarship, but I have a family feeling for it as well. My brother, Grigory Ilich . . . well, his wife's brother, Konstantin Trofimovich Lakedemonov—perhaps you know him—he had a master's degree. . . .

VOYNITSKY. Enough, Waffles. We're talking business. . . . Later. . . . (*To* SEREBRYAKOV.) Ask him. The estate was bought from his uncle.

SEREBRYAKOV. Really, why should I? For what purpose?

VOYNITSKY. It went for ninety-five thousand rubles. My father paid seventy thousand cash, which left a debt of twenty-five. Now listen closely. . . . This estate was purchased only because I waived my share of the inheritance in favor of my sister, whom I loved with all my heart. What's more, for ten years I worked like an ox to pay off the mortgage. . . .

SEREBRYAKOV. I regret I ever started this conversation.

VOYNITSKY. The estate is clear of debt and hasn't gone to seed only because of my personal efforts. And now that I've grown old, I'm to be tossed out by the scruff of my neck!

SEREBRYAKOV. I don't see what you're driving at!

VOYNITSKY. For twenty-five years I ran this estate. I worked, I forwarded you money like the most conscientious of managers, and not once in all that time did you thank me. Over those years—when I was young, and now—you paid me the same salary of five hundred rubles—pauper's wages! And not once did you think of raising it by as much as a single ruble!

SEREBRYAKOV. Ivan Petrovich, how was I to know? I'm not a practical man, I have no understanding of these matters. You might have given yourself a raise, as much as you liked.

VOYNITSKY. Why didn't I steal? Why don't you all despise me for not stealing? That would have been fair and square, and I wouldn't be a beggar today!

MARIA VASILYEVNA (*severely*). Jean!

TELEGIN (*agitated*). Vanya, my dear friend, you mustn't, you mustn't . . . I'm trembling. . . . Why spoil friendly relations? (*Kisses him.*) You mustn't.

VOYNITSKY. For twenty-five years I've buried myself with my mother behind these four walls, like a mole trapped in his burrow. . . . All our thoughts and feelings belonged to you alone. Our days were spent speaking about you, about your work. You were our pride, we spoke your name with reverence. Our nights were wasted reading journals and books for which I now have the profoundest contempt!

TELEGIN. You mustn't, Vanya, you mustn't . . . I can't bear . . .

SEREBRYAKOV (*furiously*). What is it you want?

VOYNITSKY. You were a higher order of being for us, we knew your articles by heart. . . . But now my eyes are open! I see you through and through! You write about art without understanding it in the least! All your work, which I once admired, isn't worth a damn! You pulled the wool over our eyes!

SEREBRYAKOV. Ladies and gentlemen! Restrain him. Enough is enough! I'm leaving!

YELENA ANDREYEVNA. Vanya, I insist you keep quiet! Do you hear?

VOYNITSKY. I won't keep quiet! (*Blocking* SEREBRYAKOV'S *way.*) Wait, I'm not done yet! You've ruined my life! I haven't lived, do you hear me, I haven't lived! Thanks to you I destroyed the best years of my life, turned them to ashes! You are my worst enemy!

TELEGIN. I can't . . . I just can't . . . I'm going. . . . (*Goes out in extreme agitation.*)

SEREBRYAKOV. What do you want from me? And by what right do

you speak to me in such a tone? You nonentity! If the estate is yours, then you're welcome to it. I can manage without it!

YELENA ANDREYEVNA. I'm leaving this hell immediately! (*In a scream.*) I can't bear it any longer!

VOYNITSKY. My life is over! I'm talented, intelligent, I have daring. . . . Had I lived a normal life, I might have become a Schopenhauer, a Dostoevsky. . . . What rubbish! I'm going out of my mind. . . . Mother, I'm in despair! Mother!

MARIA VASILYEVNA (*severely*). Do as Alexander says.

SONYA (*falls to her knees before the* NANNY *and presses up against her*). Nanny! Nanny!

VOYNITSKY. Mother! What am I to do? Never mind, don't answer! I know what I have to do! (*To* SEREBRYAKOV.) You'll have something to remember me by! (*Goes out through the middle door,* MARIA VASILYEVNA *after him.*)

SEREBRYAKOV. My friends, what's the meaning of this? Take that madman away! We can't remain under one roof! He lives there (*pointing to the middle door*), practically in the same room. . . . Have him move to the village, or into the wing, or I'll move. I refuse to remain in the same house with him. . . .

YELENA ANDREYEVNA (*to her husband*). We're leaving today! Arrangements must be made at once.

SEREBRYAKOV. A contemptible individual!

SONYA (*kneeling, addressing her father, anxious and tearful*). Papa, we must be compassionate! Uncle Vanya and I are so unhappy! (*Keeping a rein on her desperation.*) We must be compassionate! When you were younger, remember, Uncle Vanya and grandmother stayed up nights translating books for you, copying your papers. . . . Night after night! Uncle Vanya and I worked tirelessly, we were afraid to spend a kopek on ourselves—it was all for you. . . . We suffered for our daily bread! I'm not expressing myself well, but understand us, papa. We must be compassionate!

YELENA ANDREYEVNA (*agitated, to her husband*). Alexander, please, make it up with him. . . . I implore you.

SEREBRYAKOV. Very well, I'll talk to him. . . . I'm not making any accusations and I'm not angry, but you must agree, his behavior is, to say the least, peculiar. Very well, I'll go. (*Goes out through the center door.*)

YELENA ANDREYEVNA. Be gentle with him, calm him down. . . .
(*Goes out after him.*)

SONYA (*pressing up against the* NANNY). Nanny! Nanny!

MARINA. Never mind, my child. The geese cackle—and then they
stop. . . . They cackle—and soon it's over. . . .

SONYA. Nanny!

MARINA (*stroking her head*). Why you're shivering, as if it was cold.
There, there, my poor orphan. God is kind. A touch of lime tea, or
maybe raspberry, and it'll all pass. . . . Don't be sad, my little
orphan. . . . (*Looking at the center door, angrily.*) Shoo! Shoo! you
geese, off with you!

A shot offstage. YELENA ANDREYEVNA *can be heard screaming.*
SONYA *shudders.*

MARINA. Oh, off with you!

SEREBRYAKOV (*runs in, reeling in terror*). Keep him away from me!
Keep him away! He's gone mad!

YELENA ANDREYEVNA *and* VOYNITSKY *struggle in the doorway.*

YELENA ANDREYEVNA (*trying to take the revolver from him*). Give it
to me! Give it to me, I tell you!

VOYNITSKY. Let me go, Hélène! Let me go! (*Frees himself, runs in,
looking for* SEREBRYAKOV). Where is he? Ah, there you are!
(*Fires.*) Bang! (*Pause.*) It didn't hit him? Missed again! (*In a fury.*)
Damn, damn, damn . . . to hell with it all. . . . (*Slams the revolver
against the floor; drained, he sits down on a chair.* SEREBRYAKOV
is in a state of shock. YELENA ANDREYEVNA *leans against the wall,
feeling faint.*)

YELENA ANDREYEVNA. Take me away from this place! Take me
away, or kill me. . . . I can't stay here, I can't!

VOYNITSKY (*in despair*). Oh, what am I doing? What am I doing?

SONYA (*softly*). Nanny! Nanny!

Curtain

ACT IV   UNCLE VANYA'S *room—serves as both his bedroom and the estate office. By the window a large desk with account ledgers and various papers, an upright desk, bookcases and scales. A smaller desk for* ASTROV *with drawing materials, paints, a portfolio nearby. A starling in a bird cage. On the wall a map of Africa of no apparent use to anybody. An enormous sofa upholstered in oilcloth. On the left—a door leading to the other rooms; on the right—a door to the hall. A mat in front of the righthand door so that the peasants don't track dirt in. An autumn evening. Quiet.* TELEGIN *and* MARINA *sit facing each other, winding yarn for stockings.*

TELEGIN. Hurry up, Marina Timofeyevna, any minute now we'll be saying goodbye. They've already ordered horses.

MARINA (*trying to wind faster*). Not much left now.

TELEGIN. They're off to Kharkov. To live there.

MARINA. So much the better.

TELEGIN. They've had a scare. . . . Yelena Andreyevna says she won't stay here another hour. . . . "We just have to go away," she says. "We'll stop over in Kharkov, have a look about, and then send for our things." They're traveling light. You can see, it's not in the cards for them to live here, Marina Timofeyevna, just not in the cards. . . . Fate has something else in store for them.

MARINA. So much the better. The fuss they raised, shooting guns—shameful!

TELEGIN. Yes, a subject worthy of the brush of an artist.

MARINA. That I had never laid eyes on such goings-on! (*Pause.*) Now we'll go back to the old ways. Tea before eight, dinner at noon, evenings we'll sit down together for supper. Everything as it's supposed to be, like other people . . . the Christian way. (*Sighs.*) Sinner that I am, it's been ages since I've had noodles.

TELEGIN. Yes, they haven't cooked noodles in this house for a long time. (*Pause.*) A long time. . . . This morning, Marina

Timofeyevna, I was walking through the village and the grocer yelled after me: "Hey you, sponger!" I felt so miserable!

MARINA. Don't pay it any mind, my dear. All of us live off God. You, and Sonya, and Vanya—everyone has something to do, we all work! All of us. . . . Where's Sonya?

TELEGIN. In the garden. With the doctor, looking for Ivan Petrovich. They're afraid he'll put an end to himself.

MARINA. Where's his pistol?

TELEGIN (*in a whisper*). I hid it in the cellar!

MARINA (*with an ironical smile*). Oh, forgive us our sins!

VOYNITSKY *and* ASTROV *enter from outside.*

VOYNITSKY. Leave me alone! (*To* MARINA *and* TELEGIN.) Go away, give me at least an hour to myself! I can't stand being watched over.

TELEGIN. We're going, Vanya. (*Goes out on tiptoe.*)

MARINA. Hear the goose—honk, honk! (*Gathers up her yarn and goes out.*)

VOYNITSKY. Leave me alone!

ASTROV. With pleasure. I ought to have left some time ago, but I repeat, I'm not budging until you return what you took from me.

VOYNITSKY. I didn't take anything from you.

ASTROV. I'm serious—don't detain me. I'm late as it is.

VOYNITSKY. I said I didn't take anything. (*They sit.*)

ASTROV. No? In that case, I'll wait a while and—pardon me—but we'll have to employ force. We'll tie you up and search you. I'm perfectly serious.

VOYNITSKY. As you choose. (*Pause.*) To play the fool like that—two shots and not even one hit! I'll never forgive myself!

ASTROV. If you had an itch to do some shooting, you might just as well have put a bullet into your own head.

VOYNITSKY (*shrugging his shoulders*). Strange. I attempt murder and no one arrests me, I'm not indicted. That means they take me for a madman. (*Laughs bitterly.*) I'm mad and those who hide their mediocrity and dullness, their terrible coldness, under the mask of a professor and an intellectual wizard are not mad. And women who marry senile old men and openly deceive them are not mad. I saw you, I saw how you embraced her!

ASTROV. I confess, I put my arms around her. And here's to you. (*Thumbs his nose.*)

VOYNITSKY (*gazing at the door*). No, it's the world that's mad if it still contains the likes of you.

ASTROV. That's dumb.

VOYNITSKY. Well, I'm crazy and not responsible. I have a right to speak stupidities.

ASTROV. A shopworn ploy. You're not crazy, just a crackpot. A clown. I once considered every crank sick and abnormal, but I've come to the conclusion that the normal condition of a human being is to be a crank. You're perfectly normal.

VOYNITSKY (*covering his face with his hands*). The shame of it! If you only knew how ashamed I feel! No pain can compare with this burning sense of shame. (*In anguish.*) Unbearable! (*Leans against the table.*) What am I to do? What am I to do?

ASTROV. Nothing.

VOYNITSKY. Give me something! Oh, my God. . . . I'm forty-seven years old. Let's say I live to sixty. I have another thirteen years to go. How will I get through those thirteen years? What will I do, how will I fill them? Try to understand . . . (*convulsively squeezing* ASTROV'S *hand*) try to understand . . . if I could only live out my life in a fresh way. To wake up on a clear, calm morning and feel that you've begun life anew, that the past is forgotten, vanished into smoke. (*Weeps.*) To start a new life. . . . Tell me, where do I start? . . . How? . . .

ASTROV (*irritated*). Come off it! What's all this about a new life? Our situation—yours and mine—is hopeless.

VOYNITSKY. You think so?

ASTROV. I'm convinced of it.

VOYNITSKY. Give me something. . . . (*Pointing to his heart.*) My chest is on fire.

ASTROV (*shouts angrily*). Cut it out! (*Softening.*) In a hundred or two hundred years from now men will feel contempt for our stupid, insipid lives. Perhaps they will have found a way to be happy. As for us . . . we have only one hope left—that dreams attend us as we rest in our graves, maybe even pleasant ones. (*Sighing.*) Yes, my friend. In our entire county there were only two decent, educated men—you and me. But in some ten years this shallow life, this contemptible life, has sucked us in. Its putrid vapors have poisoned our blood, we've become as mediocre as the rest of them. (*Animatedly.*) But enough of your smoke screens. Give me back what you took from me.

VOYNITSKY. I didn't take anything.

ASTROV. You took a bottle of morphine from my medical bag. (*Pause.*) Listen, if you're determined to put an end to it, go off into the woods and shoot yourself. Only give me back my morphine. Otherwise there'll be talk. They'll imagine I offered it to you. . . . It's bad enough that I'll have to cut you open at the inquest. . . . Do you think that's fun?

SONYA *enters.*

VOYNITSKY. Leave me alone.

ASTROV (*to* SONYA). Sonya, your uncle made off with a bottle of morphine and won't return it. Tell him that's not very bright of him. Besides I haven't time to waste. I have to be on my way.

SONYA. Uncle Vanya, you took the doctor's morphine? (*Pause.*)

ASTROV. Yes. I'm certain of it.

SONYA. Return it. Why are you putting a scare into us? (*Tenderly.*) Return it, Uncle Vanya! It may be that I'm no less unhappy than you, but I don't give way to despair. I bear it and I shall keep on until my life runs out of its own accord. . . . You bear it too. (*Pause.*) Return it! (*Kisses his hands.*) My dear, good uncle, my precious uncle, return it! You're kind, I know you'll have pity on us and return it. Bear your life, uncle! Endure!

VOYNITSKY (*takes the bottle out of the desk and returns it to* ASTROV). Here, take it! (*To* SONYA.) Only we have to get to work right away, busy ourselves with something . . . otherwise I can't . . . I just can't. . . .

SONYA. Yes, yes, we must work. As soon as we see them off, we'll get down to work. . . . (*Nervously shuffles the papers on the desk.*) How we've let things slide.

ASTROV (*places the bottle in his bag and straps it up*). Now I can be on my way.

YELENA ANDREYEVNA (*entering*). So you're here, Vanya? We're leaving now. Go to Alexander, he has something to say to you.

SONYA. Do go, Uncle Vanya. (*Takes* VANYA *by the arm.*) Come along, you and papa must make it up. That's essential. (SONYA *and* VOYNITSKY *go out.*).

YELENA ANDREYEVNA. I'm leaving. (*Extends her hand to* ASTROV.) Goodbye.

ASTROV. So soon?

YELENA ANDREYEVNA. The horses are ready.

ASTROV. Goodbye then.

YELENA ANDREYEVNA. Today you promised me you would leave this house.

ASTROV. I haven't forgotten. I'm on my way. (*Pause.*) You're frightened? (*Takes her hand.*) Can it be that bad?

YELENA ANDREYEVNA. Yes.

ASTROV. Then stay! Why not? Tomorrow at the forest preserve. . . .

YELENA ANDREYEVNA. No . . . it's all settled. . . . That's why I have the courage to look you in the eye—our departure is firm. . . . I ask only one thing—think well of me. I want you to respect me.

ASTROV. Ugh! (*A gesture of impatience.*) Please, stay. Face it, there's nothing for you to do, you have no goal in life, nothing to occupy your mind. Sooner or later you'll give way to your impulses—you can't escape it. Better here than in Kharkov or some tawdry provincial town. Here, in the lap of nature . . . at least it's poetical. The autumn has been beautiful. . . . Here you have forests, decaying mansions à la Turgenev. . . .

YELENA ANDREYEVNA. How funny you are . . . I'm annoyed with you, but still . . . I'll remember you fondly. You're an interesting, original man. We'll never see each other again, since—why pretend—I was even a bit carried away by you. Well, let's shake hands and part as friends. Don't think badly of me.

ASTROV (*shaking her hand*). Yes, better that you leave. . . . (*Musing.*) You seem to be a good person, sincere, and yet there's something mysterious at the core of your character. Everyone here kept busy, worked, created something. Then you came along, and we all felt compelled to drop our pursuits and spend an entire summer fussing over your husband's gout and over you. The two of you have contaminated us with your idleness. You fascinated me, for a month now I haven't done a stitch of work; meanwhile people have fallen sick, the peasants have taken to grazing their cattle in my forests, on the young shoots. . . . Wherever you and your husband go, you leave destruction in your wake. . . . I'm joking, of course, but all the same . . . it's curious. I'm convinced that were you to stay on, the devastation would be enormous. I would be lost, and you wouldn't end up too well, either. So, leave. *Finita la commedia!*

YELENA ANDREYEVNA (*takes a pencil from his desk and hastily conceals it*). I'm taking this pencil to remember you by.

ASTROV. How strange. . . . To have known each other and suddenly, who knows why . . . never to meet again. All life is like that. . . . While we're alone, before Uncle Vanya shows up with his bouquet, let me . . . kiss you. . . . A goodbye kiss. . . . May I? (*Kisses her on the cheek.*) There . . . beautiful!

YELENA ANDREYEVNA. I wish you the best of everything. (*Glances about.*) Come what may, for once in my life! (*Embraces him impulsively. Both immediately and quickly step back.*) I must be going.

ASTROV. Go quickly. If the carriage is ready, go.

YELENA ANDREYEVNA. I think I hear them. (*Both listen.*)

ASTROV. *Finita!*

SEREBRYAKOV, VOYNITSKY, MARIA VASILYEVNA *with a book,* TELEGIN, *and* SONYA *enter.*

SEREBRYAKOV (*to* VOYNITSKY). Let bygones be bygones. After what occurred, I experienced so much, rethought so many things, that I consider myself capable of writing a dissertation on how one ought to live for the edification of posterity. I readily accept your apologies and ask you to accept mine. Adieu! (*He and* VOYNITSKY *kiss three times.*)

VOYNITSKY. You will receive the same amount as before, and punctually. Nothing has changed.

YELENA ANDREYEVNA *embraces* SONYA.

SEREBRYAKOV (*kissing* MARIA VASILYEVNA'S *hand*). *Maman.* . . .

MARIA VASILYEVNA (*kisses him*). Alexander, have your photograph taken again and send me a copy. You know how dear you are to me.

TELEGIN. Goodbye, Your Excellency! Don't forget us.

SEREBRYAKOV (*kissing his daughter*). Goodbye . . . Goodbye everybody! (*Offering his hand to* ASTROV.) I thank you for the pleasure of your company. . . . I respect your way of thinking, your enthusiasms and ardent impulses, but permit an old man to insert but a single observation into his words of farewell. Ladies and gentlemen, one must do something! One must do something! (*Bows to all.*) My best wishes! (*Goes out,* MARIA VASILYEVNA *and* SONYA *after him.*)

VOYNITSKY (*fervently kissing* YELENA ANDREYEVNA'S *hand*). Goodbye. . . . forgive me. . . . We'll never see each other again.

YELENA ANDREYEVNA (*touched*). Goodbye, my dear friend. (*Kisses him on the head and goes out.*)

ASTROV (*to* TELEGIN). Waffles, tell them, while they're at it, to harness my horses too.

TELEGIN. At your service, old friend. (*Goes out; only* ASTROV *and* VOYNITSKY *remain.*)

ASTROV (*clearing his paints from his table and putting them away in his suitcase*). Aren't you going to see them off?

VOYNITSKY. Let them . . . I . . . I can't. I'm in a bad way. Have to get busy fast. . . . Work, work! (*Rummages through papers on the desk. Pause. The sound of harness bells.*)

ASTROV. They've gone. I'll wager the professor is tickled pink. You couldn't bring him back here for love or money.

MARINA (*entering*). They've gone. (*Sits in an armchair and knits her stocking.*)

SONYA (*entering*). They've gone. (*Wipes tears from her eyes.*) God grant them a safe journey. (*To* UNCLE VANYA.) Well, Uncle Vanya, let's get to work.

VOYNITSKY. Work, I have to work. . . .

SONYA. It's been a long, long time since we sat together at this desk. (*Lights the lamp on the desk.*) Seems we're out of ink. . . . (*Takes the inkwell and goes to the cupboard to refill it.*) I feel sad now that they've gone.

MARIA VASILYEVNA (*enters slowly*). They've gone! (*Sits and buries herself in reading.*)

SONYA (*sits down at the desk and leafs through the account book*). First, Uncle Vanya, we'll do the accounts. It's terrible how they've been neglected. Just today a customer again sent for his bill. Write it out. You do one, I'll do another.

VOYNITSKY (*writing*). "To the account of . . . " (*They both write in silence.*)

MARINA (*yawning*). Time for night-night. . . .

ASTROV. Silence. Pens scratch, crickets chirp. It's warm and cozy. . . . You don't feel like leaving. (*Sound of harness bells.*) They're harnessing my horses. All that remains, my friends, is to say goodbye to you, say goodbye to my desk, and—I'm off! (*Packs his cartograms away in a portfolio.*)

MARINA. What's the rush? Sit a while.

ASTROV. I can't.

VOYNITSKY (*writing*). "And carry over a debt of two rubles, seventy-five . . . "

WORKMAN (*entering*). Mikhail Lvovich, your horses are ready.

ASTROV. I heard. (*Gives him his medical case, suitcase, and portfolio.*) Here, take these. Be careful you don't crumple the portfolio.

WORKMAN. Yes, sir. (*Goes out.*)

ASTROV. Well. . . . (*Goes to say goodbye.*)

SONYA. When shall we see you again?

ASTROV. Not before summer, I expect. Almost no chance during the winter. . . . Of course, if something should happen, let me know— I'll ride over. (*Shakes her hand.*) Thank you for your hospitality, your kindness . . . in a word, for everything. (*Goes over to the NANNY and kisses her head.*) Goodbye, Nanny.

MARINA. You're leaving without tea?

ASTROV. I don't feel like it.

MARINA. Maybe a drop of vodka then?

ASTROV (*indecisively*). Well, maybe. . . . (MARINA *goes out. Pause.*) My trace horse has gone lame. I noticed it yesterday, when Petrushka was watering her.

VOYNITSKY. She needs reshoeing.

ASTROV. I'll have to make a stop at the blacksmith's in

116 : UNCLE VANYA

Rozhestvennoye. No getting around it. (*Goes up to the map of Africa and examines it.*) The heat in Africa must be terrific now.

VOYNITSKY. Yes, most likely.

MARINA (*returns carrying a tray with a glass of vodka and bread*). Drink up. (ASTROV *drinks.*) Good health, my angel. (*Bows low.*) Have some bread too.

ASTROV. No, I'm fine . . . well, good luck to all! (*To* MARINA.) Don't see me out, Nanny. It's not necessary. (*He leaves,* SONYA *after him with a candle to see him out.* MARINA *sits down in her armchair.*)

VOYNITSKY (*writing*). "The second of February, twenty gallons of vegetable oil. . . . The sixteenth of February, another twenty gallons. . . . Buckwheat. . . . "(*Pause. The sound of harness bells.*)

MARINA. He's gone. (*Pause.*)

SONYA (*returns, places the candle on the table*). He's gone. . . .

VOYNITSKY (*counts on the abacus and writes*). "Total . . . fifteen . . . twenty-five. . . . " (SONYA *sits down and writes.*)

MARINA (*yawning*). Oh Lord, have mercy. . . .

TELEGIN *enters on tiptoe, sits by the door, and softly strums on his guitar.*

VOYNITSKY (*to* SONYA, *running his hand over her hair*). My dear child, how hard it is for me! If you only knew how hard!

SONYA. What can we do, we must live! (*Pause.*) We shall live, Uncle Vanya. We shall live through a long, long row of days, of endless evenings. We shall patiently bear the trials fate sends us. We shall work for others, now and in our old age, knowing no peace. And when our time comes, we shall die resigned. There, beyond the grave, we shall say that we suffered and wept, that our life was bitter, and God will have pity on us. And you and I, uncle, my dear sweet uncle, shall know a bright, beautiful, and gracious life. We shall rejoice and look back upon our present unhappiness lovingly, with a smile—and we shall rest. I believe, uncle, I believe passionately, with all my heart. . . . (*Falls to her knees and places her head in his hands. In a weary voice.*) We shall rest! (TELEGIN *plays softly on the guitar.*) We shall rest! We shall hear choruses of angels and see the heavens ablaze in diamonds. All the evils of this life, all our sufferings, will vanish in a sea of pity washing over the whole world. Our life will be peaceful, tender, gentle as a caress. I believe, I believe. . . . (*Wipes away his tears with a handkerchief.*) Poor, poor Uncle Vanya, you're crying. . . . (*In tears.*) You've had a joyless life, but wait, Uncle Vanya, wait. . . . We shall rest. . . . (*Embraces him.*) We shall rest! (*The* WATCHMAN *taps on his board.* TELEGIN *plays softly.* MARIA VASILYEVNA *writes in the margins of her pamphlet.* MARINA *knits her stocking.*) We shall rest!

The curtain descends slowly.

— ends the way it began
— nothing has changed

The Three Sisters

A Drama in Four Acts

CAST OF CHARACTERS

Prózorov, Andréy Sergéyevich

Natálya Ivánovna (Natásha)

his fiancée, then his wife

Olga

Másha

Irína

his sisters

Kulýgin, Fyódor Ilích

a high-school teacher, Masha's husband

Vershínin, Alexander Ignátyevich

a lieutenant colonel and battery commander

Túzenbach, Nikoláy Lvóvich

a baron and a lieutenant

Solyóny, Vasíly Vasílyevich

a staff captain

Chebutýkin, Iván Románovich

an army doctor

Fedótik, Alexéy Petróvich

a second lieutenant

Rodé, Vladímir Kárlovich

a second lieutenant

Ferapónt

a watchman from the County Board, an old man

Anfísa

a nanny, eighty years old

The action takes place in a provincial town.

ACT I

The PROZOROV *house. A living room with columns; behind the columns a ballroom. Midday. Cheerful and sunny outside. The table in the ballroom is being set for lunch.* OLGA *is wearing the dark blue uniform of a schoolteacher in a high school for girls; while pacing the room or standing still, she corrects her pupils' exercise books.* MASHA, *in a black dress and with a hat on her lap, sits reading a book.* IRINA, *in a white dress, stands absorbed in her thoughts.*

OLGA. Father died a year ago today. The fifth of May—your birthday, Irina. It was snowing, and very cold. I thought I wouldn't live through it, you lay in a faint, as if you were dead. And now a year has passed and we talk about it easily, you're wearing a white dress, your face is radiant. (*The clock chimes twelve.*) The clock struck then too. (*Pause.*) I remember: they bore father in his coffin, a band played, at the cemetery they fired a salute. He was a general, commander of a brigade, but not many people came. It was raining. A hard rain mixed with snow.

IRINA. Why dwell on it!

BARON TUZENBACH, CHEBUTYKIN, *and* SOLYONY *appear behind the columns of the ballroom, near the table.*

OLGA. It's warm today, we can keep the windows wide open, though the birches are still bare. It's eleven years since Father got his brigade and brought us here, and yet I remember it well— Moscow in early May, by now the trees are in bloom, it's warm, the city is bathed in sunshine. Eleven years have passed and I remember it all as if it were yesterday. My God! I woke up this morning, saw a flood of sunlight, saw that spring had come, and I trembled with joy. I so much long to go home.

CHEBUTYKIN. Fat chance!

TUZENBACH. Of course, it's all nonsense.

MASHA, *absorbed in her book, softly whistles a tune.*

OLGA. Don't whistle, Masha. Really, how can you! (*Pause.*) My headaches are from teaching at the high school day in and day out, then tutoring until late in the evening. And the things I brood about—it's as if I were already an old woman. Four years of teaching have sapped my strength and youth drop by drop. I have only one dream and it's growing stronger and stronger. . . .

IRINA. To go to Moscow. Sell the house, put an end to everything here, and—to Moscow. . . .

OLGA. Yes! As soon as possible, to Moscow.

CHEBUTYKIN *and* TUZENBACH *laugh.*

IRINA. Our brother will probably become a professor. Anyway, he won't go on living here. Nothing is holding us back but poor Masha.

OLGA. Masha will spend her summers with us in Moscow.

MASHA *softly whistles a tune.*

IRINA. God grant it all works out. (*Gazing out the window.*) The weather is lovely today. I don't know why I feel so carefree! This morning I remembered it's my birthday and I suddenly was so happy. I thought of my childhood, when Mama was still alive. Wonderful thoughts ran through my mind, wonderful thoughts!

OLGA. You're radiant today, more beautiful than ever. And Masha is beautiful too. Andrey would be handsome, only he's gotten fat. It doesn't suit him. And I've aged, I've become terribly thin, no doubt because I'm always so cross with the girls at school. But today I'm free, I'm at home, my head doesn't ache. I feel younger than yesterday. I'm only twenty-eight. . . . All's well, as God has willed it. Though I can't help feeling that if I were married and at home all day, that would be better. (*Pause.*) I would love my husband.

TUZENBACH (*to* SOLYONY) What drivel! I'm sick of listening to you. (*Entering the living room.*) I forgot to tell you. Our new battery commander will be paying a visit today. Colonel Vershinin. (*Sits at the piano.*)

OLGA. Well, I'd be delighted.

IRINA. Is he old?

TUZENBACH. No, not really. Forty or forty-five at the most. (*Plays the piano softly.*) Seems to be a nice fellow. Not stupid, that's for sure. Only he talks a lot.

IRINA. Is he interesting?

TUZENBACH. Oh, he's all right, only he has a wife, a mother-in-law, and two little daughters. What's more, it's his second marriage. He drops in on people and runs on about his wife and two daughters. He's bound to mention them here too. The wife's a bit loony. She wears her hair in a long pigtail like a schoolgirl, talks pretentiously, about her philosophy and such, and keeps on trying to kill herself. Obviously to provoke her husband. I would have walked out on a woman like that ages ago, but he puts up with it and merely complains.

SOLYONY (*entering from the ballroom into the living room with* CHEBUTYKIN). With one arm I can lift only fifty pounds, but with two—one hundred and eighty or even two hundred. Ergo, two men aren't twice as strong as one, but three times so, maybe even more. . . .

CHEBUTYKIN (*reading a newspaper while walking in*). For hair loss . . . an ounce of naphthaline to a half bottle of alcohol . . . dissolve and apply daily. . . . Must take a note of that! (*Makes a note in a notebook. To* SOLYONY.) As I was saying, you stick a cork into a bottle and run a glass tube through it. . . . Then take a pinch of ordinary alum. . . .

IRINA. Ivan Romanych, dear Ivan Romanych!

CHEBUTYKIN. What is it, my dear child, joy of my life?

IRINA. Tell me, why am I so happy today? I feel as if I were sailing, a wide blue sky above me, great white birds flying by. . . . Why is that? Why?

CHEBUTYKIN (*kissing both her hands tenderly*). My little white bird. . . .

IRINA. When I awoke this morning, I washed and dressed, and it suddenly struck me that the world made sense and that I knew how I ought to live. My darling doctor, I know it all. A human being must work, he must live by the sweat of his brow, whoever he is. That's the sole meaning and purpose of his life, his happiness and joy. How grand to be a worker waking at dawn to break paving stones, or a shepherd, or a teacher of little children, or a locomotive engineer. . . . Oh Lord, better not be a human being at all, better an ox or a horse, as long as you work! Anything but a young woman who gets up at noon, has her coffee in bed, and then spends two hours dressing. . . . Oh, what a terrible way to live! On a hot day you sometimes thirst for a drink, that's how I thirst for work. If I don't start getting up early and going off to a job, give me up as a friend, Ivan Romanych.

CHEBUTYKIN (*tenderly*). I shall, I shall, my dear. . . .

OLGA. Father trained us to get up at seven. Now Irina wakes at seven and lounges in bed at least to nine, just thinking. And she looks so serious! (*Laughs.*)

IRINA. You're used to regarding me as a child, so it seems funny to you when I'm serious. I'm twenty years old!

TUZENBACH. This craving for work, my God, how well I understand it! I've never worked a day in my life. I was born in St. Petersburg, that cold and idle city. My family never knew work or hardship. I remember how I would come home from military school. A footman was there to pull off my boots. I would play tricks on him, but my mother would gaze at me adoringly and be astonished when others didn't do the same. They protected me from work. Though they weren't altogether successful, not really! The time has come, a massive cloud is descending upon us, a powerful, invigorating storm is gathering. It's on its way, I feel it already close at hand, and it will soon blow away the indolence of our society, the indifference, the prejudice against work, the deadly boredom. I shall work, and in some twenty-five to thirty years everyone will work. Everyone!

CHEBUTYKIN. I won't work.

TUZENBACH. You don't count.

SOLYONY. If we're lucky you won't be around in twenty-five years. In two or three years you'll die of a stroke, or I'll explode and stick a bullet in your head, my friend. (*Takes a bottle of cologne out of his pocket and sprinkles his chest and hands.*)

CHEBUTYKIN (*laughing*). Actually I've never done anything. Since the day I left the university I haven't lifted a finger or read a single book. Just newspapers. . . . (*Pulls another newspaper out of his pocket.*) Here we are. . . . I know from the papers that there was a man called Dobrolyubov, but damned if I know what he wrote. . . . (*Sound of knocking from the floor below.*) Hear that? . . . They're calling me downstairs, someone's come to see me. I'll be right back . . . wait for me. . . . (*Hurries off, combing his beard.*)

IRINA. He's up to something.

TUZENBACH. Yes. He looked so solemn as he marched out, you can tell he's about to bring you a present.

IRINA. How annoying!

OLGA. Yes, it's dreadful. He's always making a fool of himself.

MASHA.

> *A green oak by a curving shore,*
> *Upon that oak a golden chain . . .*
> *Upon that oak a golden chain . . .*

(*Stands up and hums quietly.*)

OLGA. You're not in a good mood today, Masha. (MASHA, *humming, puts on her hat.*) Where are you going?

MASHA. Home.

IRINA. That's odd. . . .

TUZENBACH. Walking out of your sister's birthday party!

MASHA. It doesn't matter. . . . I'll be here in the evening. Goodbye, my beautiful sister. . . . (*Kisses* IRINA.) Once more, I wish you health, happiness. In the old days, when Father was alive, thirty or forty officers would show up at our birthday parties, it was lively; but today we have only a man and a half, and it's as quiet as a graveyard. . . . I'm going. . . . I'm down in the the dumps today, depressed, don't pay me any mind. (*Laughing through her tears.*) We'll chat later, for now goodbye, my sweet. I'll just go off somewhere, anywhere.

IRINA (*displeased*). Oh, you're so difficult. . . .

OLGA (*tearfully*). I know how you feel, Masha.

SOLYONY. If a man philosophizes, you get philosophistics or at least sophistics, but if a woman starts in, you're left with a bag of wind.

MASHA. What do you mean by that, you terrible, terrible man?

SOLYONY. Nothing.

> *And he no sooner made a sound*
> *Than the bear knocked him to the ground.*

(*Pause.*)

MASHA (*to* OLGA, *angrily*). Stop bawling!

ANFISA *and* FERAPONT *enter with a cake.*

ANFISA. This way, Grandpa. Go on in, your boots are clean enough. (*To* IRINA.) From the County Board, Protopopov sent it. . . . Mikhail Ivanych Protopopov, that is. . . . It's a cake.

IRINA. Thank you. And thank him for us. (*Takes the cake.*)

FERAPONT. Eh?

IRINA (*louder*). Tell him, thank you!

OLGA. Nanny, give him some cake. Ferapont, you may go, they'll let you have some cake.

FERAPONT. Eh?

ANFISA. Come along, Ferapont. Come along, Grandpa. . . . (*They go out.*)

MASHA. I don't care for that Protopopov. . . . Mikhail Potapych or Ivanych or whatever. . . . We shouldn't have invited him.

IRINA. I didn't invite him.

MASHA. Good.

CHEBUTYKIN *enters. After him a soldier with a silver samovar; a buzz of astonishment and displeasure.*

OLGA (*covering her face with her hands*). A samovar! How embarrassing! (*Goes out to the table in the ballroom.*)

All together.

IRINA. My dear, kind Ivan Romanych, how could you?

TUZENBACH (*laughing*). I told you.

MASHA. You're incorrigible.

CHEBUTYKIN. My dear girls, my lovely girls, you're very precious to me, you're all I have in the world. I'll soon be sixty. I'm an old man, a lonely, worthless old man. . . . There's nothing good about me except my love for you. If not for you, I would long since have been dead and buried. . . . (*To* IRINA.) My darling, my child, I've known you from the day you were born . . . I carried you in my arms . . . I loved your mother. . . .

IRINA. But why such an expensive present?

CHEBUTYKIN (*tearfully, angry*). Expensive present. . . . Stop that, will you? (*To the* ORDERLY.) Take the samovar in there. . . . (*Mimicking them.*) Expensive present. . . . (*The* ORDERLY *takes the samovar into the ballroom.*)

ANFISA (*on her way through the living room*). My darlings, a stranger's come, a colonel! The man's already taken off his coat, my children, he's on his way in here. Now you be nice and polite to him, Irina. . . . (*On her way out.*) And it's time lunch was served. . . . Oh, Lord!

TUZENBACH. Must be Vershinin.

VERSHININ *enters.*

TUZENBACH. Colonel Vershinin!

VERSHININ (*to* MASHA *and* IRINA). May I introduce myself: I'm Vershinin. I'm so glad, so very glad to be here with you at last. My how you've grown! My, my!

IRINA. Be seated, please. It's a pleasure for us too.

VERSHININ (*cheerfully*). I'm delighted, sincerely delighted! But there were three sisters. I remember—three little girls. Your faces I don't remember, but that your father, Colonel Prozorov, had three little girls I remember quite clearly. I saw you myself. How time flies! Oh, my! how time flies!

TUZENBACH. Colonel Vershinin is from Moscow.

IRINA. Moscow? Are you really from Moscow?

VERSHININ. Yes, from Moscow. Your father was a battery commander there, and I served as an officer in the same brigade. (*To* MASHA.) Now I seem to remember your face.

MASHA. I don't remember you!

IRINA. Olga! Olga! (*Calls to the ballroom.*) Olga, come quickly. (OLGA *enters from the ballroom into the living room.*) Colonel Vershinin is from Moscow.

VERSHININ. You must be Olga, you're the oldest. . . . And you're Masha. . . . And you're Irina—the youngest. . . .

OLGA. Are you really from Moscow?

VERSHININ. Yes. I went to school in Moscow, and began my military service in Moscow. I was stationed there for a long time. Finally I was appointed to a battery here—and, as you can see, here I am. I don't really remember you, but I do remember that there were three sisters. Your father I remember well, I can close my eyes and see him as if he were alive. I used to visit you in Moscow. . . .

OLGA. I thought I remembered everyone, but. . . .

VERSHININ. My first name is Alexander. . . . Alexander Ignatich Vershinin.

IRINA. Alexander Ignatich, from Moscow. . . . What a coincidence!

OLGA. You see, we're moving there.

IRINA. We hope to be there by autumn. It's our hometown, we were born there . . . on Old Basmannaya Street. (*Both sisters laugh joyfully.*)

MASHA. What a surprise! Meeting someone else from Moscow. (*Animatedly.*) Now I remember! Remember, Olga, at home we would talk about the lovesick major. You were a lieutenant then and you were in love. Everyone called you "major" to tease you.

VERSHININ (*laughing*). Yes, yes. . . . The lovesick major. That's true. . . .

MASHA. You only had a tiny mustache in those days. . . . Oh, how you've aged! (*Tearfully.*) How you've aged!

VERSHININ. Yes, when they called me the lovesick major, I was young and in love. Things are different now.

OLGA. But you don't have a single gray hair. You're not as young, but you're far from old.

VERSHININ. All the same, I'll soon be forty-three. Is it long since you left Moscow?

IRINA. Eleven years. But why are you crying, Masha? How silly you are. . . . (*Tearfully.*) Soon you'll have me crying, too.

MASHA. I'm all right. On what street did you live?

VERSHININ. On Old Basmannaya.

OLGA. Why, that's where we. . . .

VERSHININ. At one time I lived on Nemetskaya Street. I would walk from there to the Red Barracks. On the way there's a gloomy bridge, the water roars beneath it. Depressing for a lonely man.

(*Pause.*) But what a broad and magnificent river you have here! A marvelous river!

OLGA. Yes, only it's cold. It's so cold here, and there are mosquitoes. . . .

VERSHININ. Oh, come now! Here you have such wholesome and healthy weather, Russian weather. Forests, the river . . . and there are birches. Charming modest birches. They're my favorite trees. How pleasant to live here! Only it's peculiar that the railroad station is fifteen miles out of town. . . . And no one seems to know why.

SOLYONY. I know why. (*All look at him.*) Because if it were close it wouldn't be far, and if it were far then it wouldn't be close. (*Awkward silence.*)

TUZENBACH. Solyony will have his little jokes.

OLGA. Now I remember you.

VERSHININ. I knew your mother.

CHEBUTYKIN. A lovely woman, may she rest in peace.

IRINA. Mama is buried in Moscow.

OLGA. In the Novo-Devichy cemetery. . . .

MASHA. Who would believe it?—I've already begun to forget her. People won't remember us either. We'll be forgotten.

VERSHININ. Yes. We'll be forgotten. That's the way things are, there's nothing to be done about it. What we regard as serious, significant, quite important—a time will come and it will be forgotten or seem unimportant. (*Pause.*) And the curious thing is that we can't at all know what will be considered great and valuable and what will be thought contemptible or even absurd. Didn't the discoveries of Copernicus or, say, Columbus, at first seem pointless and ridiculous, while the inane scribblings of some crank were taken for the truth? And it may be that our present life, reconciled to it as we are, will someday seem strange, difficult, foolish, not as pure as it should have been. Perhaps even sinful. . . .

TUZENBACH. Who knows? Maybe people will say our way of life was great and remember it with respect. We don't practice torture nowadays, there are no executions or invasions. And yet there's so much suffering!

SOLYONY (*in a high-pitched voice*). Cheep, cheep, cheep. . . . Keep the baron on bread and water, as long as you let him make his speeches.

TUZENBACH. Solyony, please, leave me alone. . . . (*Changes his seat.*) It's getting to be a bore.

SOLYONY. Cheep, cheep, cheep. . . .

TUZENBACH. The suffering we see today—and there's so much of it!—it's at least a sign of the moral level society has reached.

VERSHININ. Yes, yes, of course.

CHEBUTYKIN. Baron, you just said they'll call our life great, but all the same people are small. . . . (*Stands.*) Just see how tiny I am. To console me they tell me my life is great and makes sense. (*A violin plays in the wings.*)

MASHA. That's Andrey, our brother.

IRINA. He's the scholar of the family. He'll probably be a professor. Papa was a soldier, but his son has chosen an academic career.

MASHA. It's what Papa wanted.

OLGA. We've been teasing him today. It seems he's in love.

IRINA. With a local girl. Most likely she'll be here today.

MASHA. The way she dresses! It's not only grotesque and unfashionable, it's downright pathetic. A queer skirt of gaudy yellow with some sort of vulgar fringe, and on top of that a red blouse. And cheeks that have been scrubbed white! Andrey isn't in love—I won't believe it for a moment. After all, he has taste. He's just teasing us and playing the fool. Yesterday I heard she's marrying Protopopov, the chairman of the County Board. And a good thing too. (*To the side door.*) Andrey dear, come in here for a minute.

ANDREY *enters.*

OLGA. My brother, Andrey Sergeyich.

VERSHININ. Vershinin.

ANDREY. Prozorov. (*Wipes his sweating face.*) Are you the new battery commander?

OLGA. Just imagine, Colonel Vershinin is from Moscow.

ANDREY. Really? Congratulations. Now my sisters won't give you a moment's peace.

VERSHININ. I've already managed to bore your sisters thoroughly.

IRINA. Let me show you the picture frame Andrey gave me as a gift today! (*Shows it.*) He made it all by himself.

VERSHININ (*examining the frame and not knowing what to say*). Yes. . . . It's quite, er, quite. . . .

IRINA. And the frame above the piano, he made that too. (ANDREY *waves his hand impatiently and moves away.*)

OLGA. He's our scholar, he plays the violin, does woodwork—in short, a jack-of-all-trades. Andrey, don't go! He has a way of always walking off. Andrey, come here! (MASHA *and* IRINA *take him by the arms and, laughing, bring him back.*)

MASHA. Come on, come on.

ANDREY. Leave me alone, please.

MASHA. What a silly boy you are! We once called Colonel Vershinin the lovesick major and he didn't mind a bit.

VERSHININ. Not a bit!

MASHA. And I'd like to call you the lovesick violinist!

IRINA. Or the lovesick professor!

OLGA. He's in love! Our Andrey is in love!

IRINA (*applauding*). Bravo! Bravo! Encore! Our Andrey is in love!

CHEBUTYKIN (*comes up to* ANDREY *from behind and wraps both arms around his waist*).

> *Nature made earth our home*
> *For happy love alone.*

(*Laughs loudly, all the time holding onto his newspaper.*)

ANDREY. All right, that's enough. . . . (*Wipes off his face.*) I didn't sleep a wink last night and I'm not myself. I read till four, then went to bed, but it was no use. Kept thinking about one thing and another, and before I knew it, it was dawn and the sunlight came pouring into my room. There's an English book I'd like to translate this summer.

VERSHININ. So you know English?

ANDREY. Yes. My father, may he rest in peace, loaded us down with education. It's a funny thing, actually silly, but I must admit that after his death I started to put on weight and in a year I've filled out, as if my body had been freed of a heavy burden. Thanks to my father, my sisters and I know French,

German, and English, and Irina also speaks Italian. But at what a price!

MASHA. Knowing three languages in this town is an unnecessary luxury. Not even a luxury but a useless appendage, like a sixth finger. We know many useless things.

VERSHININ. Come now! (*Laughs.*) Useless things! Can there really be a town so dull and dreary as to have no place for intelligent, educated men and women? Let's suppose that among the hundred thousand inhabitants of this town, backward and crude as it is, there are only three like you. It goes without saying that you won't prevail against the ignorant masses surrounding you. Over the course of your lives you must gradually give way and be swallowed up by that crowd of a hundred thousand. Life will crush you. But you won't vanish without a trace, without having an impact. After you're gone perhaps another six like you will appear, then twelve, and so on, until at last your kind will be the majority. In two or three hundred years life on this earth will be beautiful beyond our wildest dreams, it will be astonishing. A human being needs a life like that, and if he doesn't have it yet, he must feel it in his heart. He must wait, dream, prepare for it. He has to have greater vision and knowledge than his father or grandfather ever had. (*Laughs.*) And you complain of knowing useless things!

MASHA (*taking off her hat*). I'm staying for lunch.

IRINA (*sighing*). Someone should write all that down. (ANDREY *has slipped out unobserved.*)

TUZENBACH. You say that after many years life will be beautiful and wonderful. I agree. But in order to play a part in that life, even from a distance, we must get ready for it, we must work. . . .

VERSHININ (*rises*). Yes. But how many flowers you have here! (*Looking about.*) And your apartment is lovely. How I envy you! I've spent my life knocking about cramped quarters, the kind that have only two chairs, a sofa, and a stove belching smoke. Flowers like these are just what has been missing from my life. . . . (*Rubbing his hands.*) Oh, well!

TUZENBACH. Yes, we must work. You're probably thinking, the German is getting sentimental again. But you have my word for it, I'm Russian. I don't even speak German. My father belonged to the Russian Orthodox Church. . . . (*Pause.*)

VERSHININ (*pacing*). I often wonder, what if we could start life over knowing what we know now? If our first life was, so to speak, a rough draft and the second—the final copy! I imagine each of us would try not to repeat himself. At the very least he would create new surroundings for himself, an apartment like this, with flowers, a sea of light. . . . I have a wife, two little girls, my wife is not well, and so on and so forth. Now if I were to start my life over, I wouldn't marry. . . . No, a thousand times no!

KULYGIN (*enters in a schoolteacher's uniform; steps up to* IRINA). My dear sister-in-law, permit me to congratulate you on your birthday and convey from the bottom of my heart my sincerest wishes for your health and happiness and everything else one may wish a girl of your years. And permit me to present you this volume as a gift. (*Gives her a book.*) The fifty-year history of our high school, composed by yours truly. A mere trifle. I wrote it because I had nothing better to do, but all the same, do read it. Good morning, ladies and gentlemen! (*To* VERSHININ.) May I introduce myself: Kulygin, teacher in the local high school, civil servant of the seventh rank. (*To* IRINA.) Here you will find the names of everyone who graduated from our school over the last fifty years. *Feci quod potui, faciant meliora potentes.* (*Kisses* MASHA.)

IRINA. But you gave me the same book at Easter.

KULYGIN (*laughs*). Impossible! In that case, give it back. Or better yet, give it to the colonel. Take it, colonel. You can read it when you're feeling bored.

VERSHININ. Thank you. (*Prepares to leave.*) I'm very happy to have met . . .

OLGA. You're not leaving, are you? Don't go!

IRINA. Stay and have lunch with us. Please.

OLGA. Please, do!

VERSHININ (*bows*). It seems I've dropped in on your birthday party. Forgive me, I had no idea. I haven't offered my congratulations. . . . (*Goes with* OLGA *to the ballroom.*)

KULYGIN. Today is Sunday, ladies and gentlemen, the day of rest, so let us rest, let us enjoy ourselves, everyone in conformity with his age and position. The carpets must be taken up for the summer and put away until winter. . . . We sprinkle them first with insect powder or mothballs. . . . The Romans were healthy because they knew how to work, how to rest, they had *mens sana in corpore sano.* Their life ran in well-established forms. Our principal says that the chief thing in life is form. . . . Whatever loses its form, dies. It's the same in our everyday affairs. (*Takes* MASHA *by the waist, laughing.*) Masha loves me. My wife loves me. And the window curtains go into storage along with the carpets. . . . I'm cheerful today, in excellent spirits. Masha, we're due at the principal's at four o'clock this afternoon. They've planned an outing for the teachers and their families.

MASHA. I'm not going.

KULYGIN (*pained*). Masha darling, why not?

MASHA. We'll discuss it later. . . . (*Angrily.*) All right, I'll go, only let me be, please. . . . (*Walks away.*)

KULYGIN. And afterward we'll spend the evening at the principal's. Despite his poor health he does his best to be sociable. A man of excellent qualities, of sterling character. A magnificent human being. Yesterday, after our staff meeting, he said to me, "I'm tired, Fyodor Ilich! I'm tired." (*Looks up at the wall clock, then at his own watch.*) Your clock is seven minutes fast. Yes, those were his very words—"I'm tired." (*A violin plays offstage.*)

OLGA. My friends, come along please, lunch! There's pie!

KULYGIN. Oh, my dear Olga, dear, dear Olga! Yesterday I worked from sunup to eleven in the evening. I was exhausted, and today I'm happy. (*Goes to the table in the ballroom.*) Dear, dear Olga.

CHEBUTYKIN (*stuffs his newspaper into his pocket, combs out his beard*). Pie? Splendid!

MASHA (*to* CHEBUTYKIN, *sternly*). Mind, not a drop today. Do you hear me? It's bad for you.

CHEBUTYKIN. Oh, come on! All that's in the past. I haven't gotten soused for two years now. (*Impatiently.*) Besides, what does it matter!

MASHA. All the same, don't you dare drink. Don't you dare. (*Angrily, but so her husband doesn't hear.*) Damn it, another boring evening at the principal's.

TUZENBACH. I wouldn't go if I were you. . . . It's as easy as that.

CHEBUTYKIN. Don't go, my pet.

MASHA. Oh sure, don't go. . . . This damned life, it's more than I can bear. . . . (*Goes into the ballroom.*)

CHEBUTYKIN (*goes up to her*). Now, now!

SOLYONY (*on his way to the ballroom*). Cheep, cheep, cheep. . . .

TUZENBACH. That'll do, Solyony. Give it a rest!

SOLYONY. Cheep, cheep, cheep. . . .

KULYGIN (*cheerfully*). Your health, colonel. I'm a schoolteacher, one of the family here . . . Masha's husband. She's a good woman. . . .

VERSHININ. I'll have a glass of that dark vodka. (*Drinks.*) Cheers! (*To* OLGA.) It's so good to be here!

Only IRINA *and* TUZENBACH *remain in the living room.*

IRINA. Masha is in a bad mood today. She married at eighteen, when she thought he was a very intelligent man. It hasn't worked out. He's very kind but not very intelligent.

OLGA (*impatiently*). Andrey, are you coming!

ANDREY (*from offstage*). Coming. (*Enters and goes up to the table.*)

TUZENBACH. What are you thinking about?

IRINA. Oh, nothing in particular. I don't care for that Solyony of yours. He frightens me. He says such stupid things. . . .

TUZENBACH. He's a strange man. I'm sorry for him, peeved too, but mostly sorry. I think he's shy. . . . When we're alone together he can be quite clever and friendly, but in company he's rude and hotheaded—ready for a duel at the drop of a hat. Don't go yet, wait till they're seated at the table. Give me a moment with you. What are you thinking about? (*Pause.*) You're twenty, I'm not yet thirty. How many years are ahead of us! A long, long row of days and nights filled with my love for you. . . .

IRINA. Don't speak to me of love, Nikolay.

TUZENBACH. I have an unquenchable thirst for life, for struggle, for work. That thirst has become one with my love for you, Irina. You're beautiful, and because of you I find life beautiful! What are you thinking about?

IRINA. You say life is beautiful. But what if it only seems so! We three sisters, life hasn't yet been beautiful for us. It has smothered us under a tangle of weeds. . . . I have tears in my eyes. I really shouldn't. . . . (*Quickly wipes her face and smiles.*) We must work, work. That's why we're so cheerless and have such a gloomy view of life. Because we don't work. Our ancestors despised work.

NATASHA (*enters, wearing a pink dress with a green sash*). They've already sat down to lunch. . . . I'm late. . . . (*Steals a glance at her mirror, fixes herself up.*) My hair seems all right. (*Noticing* IRINA.) Congratulations, my dear Irina! (*Gives her a vigorous and prolonged kiss.*) You have so many guests, I feel out of place. . . . Good morning, baron.

OLGA (*entering the living room*). Well, if it isn't Natasha. Hello, my dear. (*They kiss.*)

NATASHA. Congratulations on Irina's birthday. You have so many people here, I'm terribly nervous. . . .

OLGA. Don't be silly, they're all friends. (*In a low voice, horrified.*) You're wearing a green sash! That won't do, my dear!

NATASHA. Is green a sign of bad luck?

OLGA. No, it just doesn't go with your dress . . . it looks peculiar.

NATASHA (*tearfully*). Does it? But it's not really green, it's more of a neutral color. (*Follows* OLGA *into the ballroom.*)

All are seated for lunch; no one remains in the living room.

KULYGIN. Irina, I wish you a good man. It's high time you were married.

CHEBUTYKIN. And I wish you a nice young man, Natasha.

KULYGIN. Natasha already has a boyfriend.

MASHA (*bangs her fork against her plate*). I'm going to have a glass of wine! Eat, drink, and be merry, I say. We live only once!

KULYGIN. C minus for behavior.

VERSHININ. A delicious liqueur. What is it made from?

SOLYONY. Cockroaches.

IRINA (*in a tearful voice*). Ugh, how disgusting!

OLGA. For supper we're going to have roast turkey and apple pie. Thank heavens, I'm home all day today, and for the evening too. . . . Come again this evening, my friends.

VERSHININ. Am I invited?

IRINA. Of course.

NATASHA. They're very informal here.

CHEBUTYKIN.

> *Nature made earth our home,*
> *For happy love alone!*

Laughs.

ANDREY (*angrily*). Cut it out! Aren't you all sick of it by now?

FEDOTIK *and* RODÉ *appear with a large basket of flowers.*

FEDOTIK. They've already started lunch.

RODÉ (*loudly, with guttural speech*). They've started lunch? So they have. . . .

FEDOTIK. Hold it, please! (*Snaps a picture.*) That's one! Wait, just one more. . . . (*Snaps another.*) That's two! Done! (*They pick up the basket and enter the ballroom where they are greeted noisily.*)

RODÉ (*loudly*). Many happy returns. The best of everything, the very best! The weather today is delightful, just splendid. All morning I was tramping about with the boys. I teach gymnastics in the high school. . . .

FEDOTIK. You can move now, Irina, it's all right! (*Snapping a photograph.*) You're very attractive today. (*Takes a top out of his pocket.*) By the way, I've got a top here. . . . It makes an amazing sound. . . .

IRINA. How charming!

MASHA.

> *A green oak by a curving shore,*
> *Upon that oak a golden chain . . .*
> *Upon that oak a golden chain . . .*

(*Tearfully.*) Why do I keep saying that? Those words have been haunting me since early morning. . . .

KULYGIN. Thirteen at table!

RODÉ. My friends, do you really put any stock in such superstitions? (*General laughter.*)

KULYGIN. Thirteen at table means someone here is in love. Not you by any chance, doctor. . . . (*Laughter.*)

CHEBUTYKIN. I'm an old sinner, but why Natasha blushed is beyond me. . . .

Loud laughter. NATASHA *runs from the ballroom into the living room,* ANDREY *in pursuit.*

ANDREY. Stop, don't pay them any mind! Wait . . . wait, please.

NATASHA. I'm so embarrassed. . . . I don't know what's wrong with me. They're all laughing at me. Leaving the table like that, it was bad manners—I know that—but I couldn't help it . . . I couldn't help it. (*Hides her face in her hands.*)

ANDREY. My darling, please, I beg you, don't be upset. Trust me, they're only joking, they mean well. My darling, my sweet, they're all kind, good-hearted people. They love us both. Come to the window. They can't see us here. (*Glances about.*)

NATASHA. I'm not used to being among educated people!

ANDREY. O how young you are, wonderfully, beautifully young! My darling, my dearest, don't be so upset! . . . Trust me, trust me. . . . I'm so happy, my heart is brimming over with love and joy. . . . They can't see us! They can't see us! Why, why did I fall in love with you, when did I fall in love—oh, I don't understand a blessed thing. My darling, my sweet, my angel, be my wife! I love you, I love you . . . as I've never loved anyone before. . . . (*They kiss.* TWO OFFICERS *enter and, seeing them kissing, stand surprised.*)

Curtain

ACT II

The same set as Act I. Eight o'clock in the evening. Offstage the faint sounds of an accordian being played on the street. No lighting. NATASHA *enters in a housecoat carrying a candle. She stops at the door leading to* ANDREY'S *room.*

NATASHA. Andrey, what are you up to? Reading again? Never mind, I was only. . . . (*Goes to another door, opens it, looks in, and closes it.*) Did someone leave a light burning?

ANDREY (*enters with a book in his hand*). What are you doing, Natasha?

NATASHA. Checking the lights. . . . It's Carnival Week, the servants are in such a state, I have to stay on my toes, anything might happen. Late last night I was passing through the dining room, and a candle was burning. Who lit it? I couldn't for the life of me find out. (*Sets the candle down.*) What time is it?

ANDREY (*looking at his watch*). A quarter past eight.

NATASHA. Olga and Irina aren't home yet. The poor things—still at work. Olga went to a teacher's meeting, and Irina's at the telegraph office. . . . (*Sighs.*) Only this morning I was saying to your sister, "Take care of yourself, Irina, my dear." But she won't listen. A quarter past eight, you say. I'm afraid our Bobik isn't well. Why is he so cold? Yesterday he ran a fever and today he's cold all over . . . I'm so anxious!

ANDREY. It's nothing, Natasha. The boy's fine.

NATASHA. All the same, we ought to watch his diet. I'm worried. And at nine o'clock people in carnival masks are supposed to show up. We shouldn't let them in, Andrey.

ANDREY. Well, I don't know about that. After all, they were invited.

NATASHA. This morning my darling baby woke up, he looked at me, and all of a sudden, he smiled. You see, he knows me. "Bobik," I said, "Good morning. Good morning, sugar plum!" And he laughed. Children understand, they understand everything. So, Andrey, I'll tell them not to admit the carnival people.

ANDREY (*indecisively*). But that's up to my sisters. It's their home.

NATASHA. Of course, it's theirs too. I'll speak to them. They're so nice. . . . (*Starts to go.*) I've ordered some yogurt for supper. The doctor says you're to keep to your yogurt diet, otherwise you'll never lose weight. (*Stops.*) Bobik is cold. I'm afraid his room may be too chilly for him. We really ought to put him in another room, at least until the weather warms up. Now Irina's room is perfect for a baby—it's dry, sunny all day. I'll have to tell her she can share a room with Olga for a while. . . . Anyhow, she's never at home during the day, she only sleeps here. . . . (*Pause.*) Andrey my pet, why don't you say something?

ANDREY. Oh, I was just thinking. . . . Besides, there's nothing to say. . . .

NATASHA. Hmm. . . . There was something else. . . . Oh, yes. Ferapont has come from the County Board, he asked for you.

ANDREY (*yawning*). Send him in.

NATASHA *goes out.* ANDREY, *bending over the candle she has forgotten, reads his book.* FERAPONT *comes in. He's wearing a tattered old coat with a raised collar; his ears are muffled.*

ANDREY. Hello, old friend. Well, what is it?

FERAPONT. The chairman sent a book and some sort of papers. Here you are, sir. . . . (*Gives him the book and a parcel.*)

ANDREY. Thanks. Fine. But why have you come so late? It's already past eight.

FERAPONT. How's that?

ANDREY (*louder*). I said, it's late. Going on nine o'clock.

FERAPONT. So it is. When I came it was still light, but they wouldn't let me in. The master, they say, is busy. Well, what of it? If he's busy, he's busy. I'm in no rush. (*Imagining that* ANDREY *has asked him something.*) How's that?

ANDREY. Nothing. (*Looking over the book.*) Tomorrow's Friday, the office is closed, but I'll drop by anyhow . . . find something to do. . . . Boring at home. . . . (*Pause.*) Grandpa, it's strange the way things change, the tricks life plays on you. Today I was bored, at loose ends, so I picked up this book—my old university lectures— and I burst out laughing. . . . My God, I'm the secretary of a County Board, the same board where Protopopov is chairman. I'm a secretary, and the most I can hope for is to become a full-fledged member! Andrey Prozorov—a member of a County Board!

Andrey Prozorov—who night after night dreams of being a professor at the University of Moscow, a celebrated scholar, the pride of all Russia!

FERAPONT. I wouldn't know, sir. . . . I don't hear too good. . . .

ANDREY. If you could hear, I probably wouldn't be saying these things to you. I have to talk to someone. My wife doesn't understand me, I'm afraid of my sisters, afraid they'll laugh at me, make me feel ashamed. . . . I don't drink, taverns don't interest me, but right now, my friend, what I wouldn't give to be in Moscow, enjoying myself at Testov's or the Bolshoy Moskovsky.

FERAPONT. Just now at the board office a contractor was saying as how in Moscow some tradesmen was eating pancakes. One of them ate forty pancakes and dropped dead. Forty, or maybe it was fifty. I can't remember.

ANDREY. In Moscow you'll find yourself in a restaurant, the room is gigantic, you don't know anybody and no one knows you. Yet you don't feel out of place. And here you know everybody and everybody knows you and you're alone, all alone. . . . Alone and lonely.

FERAPONT. How's that? (*Pause.*) And that contractor—now maybe he's lying—but he says there's a rope stretched across all Moscow.

ANDREY. What for?

FERAPONT. I wouldn't know. That's what the contractor says.

ANDREY. Ridiculous. (*Reads his book.*) Have you ever been in Moscow?

FERAPONT (*after a pause*). Can't say as I have. It wasn't God's will. (*Pause.*) Can I go now, sir?

ANDREY. Yes. Take care. (FERAPONT *goes out.*) Be well. (*Reading.*) Come tomorrow morning for these papers. . . . Go along now. (*Pause.*) He's gone. (*A bell rings.*) Yes, work to be done. . . . (*Stretches and slowly makes his way to his room.*)

Offstage the nanny sings, rocking the baby. MASHA *and* VERSHININ *enter. While they speak a maid lights a lamp and candles.*

MASHA. I don't know. (*Pause.*) I really don't know. Of course, habit means a great deal. For example, after father died, it took us a long time to get used to doing without orderlies. But apart from habit, what I'm saying seems quite fair. Perhaps it's not that way in other places, but in our town the most decent, honest, and cultivated people are the military.

VERSHININ. I'm a bit thirsty. Tea would be nice.

MASHA (*glancing at the clock*). They'll be serving soon. I got married when I was eighteen. I was afraid of my husband because he was a teacher, and I was barely out of school. He seemed terribly clever, well-educated, an important person. It hasn't turned out that way . . . regrettably.

VERSHININ. Yes . . . that's so.

MASHA. It's not my husband, I've gotten used to him. But most civilians are coarse, disagreeable, and rude. Coarseness in people upsets me, I find it offensive. I'm pained when I meet a person who lacks delicacy, who isn't as gentle and courteous as he might be. When I happen to be among schoolteachers, colleagues of my husband, I'm just miserable.

VERSHININ. Yes. . . . But in my view there's not much to choose between civilians and military men, in this town at any rate. Two sides of the same coin! Just listen to any one of the local educated classes, civilian or military—he'll tell you he's fed up with his wife, fed up with his house, fed up with his property, even with his horses. . . . It's in a Russian's blood to let his thoughts soar high, but tell me, why does his life fall so short? Why?

MASHA. Why?

VERSHININ. Why is he sick of his wife and children and why are they sick of him?

MASHA. You're out of sorts today.

VERSHININ. Maybe. I haven't eaten since this morning. My daughter is ailing, and when my girls aren't well, I can't shake off my worries. I feel to blame for the kind of mother they have. Oh, if you only had seen her this morning! What a contemptible creature! We started trading insults at seven o'clock and at nine I slammed the door and stalked out. (*Pause.*) I never talk about it. It's curious, but I complain only to you. (*Kisses her hand.*) Don't be angry with me. Besides you I have no one, no one. . . . (*Pause.*)

MASHA. That noise in the stove. Just before father died the wind howled in the chimney. The same sound.

VERSHININ. Are you superstitious?

MASHA. Yes.

VERSHININ. How strange. (*Kisses her hand.*) You're a beautiful, wonderful woman. Beautiful and wonderful! It's dark but I can see the light in your eyes.

MASHA (*moves to another chair*). There's more light here.

VERSHININ. I love you, love you, love . . . I love your eyes, the way you move, I dream of you. . . . You're a beautiful woman, a magnificent woman!

MASHA (*laughing softly*). When you say those words, I have to laugh, though I'm frightened. Please, don't say them again. . . . (*In a low voice.*) Go ahead, say them, I don't mind. . . . (*Covers her face with her hands.*) I really don't mind. Someone's coming. Quick, change the subject. . . .

IRINA *and* TUZENBACH *enter from the ballroom.*

TUZENBACH. I have a three-headed name: Baron Tuzenbach-Krone-Altschauer, but I'm really Russian, a member of the Orthodox Church, the same as you. There's little that's German about me—perhaps only my patience, this stubborn persistence which bores you so. Every evening I see you home.

IRINA. I'm worn out!

TUZENBACH. And for the next ten or twenty years I'll keep on going to the telegraph office to walk you home, until you drive me away. . . . (*Delighted at noticing* MASHA *and* VERSHININ.) Is that you? Hello.

IRINA. Home at last. (*To* MASHA.) A moment ago some woman dropped in to telegraph her brother in Saratov. Her son had just died, but she couldn't for the life of her recall the address. So she sent it off without an address, just "to Saratov." She was crying. And for no reason at all I was rude to her. I told her, "I have no time for that sort of thing." Stupid of me. Are the carnival people coming today?

MASHA. Yes.

IRINA (*sits in an armchair*). I'll rest a while. I'm tired.

TUZENBACH (*smiling*). When you come back from work, you look so tiny, so pathetic. . . . (*Pause.*)

IRINA. I'm tired. I don't like working in the telegraph office, I don't like it at all.

MASHA. You've become thinner. . . . (*Whistles.*) And you look younger. Like a little boy.

TUZENBACH. It's her hairdo.

IRINA. I must find another job. This one's not for me. The things I dreamed of, what I so much wanted—they just aren't there. It's sheer drudgery, there's no poetry in it, no intellectual stimulation. . . . (*A knock on the floor from below.*) The doctor's knocking. (*To* TUZENBACH.) Answer him, dear. I can't . . . I'm tired. . . . (TUZENBACH *knocks on the floor.*) He'll come up in a moment. Something ought to be done. Yesterday the doctor and our Andrey were at the club and lost at cards again. They say Andrey lost two hundred rubles.

MASHA (*indifferently*). Well, what's to be done about it now?

IRINA. He lost two weeks ago, and in December too. If he'd only gamble away everything at once then maybe we'd get out of this town. My God, my God! Every night I dream of Moscow, it's as if I'd gone completely mad. (*Laughs.*) We're going to Moscow in June, that leaves . . . February, March, April, May . . . almost half a year!

MASHA. Natasha mustn't find out about his losses.

IRINA. I don't imagine she cares.

CHEBUTYKIN, *who has just gotten out of bed from an after-dinner nap, enters the ballroom, combs out his beard, then sits at the table, pulling a newspaper out of his pocket.*

MASHA. There he is. . . . Has he paid his rent?

IRINA (*laughing*). No. Not a kopek for six months. He must have forgotten.

MASHA (*laughs*). The way he sits, how pompous! (*Everyone laughs. Pause.*)

IRINA. Why are you so quiet, Alexander Ignatich?

VERSHININ. I really don't know. I'd like some tea. My kingdom for a cup of tea! I haven't had a bite since this morning.

CHEBUTYKIN. Irina!

IRINA. What do you want?

CHEBUTYKIN. Come here, please. *Venez ici.* (IRINA *goes over to the table and sits.*) I can't manage without you. (IRINA *lays out the cards for solitaire.*)

VERSHININ. Well, if there's to be no tea, let's at least have a little discussion.

TUZENBACH. Let's. What about?

VERSHININ. What about? We can dream . . . let's say, about what life will be like two or three hundred years from now, after we're long dead and buried.

TUZENBACH. All right. . . . In the future men will fly in balloons, wear their coats cut in a new style, perhaps discover a sixth sense and develop it. But life will be exactly the same—difficult, full of mystery, and happy. And a thousand years from now people will still be moaning: "Oh, how hard life is!" And they will still fear death and not want to die.

VERSHININ (*reflecting*). How should I put it? It seems to me that everything on earth must gradually change, and is already changing before our eyes. In two or three hundred years, in a thousand years—the time doesn't matter—men will finally see the dawn of a fresh and happy life. Of course, we won't play a part in that new way of life, but we're living for it now, working for it, and yes, suffering. We are creating it—and that's our only purpose in life or, as you might say, our happiness.

MASHA *laughs softly.*

TUZENBACH. What's wrong?

MASHA. I don't know. I've been laughing all day.

VERSHININ. I graduated the same school as you, but I didn't go on to the military academy. I read a good deal, though I'm not too good at choosing books and perhaps don't always read the right things. But the more I live, the more I want to know. My hair is turning gray, I'm almost an old man now, but I know so little, oh, so very little! Still I believe I know what really counts, know it in my bones. I'd so much like to prove to you that there's no such thing as happiness, we won't find it, and we ought not find it. . . .

We have to work and keep on working, that's all. Happiness is the lot of our distant descendants. (*Pause.*) If it's not in store for me, then at least my children's children will have it.

FEDOTIK *and* RODÉ *appear in the ballroom. They sit and sing softly, one of them strumming on a guitar.*

TUZENBACH. According to you, I can't even dream of happiness! But what if I am happy!

VERSHININ. You're not.

TUZENBACH (*throwing up his hands and laughing*). It's obvious we don't understand one another. Well, how do I convince you? (MASHA *laughs softly. He points a finger at her.*) Go on, laugh! (*To* VERSHININ.) Forget about your two or three hundred years. In a million years life will be what it's always been. It doesn't change, but stays on the same course, following its own laws. Laws you have nothing to do with. Anyhow, you'll never know them. The birds—cranes, for example—just fly. Ideas may flit through their heads, either sublime or petty, but they'll keep on flying, without knowing where or why. They fly and they'll go on flying, no matter how many philosophers hatch among them. Let them chirp about whatever philosophy they like, as long as they fly. . . .

MASHA. Yet there's a meaning to it all?

TUZENBACH. Meaning. . . . Look, it's snowing. Where's the meaning in that? (*Pause.*)

MASHA. It seems to me that a human being must have faith, or look for something to believe in. Otherwise his life is empty and hollow. . . . To live and not know why the cranes fly, why children are born, why stars sparkle in the sky. . . . Either you know why you're alive, or it's all futile, not worth a rap. (*Pause.*)

VERSHININ. It's a pity I'm not young any more. . . .

MASHA. As Gogol says, "My friends, life in this world is a bore!"

TUZENBACH. And as I say, "My friends, arguing with you is an ordeal!" I give up.

CHEBUTYKIN (*reading from his newspaper*). Balzac was married in Berdichev. (IRINA *hums softly.*) Have to make a note of that. (*Writes in his notebook.*) "Balzac was married in Berdichev."

IRINA (*musing, as she lays out the cards*). Balzac was married in Berdichev.

TUZENBACH. The die is cast. Masha, do you know I've handed in my resignation?

MASHA. So I heard. Nothing good will come of it. I don't like civilians.

TUZENBACH. All the same. . . . (*Stands.*) A fine officer I make. I'm not much to look at. Anyhow, it makes no difference. . . . I'm going to get a job. At least one day in my life I'll work. I'll come home in the evening dead tired, plop into bed, and sleep like a log. (*Going off to the ballroom.*) I bet working people sleep well!

FEDOTIK (*to* IRINA). I bought some crayons for you at Pyzhikov's on Moscow Street. And this little pocket knife. . . .

IRINA. You treat me like a child, but I'm grown up now. . . . (*Gaily takes the crayons and knife.*) How charming!

FEDOTIK. And I bought myself a knife. . . . Look . . . one blade, another blade, and here's a third. These are scissors, this is to clean out your ears, and this one's to clip your fingernails. . . .

RODÉ (*loudly*). Doctor, how old are you now?

CHEBUTYKIN. Me? Thirty-two. (*General laughter.*)

FEDOTIK. Now let me show you another kind of solitaire. . . . (*Lays out the cards.*)

The samovar is brought in. ANFISA *attends to it. A moment later* NATASHA *comes in and also busies herself at the table.* SOLYONY *enters and, after greeting the others, sits at the table.*

VERSHININ. Quite a wind out there!

MASHA. Yes. I'm sick of winter. I've already forgotten what summer is like.

IRINA. The cards are turning up right. That means we'll go to Moscow.

FEDOTIK. No, they're not. See, the eight is on the two of spades. (*Laughs.*) That means no Moscow for you.

CHEBUTYKIN (*reading from the newspaper*). "Tsitsihar. A smallpox epidemic is raging in the city."

ANFISA (*going up to Masha*). Tea is ready, Masha my dear. (*To*

VERSHININ.) Come, sir. . . . Excuse me, I've forgotten your name. . . .

MASHA. Bring it here, Nanny. I'm not going in there.

IRINA. Nanny!

ANFISA. Coming, coming!

NATASHA (*to* SOLYONY). Babies understand you perfectly. "Hello, Bobik," I say to him. "Hello, sweetie." And he looks at me in that special way of his. You may think I'm just being a mother, but that's not so, not at all, you can be certain of that. Bobik is an extraordinary child.

SOLYONY. If he were my kid I'd fry him in a pan and eat him. (*Takes his glass, goes into the living room, and sits in a corner.*)

NATASHA (*covering her face with her hands*). Oh you rude, ill-mannered man!

MASHA. A happy person doesn't notice whether it's summer or winter. If I lived in Moscow I don't think I'd care about the weather. . . .

VERSHININ. The other day I was reading the prison diary of a French minister convicted in the Panama swindle. The way he talks about the birds he saw through the prison window—the enthusiasm and excitement! When he was a minister he didn't notice them, and now that he's free, he takes as little stock of them as before. You won't notice Moscow either when you're living there. Happiness is elsewhere. We never have it, we only long for it.

TUZENBACH (*taking a box from the table*). What happened to the candy?

IRINA. Solyony ate them.

TUZENBACH. All of them?

ANFISA (*pouring tea*). A letter for you, sir.

VERSHININ. For me? (*Takes the letter.*) It's from my daughter. (*Reads.*) Yes, of course. . . . Excuse me, Masha, I'll leave quietly. I won't be having tea. (*Stands up, agitated.*) The same old story. . . .

MASHA. What is it? Or is it personal?

VERSHININ (*softly*). My wife has taken poison again. I have to go. I'll slip out so nobody notices. All this is terribly unpleasant. (*Kisses her hand.*) My darling, you're so lovely, so marvelous . . . I'll go this way. I won't make a sound. . . . (*Goes out.*)

ANFISA. Where's the gentleman gone? I just poured his tea. . . . Did you ever see the likes of it!

MASHA (*losing her temper*). Stop it! The way you pester people, you won't give us a moment's peace. . . . (*Goes with her cup to the table.*) I've had it with you, old woman!

ANFISA. But why are you upset, Masha darling?

ANDREY (*from offstage*). Anfisa!

ANFISA (*mimicking him*). Anfisa! He just sits there and . . . (*Goes off.*)

MASHA (*at the table in the ballroom, angry*). Make some room for me! (*Scatters the cards on the table.*) Sprawling all over the place with your stupid cards! Drink your tea!

IRINA. You're in a nasty mood, Masha.

MASHA. If I'm in a nasty mood, then don't talk to me. Just leave me alone!

CHEBUTYKIN (*laughing*). Leave her alone, leave her alone. . . .

MASHA. You're sixty years old but you're like a little boy, always prattling some goddamn gibberish.

NATASHA (*sighs*). My dear Masha, why must you use such expressions in your conversation? An attractive woman like you. . . . I'll be frank—if not for your language you would be thoroughly charming even in the best society. *Je vous prie, pardonnez moi, Marie, mais vous avez des manières un peu grossières.*

TUZENBACH (*restraining his laughter*). Let me have. . . . Let me have . . . I think there's some cognac over there. . . .

NATASHA. *Il paraît, que mon Bobik déjà ne dort pas.* Bobik is awake. He's not well today. I'm going in to him. Excuse me. . . . (*Goes out.*)

IRINA. Where did Colonel Vershinin go?

MASHA. Home. Another one of those bizarre episodes with his wife.

TUZENBACH (*a cognac decanter in hand, goes up to* SOLYONY). You're off by yourself again, brooding—the devil knows about what. Come on, let's make it up. Have a cognac with me. (*They drink.*) I'll probably have to spend the night pounding away at the piano. Some trash that passes for music. . . . Well, that's the way it goes.

SOLYONY. Why make it up? We haven't quarreled.

TUZENBACH. You alway give me the feeling something has happened between us. I can't help saying it, but you're a strange one.

SOLYONY (*declaiming*). "I'm strange, who is not strange! Be not angry, Aleko!"

TUZENBACH. What does Aleko have to do with it? . . . (*Pause.*)

SOLYONY. When I'm together with someone, I'm all right, like everybody else, but in company I feel depressed, ill at ease . . . and I say all sorts of dumb things. Nevertheless, I'm a good deal more honest and decent than a lot of people I know. And I can prove it.

TUZENBACH. I often feel annoyed with you, you're always picking on me in front of other people, but for some reason I'm drawn to you. Well, no matter what, I'm getting plastered tonight. Drink up!

SOLYONY. Fine. (*They drink.*) I've never had anything against you, baron. It's just that my character is like Lermontov's. (*Softly.*) They say I even look a bit like Lermontov. . . . (*Takes a flask of cologne out of his pocket and sprinkles his hands.*)

TUZENBACH. I'm resigning my commission and that's the end of it! I've been mulling it over for five years now and I finally made up my mind. I'm going to get a job.

SOLYONY (*declaiming*). "Be not angry, Aleko. . . . Forget, forget your dreams."

While they're talking, ANDREY *quietly enters with a book and sits by a candle.*

TUZENBACH. I'll work.

CHEBUTYKIN (*going into the living room with* IRINA). And it was genuine Caucasian food too—onion soup, and for the meat course, something called *chekhartma.*

SOLYONY. *Cheremsha* isn't meat. It's a vegetable, a bit like our onion.

CHEBUTYKIN. No, my friend, *chekhartma* isn't an onion; it's roast lamb.

SOLYONY. And I say *cheremsha* is onion.

CHEBUTYKIN. And I say *chekhartma* is lamb.

SOLYONY. And I say *cheremsha* is onion.

CHEBUTYKIN. What am I arguing with you for! You've never been to the Caucasus and you've never eaten *chekhartma*.

SOLYONY. I've never eaten it because I can't stomach it. *Cheremsha* stinks like garlic.

ANDREY (*imploringly*). Enough, you two! Have a heart!

TUZENBACH. When are the carnival people coming?

IRINA. They promised to be here by nine. Any minute now.

TUZENBACH (*embraces* ANDREY, *sings*). "Oh, my porch, my porch, my brand new porch. . . . "

ANDREY (*dances and sings*). "My brand new porch, my porch of maple wood. . . . "

CHEBUTYKIN (*dances*). "Oh, lovely carvings!" (*Laughter.*)

TUZENBACH (*kisses* ANDREY). Damn it, Andrey, let's have a drink. To our friendship. The two of us together, Andrey, we're off to Moscow, to the university.

SOLYONY. Which one? There are two universities in Moscow.

ANDREY. There's only one university in Moscow.

SOLYONY. And I say two.

ANDREY. Make it three. The more the merrier.

SOLYONY. There are two universities in Moscow! (*Murmurs of protest and hissing.*) There are two universities in Moscow—the old one and the new one. And if you don't like listening to me, if what I'm saying irritates you, I can keep silent. I can even go into another room. . . . (*Goes out.*)

TUZENBACH. Bravo! Bravo! (*Laughs.*) Ladies and gentlemen, grab your partners. I'm going to play now! A funny fellow, that Solyony. (*Sits at the piano and plays a waltz.*)

MASHA (*waltzes by herself*). The baron's drunk, the baron's drunk, the baron's drunk!

NATASHA (*comes in, to* CHEBUTYKIN). Doctor Chebutykin! (*She says something to* CHEBUTYKIN *and then quietly goes out.* CHEBUTYKIN *taps* TUZENBACH *on the shoulder and whispers something to him.*)

IRINA. What's wrong?

CHEBUTYKIN. It's time we left. Be well.

TUZENBACH. Yes, time to go. Good night.

IRINA. But you can't. . . . What about the carnival people?

ANDREY (*embarrassed*). They're not coming. You see, my dear,

Natasha says Bobik isn't feeling too well and that's why. . . . To cut it short, I don't know why and I really don't give a damn.

IRINA (*shrugging her shoulders*). Bobik's not feeling well!

MASHA. Well, that's that! If we're being thrown out, we might as well leave. (*To* IRINA.) It's not Bobik who's sick, but his mother. . . . Up here. (*Taps her forehead.*) Common trash!

ANDREY *goes off to his room through the door on the right.* CHEBUTYKIN *follows. The others take leave of each other in the ballroom.*

FEDOTIK. A shame! I was looking forward to spending the evening here, but if the little baby's sick, then of course. . . . Tomorrow I'll bring him a little toy. . . .

RODÉ (*loudly*). I made a point of taking a nap after dinner, I thought I'd be dancing all night. After all, it's only nine o'clock!

MASHA. We can talk it over outside. Decide what we want to do.

Voices saying, "Goodbye! Good night. Take care of yourself." TUZENBACH'S *cheerful laughter. All go out.* ANFISA *and a maid clear the table, put out the lights.* ANFISA *sings offstage.* ANDREY, *in an overcoat and hat, and* CHEBUTYKIN *enter quietly.*

CHEBUTYKIN. I never got around to getting married. For one thing, my life has sped by like a flash of lightning. Also, I was head over heels in love with your mother. And she was married to someone else. . . .

ANDREY. A man shouldn't marry. Marriage is a bore.

CHEBUTYKIN. That may be so, but there's always loneliness. You can dress it up with fancy words, but loneliness, my boy, is a terrible thing. . . . Though when you come right down to it, of course nothing really matters!

ANDREY. Let's hurry.

CHEBUTYKIN. What's the rush? We've got time.

ANDREY. I'm afraid my wife will stop us.

CHEBUTYKIN. Ah!

ANDREY. I won't play today, only watch. I'm not feeling too well.

... I'm having trouble breathing. Is there anything I can do for it, Ivan Romanych?

CHEBUTYKIN. Why ask me! I can't remember, my boy. I just don't know.

ANDREY. Let's go through the kitchen. (*They go out.*)

The doorbell rings, then rings again. Voices. Laughter.

IRINA (*enters*). Who is it?

ANFISA (*in a whisper*). The carnival people! In masks. (*A ring.*)

IRINA. Tell them no one's home, Nanny. Ask them to excuse us.

ANFISA *goes out.* IRINA *paces the room, absorbed in her thoughts. She is upset.* SOLYONY *enters.*

SOLYONY (*perplexed*). No one's here. . . . Where is everybody?

IRINA. They've gone home.

SOLYONY. Peculiar. You're the only one here?

IRINA. Yes. (*Pause.*) Goodbye.

SOLYONY. Just now I was a bit indiscreet, tactless. But you're not like the others. You're special, you're innocent, you see through to the truth. . . . You're the only one who can understand me, only you. I love you, I love you deeply, boundlessly. . . .

IRINA. Goodbye! Go now.

SOLYONY. I can't live without you. (*Following her.*) Oh, my happiness! (*Through tears.*) My bliss! Splendid, lovely, dazzling eyes. I've never met a woman with such eyes. . . .

IRINA (*coldly*). Stop it, Captain Solyony!

SOLYONY. It's the first time I've ever spoken of my love for you. It's as if I'm not here on this earth, but on some other planet. (*Rubs his forehead.*) But what does it matter? Of course, I can't force you to love me. . . . But I won't tolerate any lucky rivals. . . . I won't. . . . On my word of honor, I'll kill anyone who dares. . . . Oh, marvelous creature!

NATASHA *passes by with a candle.*

NATASHA (*peeps in one door, then another; passes by the door to her husband's room*). Andrey's in there. Let him go on reading. Captain Solyony! I didn't realize you were here. Excuse my appearance.

SOLYONY. Who cares! Goodbye. (*Goes out.*)

NATASHA. You must be tired. Dear, poor girl! (*Kisses* IRINA.) You really ought to go to bed earlier.

IRINA. Is Bobik asleep?

NATASHA. Yes. But he's restless. By the way, my dear, I've been meaning to tell you, but either you're out or I'm too busy. . . . In my opinion the nursery is too cold and damp for little Bobik. Now your room would be just perfect for a baby. My sweet, my pet, do move in with Olga for a while!

IRINA (*uncomprehending*). Move where?

Sounds of a troika with bells ringing driving up to the house.

NATASHA. You and Olga can share a room for the time being and Bobik will have your room. He's such a dear. Today I said to him, "Bobik, you're mine. Mine!" And he looked at me with those cute little eyes of his. (*A ring.*) That must be Olga now. She's quite late! (*A* MAID *approaches* NATASHA *and whispers in her ear.*) Protopopov, you say. Isn't he hilarious! Protopopov is here. He wants me to go for a ride in his troika. How silly these men are. . . . (*A ring.*) Someone else is at the door. Maybe I will go for a little drive, for fifteen minutes or so. . . . (*To the* MAID.) Tell him I'll be right there. (*A ring.*) The doorbell again. . . . Now that must be Olga. (*She goes out.*)

The MAID *runs off.* IRINA *sits wrapped in thought.* KULYGIN *and* OLGA *enter,* VERSHININ *after them.*

KULYGIN. Well, how do you like that! They said there would be a party.

VERSHININ. That's odd. I left just a while ago, about a half hour. They were waiting for the carnival people. . . .

IRINA. They all left.

KULYGIN. Masha too? Where can she have gone? And what's Protopopov doing in his troika? Who's he waiting for?

IRINA. Better not ask. . . . I'm tired.

KULYGIN. Oh, you naughty girl.

OLGA. The teachers' meeting just ended. I'm completely drained. Our headmistress is ill, and I'm to take her place. My head is splitting. Oh, my head, my poor head. . . . (*Sits.*) Andrey lost two hundred rubles at cards last night. . . . The whole town is talking about it. . . .

KULYGIN. The meeting tired me out too. (*Sits.*)

VERSHININ. Today my wife took it into her head to give me a scare, she almost poisoned herself. It turned out all right though, and I'm relieved, I can breathe easy now. . . . So, we have to leave, do we? Well then, I wish you all good night. Kulygin, let's go someplace, the two of us! I can't stay at home, I just can't. . . . Let's go!

KULYGIN. I'm not up to it. Go yourself. (*Stands.*) I'm exhausted. Has my wife gone home?

IRINA. She must have.

KULYGIN (*kisses* IRINA'S *hand*). Good night. For the next two days we can relax. All the best! (*Starts to go.*) I'd love a cup of tea. I was counting on spending the evening in pleasant company and—*o fallacem hominum spem!* . . . Accusative case for exclamations! . . .

VERSHININ. So I'm to go alone. (*He and* KULYGIN *go out.*)

OLGA. My head is killing me, oh, my head. . . . Andrey lost. . . . The whole town is talking. . . . I'm going to lie down. (*Starts to go.*) Tomorrow I'm free, the day after tomorrow—also free. . . . How my head aches, oh my head. . . . (*Goes out.*)

IRINA (*alone*). They've all gone. No one's left.

The sound of an accordian from the street; the NANNY *is singing.*

NATASHA (*crosses the ballroom in a fur coat and fur cap, the* MAID *behind her*). I'll be back in a half hour. I'm just off for a short spin. (*Goes out.*)

IRINA (*alone, longingly*). Moscow! Moscow! Moscow!

Curtain

ACT III

OLGA's and IRINA's *room. On the left and right, beds with screens around them. After two in the morning. Offstage, a fire alarm for a fire that has been going on for some time. It is apparent that no one in the house has gone to bed.* MASHA *is lying on a sofa, as usual in a black dress.* ANFISA *and* OLGA *enter.*

ANFISA. They're under the staircase. . . . I say to them, "Come on upstairs, you can't just sit there like that." They're crying. "Papa," they say, "we don't know where Papa is. We pray to God he hasn't burned up in the fire." The things they've gotten into their heads! And there are others in the yard . . . also in their pajamas.

OLGA (*taking clothes out of the wardrobe*). Take this gray dress. . . . And this one. . . . The blouse too. . . . And this skirt, Nanny. My God, how awful! All of Kirsanovsky Street burned to the ground, it seems so anyhow. . . . Take this. . . . And this. . . . (*Tosses clothes into her arms.*) The Vershinins, poor things, had a terrible scare. . . . Their house barely escaped. They'll have to spend the night here . . . we can't let them go home. . . . At Fedotik's place everything went up in smoke, the poor fellow has nothing left. . . .

ANFISA. You'd better call Ferapont, Olga. I can't manage all this by myself. . . .

OLGA (*rings*). Nobody answers when I ring. . . . (*Speaks toward the door.*) Come in, whoever's out there! (*Through the open door can be seen a window red from the glow of the fire. Sounds of a fire engine passing the house.*) How horrible! And how it tires one! (FERAPONT *enters.*) Take this downstairs. . . . The Kolotilin girls are under the staircase. . . . Give it to them. And this, too. . . .

FERAPONT. Very well, miss. In 1812 Moscow burned down, too. By God, the French were in for a surprise!

OLGA. Go along now.

FERAPONT. Yes, miss. (FERAPONT *goes out.*)

OLGA. Nanny, dearest, give them everything. We don't need it, give it all away, Nanny. I'm worn out, I can barely stand on my feet. . . . We just can't let the Vershinins go home. . . . The girls will sleep in the living room, and the colonel downstairs with Baron Tuzenbach. Fedotik can also stay in the baron's room, or maybe in the ballroom. The doctor would start drinking at a time like this! He's dead drunk, we can't have anyone in with him. And put up Vershinin's wife in the living room, too.

ANFISA (*exhausted*). Olga dearest, don't send me away! Don't send me away!

OLGA. Don't be silly, Nanny. No one's sending you away.

ANFISA (*laying her head on* OLGA'S *breast.*) My darling, my precious, I work, I work as hard as I can. . . . If I get too weak, they'll say, "Go away!" But where do I go? Where? I'm over eighty years old. Eighty-one, in fact. . . .

OLGA. Sit down, Nanny. . . . You're tired, you poor woman. . . . (*Seats her.*) Now rest a bit, my sweet. How pale you are!

NATASHA (*enters*). They're saying a relief committee ought to be set up as soon as possible to assist victims of the fire. A splendid idea, I say. We should always help the less fortunate—that goes with being rich. Bobik and Sofochka are sound asleep, as if nothing had happened. We have a mob here now, people wherever you turn, the house is crammed. Influenza is spreading through the town, I'm afraid the children might catch it.

OLGA (*not listening to her*). You can't see the fire from this room, it's peaceful here. . . .

NATASHA. Yes. . . . I must be a mess. (*In front of a mirror.*) They say I've put on weight . . . but it's not so! Not in the least! Masha's asleep, the poor girl's exhausted. . . . (*To* ANFISA, *coldly.*) Don't you dare remain seated in my presence! Stand up! And now get out of here! (ANFISA *goes out. Pause.*) Why you hold on to that old woman is beyond me!

OLGA (*taken aback*). I'm sorry but I also fail to understand. . . .

NATASHA. She's of no use here. She's a peasant, she belongs in the country. . . . The way you pamper her! I like a house that's run properly! A house that has no dead wood in it. (*Patting* OLGA'S *cheek.*) Poor child, you're tired! Our headmistress is tired! You know, when my little Sofochka grows up and goes to high school, I'll be intimidated by you.

OLGA. I'm not going to be the headmistress.

NATASHA. But they're appointing you, Olga. It's all settled.

OLGA. I'll turn them down. I can't . . . I'm not up to it. . . . (*Drinks a glass of water.*) You were so rude to Nanny just now. . . . I'm sorry, but the state I'm in . . . I can't bear it. . . . It even made me feel faint.

NATASHA (*agitated*). I beg your pardon, Olga, excuse me. . . . I didn't mean to upset you.

MASHA *gets up, takes her pillow, and walks off angrily.*

OLGA. Please, try to understand. . . . Perhaps the way we were brought up was unusual, but I can't bear that sort of thing. When I see people treated badly it depresses me. I feel ill . . . and my heart just sinks!

NATASHA. Forgive me. . . . (*Kisses her.*)

OLGA. The slightest rudeness, even a tactless word, distresses me. . . .

NATASHA. I often say things I shouldn't, that's so, but you must agree, my dear, she can just as well live in the country.

OLGA. She's been with us for thirty years.

NATASHA. But now she's too old to work! Either I don't understand you or you refuse to understand me. She's incapable of doing a day's work. All she does is sleep or sit around.

OLGA. Then let her sit.

NATASHA (*astonished*). What do you mean, "let her sit"? She's a servant! (*Tearfully.*) I don't know what to make of you, Olga. I employ a nurse and a wet nurse, we have a maid, a cook. . . . What in the world do we need that old woman for? What for, I ask you? (*A fire alarm from offstage.*)

OLGA. I've aged ten years tonight.

NATASHA. We have to get things straight, Olga. Once and for all. . . . You're away at school, I'm at home. You have your teaching, I run the house. And if I make some comments about the servants, I know what I'm talking about. I know what I'm ta..lk..ing about! . . . I want that thieving old hag out of here by tomorrow morning. . . . (*Stamping her feet.*) The old witch! . . . And don't you dare cross me! Don't you dare! (*Catching herself.*) Now Olga, if you don't move downstairs, we'll always be quarreling. That would be just dreadful.

KULYGIN (*enters*). Where's Masha? It's time we went home. They say the fire is dying down. (*Stretching.*) Only one neighborhood burned up, though there was a strong wind and at first it seemed the whole town was in flames. (*Sits.*) I'm exhausted. Olga, my dear . . . I often think if not for Masha, I would have married you. You're very kind. . . . I'm just done in. (*Listens attentively.*)

OLGA. What is it?

KULYGIN. The doctor would pick a time like this for one of his drinking bouts. He's roaring drunk. As if in spite! (*Stands.*) I think he's coming this way. . . . Do you hear? Yes, that's him. . . . (*Laughs.*) Yes, he's quite a character! . . . I'm going to hide. (*Goes to the cupboard in the corner.*) Our daredevil!

OLGA. He hasn't touched a drop for two years and at a time like this he goes and gets drunk. . . . (*Goes with* NATASHA *to the back of the room.*)

CHEBUTYKIN (*enters, steady on his feet as if sober. He crosses the room, stops, looks about, then goes to the washstand and starts to wash his hands. Sullenly*). The hell with them . . . every damn one of them. . . . They take me for a doctor, think I can cure whatever ails them, and I haven't the foggiest idea what I'm doing. I've forgotten everything I ever knew. It's all slipped away, all of it. (OLGA *and* NATASHA *go out, without his noticing them.*) Damn 'em. Last Wednesday in Zasyp I treated a woman— she didn't pull through and it was my fault. Yes. . . . Twenty-five years ago I knew a thing or two, but now I remember nothing. Nothing. . . . My mind's a blank, my feelings have turned to ice. Maybe I'm not even a man, maybe I'm only pretending I have arms and legs . . . and a head. Maybe I don't really exist, and I only imagine I'm walking, eating, sleeping. (*Weeps.*) Oh, if only I didn't exist! (*Stops crying; sullenly.*) Ah, who the hell knows! . . . The other day they were throwing around names at the club . . . Shakespeare, Voltaire. . . . I've never read them, not a word, but I put on a face as if I had. And the others played the same game. Petty! Despicable! And that woman I did in on Wednesday came to mind . . . it all came back, and I felt rotten, loathsome, as if my insides were twisted out of shape. . . . So I went off and got plastered. . . .

IRINA, VERSHININ, *and* TUZENBACH *enter;* TUZENBACH *is wearing new and fashionable civilian clothes.*

IRINA. Let's sit for a while. No one will come in here.

VERSHININ. If it weren't for the soldiers, the whole town would have gone up in smoke. Brave fellows! (*Rubs his hands in pleasure.*) The salt of the earth! Heroes, every last one of them!

KULYGIN (*approaching them*). What time is it, my friends?

TUZENBACH. Going on four. It's getting light.

IRINA. They're all in the ballroom. No one's leaving. Your Solyony's there too. . . . (*To* CHEBUTYKIN.) You should go to bed, doctor.

CHEBUTYKIN. I'm all right. . . . Thanks! (*Combs out his beard.*)

KULYGIN (*laughs*). You've had a drop too much, doctor! (*Slaps him on the shoulder.*) To the head of the class! *In vino veritas,* as the Romans put it.

TUZENBACH. I've been asked to arrange a benefit concert for the victims.

IRINA. But who is there to . . . ?

TUZENBACH. We could pull it off if we wanted to. If you ask me, Masha plays the piano beautifully.

KULYGIN. She does play beautifully!

IRINA. She's forgotten by now. She hasn't played for three years . . . maybe four.

TUZENBACH. No one in this town appreciates music, absolutely no one. But I do, and you have my word for it, Masha plays splendidly, almost with genius.

KULYGIN. You're right, baron. I love my Masha very much. She's a fine girl.

TUZENBACH. To play so beautifully when you're aware that no one, absolutely no one understands you!

KULYGIN (*sighing*). Yes. . . . But would it be proper for her to take part in a concert? (*Pause.*) I . . . I really know nothing about such matters. Maybe it would even be a good thing. Our principal is a decent fellow, quite decent. He's very clever, but he has his opinions. . . . Of course, it's none of his business, but, if it's what you want, I guess I could speak to him.

CHEBUTYKIN *picks up a porcelain clock and examines it.*

VERSHININ. I'm covered with ashes from the fire. I look like a mess. (*Pause.*) Yesterday I overheard a rumor about our brigade being transferred. Somewhere far from here. Some say Poland, others Siberia.

TUZENBACH. I heard it too. Well, the town will be empty.

IRINA. We'll leave too!

CHEBUTYKIN (*drops the clock, which smashes*). Smashed to smithereens! (*Pause. Everyone is distressed and ill at ease.*)

KULYGIN (*picking up the fragments*). Breaking such an expensive object! Oh, Doctor Chebutykin, Doctor Chebutykin! F minus for behavior!

IRINA. That clock belonged to my mother.

CHEBUTYKIN. Maybe . . . if you say so. Maybe I didn't break it but it only seems that I broke it. Maybe we only imagine we exist, but we really don't. I don't know anything, no one knows anything. (*Standing at the door.*) What are you looking at? Natasha's having an affair with Protopopov and you don't see it. . . . You sit here, blind as bats, and Natasha's having an affair with Protopopov. . . . (*Sings.*) "Oh, won't you take this juicy fruit from me." . . . (*Goes out.*)

VERSHININ. Yes. . . . (*Laughs.*) How strange it all is! (*Pause.*) When the fire broke out, I ran home as fast as my legs would carry me. I saw that our house was safe and sound, there was no danger, but my little girls were at the front door in their underwear. Their mother was nowhere to be seen, people were bustling about, horses and dogs darting by. Anguish, terror, a cry for help—whatever it was, it was etched on those children's faces. When I saw those faces, my heart sank. My God, I thought, what those girls still have to go through over the course of their lives! I picked them up and ran, thinking all the while—what else does the world hold in store for them! (*Fire alarm. Pause.*) I got back, their mother was here, hysterical and angry. (MASHA *returns, carrying her pillow, and sits on the sofa.*) My girls at the front door in their underwear, barefoot, the street a sheet of red flame, the terrible uproar—it set me to thinking that something similar must have taken place many years ago when our enemies made a sudden raid, plundering and setting towns to the torch. . . . But really, what a difference between then and now! And before long, say in some two or three hundred years, people will look back at our present life with a mixture of horror and amusement. The way we live today will seem cumbersome and difficult, very wrong, even strange. Oh, no doubt about it, life is going to be wonderful, wonderful! (*Laughs.*) Excuse me, there I go again. But let me continue, my friends. I'd very much like to do a little philosophizing. I'm in the mood. (*Pause.*) The town seems to be asleep. As I was saying, life will be wonderful. Surely you can imagine it. . . . Now there are only three of you in this town, in the following generations there will be more, then even more. A time will come when everything will change, people will follow your example, they'll live like you. Then you too will become outdated, men and women even better than you will spring up on this earth. (*Laughs.*) I'm in a rare mood today. Damn it all, I want to live. . . . (*Sings.*)

> *Love binds us all, both young and old,*
> *Its passions make us brave and bold.*

MASHA. Tram-tam-tam. . . .

VERSHININ. Tram-tam. . . .

MASHA. Tra-ra-ra?

VERSHININ. Tra-ta-ta. (*Laughs.*)

FEDOTIK (*enters dancing*). Burnt up. Burnt up. Everything in ashes! (*Laughter.*)

IRINA. That's not much of a joke. Have all your things really burned?

FEDOTIK (*laughs*). To ashes! Not a scrap left. My guitar burnt, my photography equipment burnt, my correspondence. . . . The notebook I meant to give you—burnt.

SOLYONY *enters.*

IRINA. No, Captain Solyony, please leave. You can't come in here.

SOLYONY. How come the baron can and I can't?

VERSHININ. We really should be going. What's happening with the fire?

SOLYONY. They say it's dying down. But I find it quite peculiar that the baron can stay and I can't. (*Takes out a bottle of cologne and sprinkles himself.*)

VERSHININ. Tram-tam-tam.

MASHA. Tram-tam.

VERSHININ (*laughs, to* SOLYONY). Let's go to the ballroom.

SOLYONY. Very well. I'll make a note of that.

> *The moral might be made more clear,*
> *But would upset the geese, I fear.*

(*Looking at* TUZENBACH.) Cheep, cheep, cheep. . . . (*Goes out with*
VERSHININ *and* FEDOTIK.)

IRINA. The room stinks from that Solyony's cologne. . . . (*Puzzled.*)
The baron's asleep! Baron! Baron!

TUZENBACH (*waking up*). How tired I am. . . . The brickyard. . . .
No, I'm not talking in my sleep. As a matter of fact, I'm going to
the brickyard soon, I have a job there. . . . I've already talked it
over with them. (*To* IRINA, *tenderly.*) You're so pale, so beautiful.
Enchanting. . . . It's as if your paleness were a bright light
illuminating the darkness. . . . You're sad, you're dissatisfied with
life. . . . Oh, join me, we'll work side by side!

MASHA. Go away, Nikolay.

TUZENBACH (*laughs*). So you're here too? I didn't notice you. (*Kisses*
IRINA's *hand.*) I'm going. Goodbye. As I look at you now, I
remember that day, long long ago—it was your birthday—you
were so cheerful and lively then. You spoke of the joy of work. . . .
And I dreamed of such a happy life before us! Where is it? (*Kisses
her hand.*) You have tears in your eyes. Go to bed, the sun is
coming up. . . . It's already morning. . . . If only I could give my
life to you!

MASHA. Nikolay, go away! Really. . . .

TUZENBACH. I'm going. . . . (*Goes.*)

MASHA (*lies down*). Are you asleep, Fyodor?

KULYGIN. Eh?

MASHA. You'd better go home.

KULYGIN. My dear Masha, my sweet Masha. . . .

IRINA. She's exhausted. Let her rest, Fyodor.

KULYGIN. I'll go in a minute. . . . My good wife, my nice wife . . . I
love you, my one and only. . . .

MASHA (*irritated*). *Amo, amas, amat, amamus, amatis, amant.*

KULYGIN (*laughs*). Yes, she's amazing. It's seven years since we got married and it seems only yesterday. Honestly. Yes indeed, you're an amazing woman. I'm content, I'm content, I'm content!

MASHA. I'm bored, I'm bored, I'm bored. . . . (*Sits up.*) I can't stop thinking about it. . . . Just outrageous! It's become an obsession, I have to get it off my chest. I mean Andrey. . . . He's mortgaged the house, and his wife's snapped up the money. The house doesn't belong to him, but to the four of us! He ought to realize that, if he's at all honest.

KULYGIN. Why get upset, Masha! What's it to you? Andrey's up to his neck in debt. Let him do what he wants.

MASHA. Still, it's disgraceful. (*Lies down.*)

KULYGIN. We're not poor. I have my job in the high school, I give private lessons. . . . I'm an honest man. An ordinary man. . . . *Omnia mea mecum porto,* as the saying goes.

MASHA. I don't want anything for myself, but the injustice of it makes my blood boil. (*Pause.*) Go home, Fyodor.

KULYGIN (*kisses her*). You're tired, rest for half an hour or so. I'll sit out there and wait. Sleep a while. . . . (*He starts to go.*) I'm content, I'm content, I'm content! (*Goes out.*)

IRINA. Yes, it's true, our Andrey isn't the man he once was. Living with that woman has added years to his life. He's gone to seed. Not too long ago he was studying to become a professor, and yesterday he boasted that at last he made it to the County Board. He's a member, and Protopopov's the chairman. . . . The whole town is buzzing about it. They laugh behind his back, and he's the only one who doesn't see what's going on. . . . Everybody dashed off to the fire, and he stayed in his room dead to the world. All he does is scrape away on his violin. (*Nervously.*) Oh, it's awful, just awful! (*Weeps.*) I can't bear it any longer! . . . I can't, I just can't! . . . (OLGA *comes in and tidies up around her dressing table.* IRINA *sobs loudly.*) You ought to send me packing. Toss me out. Toss me out! I can't take it any more! . . .

OLGA (*frightened*). What is it? What is it, my darling?

IRINA (*sobbing*). Where has it all gone? Where? Where? Oh, my God, my God! I've forgotten everything, everything . . . my head's spinning. . . . I can't remember how to say "window" in Italian, or "floor." I've forgotten everything, every day I forget something else, my life's slipping away, it won't ever come back, we'll never get to Moscow, never . . . I can see that now. . . .

OLGA. Dear, dear Irina.

IRINA (*trying to control herself*). Oh, I'm so unhappy. . . . I can't work, and I won't work. I'm fed up, fed up! I was a telegraph clerk, now I have a job at the Town Council, and I hate it. The things they give me to do only fill me with contempt. . . . I'm twenty-three years old, I've been working for a long time now. My brain has dried up, I've grown thin, lost my looks, turned old, and I've nothing to show for it, nothing at all. Not a drop of satisfaction. Time passes, and I feel myself drifting further and further away from a life that would be genuine and beautiful and heading for an abyss. I'm in despair, despair! I don't know why I go on living, why I haven't killed myself before now. . . .

OLGA. Don't cry, my dear, don't cry. It pains me.

IRINA. I'm not crying, I'm not crying. . . . See, I'm not crying any more. I've cried enough . . . enough!

OLGA. My darling, I say this as a sister, as a friend, if you want my advice, marry the baron! (IRINA *weeps softly*.) You respect him, don't you? You think highly of him. . . . It's true he's not good-looking, but he's decent, honest. . . . After all, people don't marry for love but because it's their duty. At least, I think so. I would marry without love. I would marry anyone who asked, as long as he was a decent man. Even if he were old. . . .

IRINA. I was always waiting, we would move to Moscow, there I would meet my true love. I dreamed of him, in my dreams I loved him. . . . But it all turned out to be an empty bubble. . . .

OLGA (*embracing her sister*). My darling, beautiful sister, I understand. When the baron left the army and showed up in civilian clothes, he looked so ungainly it brought tears to my eyes. . . . He asked me why I was crying. What could I say! But if it were God's will that he marry you, I would be happy. That would be altogether different.

NATASHA, *carrying a candle, walks across the stage, from the door on the right to the door on the left, without speaking.*

MASHA (*sitting up*). The way she walks, you'd think she started the fire.

OLGA. Masha, you're silly. The silliest one in the family. Forgive me for saying so. (*Pause.*)

MASHA. My sisters, I have a confession to make. I'm having a bad time of it. I'll confess to you and nobody else, ever. . . . Just a moment. (*Softly.*) It's my secret, but you ought to know. . . . I can't keep it to myself. . . . (*Pause.*) I'm in love, I love . . . I love that man. . . . He was here just now. . . . Well, what's the use? In a nutshell, I love Vershinin. . . .

OLGA (*goes behind the screen*). Don't say another word. Anyhow, I'm not listening.

MASHA. What can I do? (*Clutches her head.*) At first I found him a bit strange, then I felt sorry for him . . . finally I fell in love . . . I fell in love with his voice, the way he talks, his unhappiness, his two little girls. . . .

OLGA (*from behind the screen*). I'm still not listening. Say any foolishness you like, it doesn't matter, I won't hear.

MASHA. You're the silly one, Olga. I love—then that's my fate, my destiny. . . . And he loves me. . . . Terrifying, isn't it! Wrong of me? (*Draws* IRINA *to her by the hand.*) Oh, my dearest. . . . How will we get through our lives? What will become of us? . . . When you read some novel it all seems old hat, as plain as day. But go fall in love yourself and you see that nobody knows anything, each of us has to make her own choice. . . . My dear, sweet sisters . . . I've made a clean breast of it, now I'll shut up. I'll be like Gogol's madman . . . "Silent" . . . "Silent."

Enter ANDREY, FERAPONT *after him.*

ANDREY (*angrily*). What do you want? I can't make sense of it.

FERAPONT (*in the doorway, impatiently*). I've said it ten times already.

ANDREY. For starters, I'm "sir" to you!

FERAPONT. The firemen, sir, ask your permission to drive to the river by way of the garden. Otherwise they have to go roundabout. It's a pain in the neck, sir.

ANDREY. Very well. Tell them it's all right. (FERAPONT *goes out.*) I've had it with them. Where's Olga? (OLGA *appears from behind the screen.*) I was looking for you. Let me have the key to the cupboard. I lost mine. The small key. (OLGA *gives him the key without speaking.* IRINA *goes behind the screen to her part of the room. Pause.*) Quite a fire. Tremendous! But it's dying down now. Damn it, that Ferapont got my goat and made me blurt out something foolish. . . . Ordered him to call me "sir." (*Pause.*) Why don't you speak, Olga? (*Pause.*) It's high time you cut out this nonsense. You've no reason to sulk like this. . . . You're here, Masha. And Irina's here too. Fine! We can clear the air once and for all. What do the three of you have against me? What?

OLGA. Stop it, Andrey. We'll discuss it tomorrow. (*Agitated.*) It's been an agonizing night!

ANDREY (*very distressed*). Don't get upset. I ask you quite calmly, what do you have against me? You can be frank.

VERSHININ (*from offstage*). Tram-tam-tam!

MASHA (*stands; loudly*). Tra-ta-ta! (*To* OLGA.) Good night, Olga. Be well. (*Goes behind the screen, kisses* IRINA.) Sweet dreams. . . . Good night, Andrey. Go away. They're exhausted . . . you can have your talk tomorrow. . . . (*She goes out.*)

OLGA. Really, Andrey, let's put it off till tomorrow. . . . (*Goes behind the screen to her part of the room.*) It's time we were asleep.

ANDREY. I'll say what's on my mind and go. . . . To begin with, you all have it in for Natasha. I've been aware of it since the day of my wedding. My wife, if you're interested, is an excellent woman, decent, straightforward, she has high principles—at least that's what I think. I love and respect my wife—do you understand? respect!—and I insist that others respect her as well. I repeat— she's decent and honest and all your objections are so much nit-picking. . . . (*Pause.*) Secondly, you seem to be angry because I'm not a professor and a scholar. But I have a position on the County Board, I'm a full-fledged member, and I consider my duties there every bit as important and sacred as serving science. I'm a member of the County Board and, in case you're interested, I'm proud of it. . . . (*Pause.*) In the third place . . . there's something else. . . . I've mortgaged the house without asking your permission. . . . It was wrong of me, I admit it, and I'm sorry. My debts drove me to it—thirty-five thousand rubles. . . . I'm not gambling anymore, I gave it up some time ago. But the chief thing I can say to justify myself is that you girls have father's pension, while I've had no such . . . I mean, I have no income. . . . (*Pause.*)

KULYGIN (*at the door*). Masha's not here? (*Anxiously.*) Where can she be? How odd. . . . (*Goes out.*)

ANDREY. They're not listening. Natasha is an excellent, honest woman. (*Paces the stage in silence, then stands still.*) When I got married, I thought we would be happy . . . we would all be happy. . . . Oh, my God. . . . (*Weeps.*) My dear sisters, my darling sisters, don't believe a word I've said, don't believe. . . . (*Goes out.*)

KULYGIN (*at the door, anxiously*). Where's Masha? Masha isn't here? Something's fishy. (*Goes out.*)

Fire alarm. An empty stage.

IRINA (*from behind the screen*). Olga, who's that knocking on the floor?

OLGA. It's the doctor. He's drunk.

IRINA. What a night! Nerve-wracking! (*Pause.*) Olga! (*Peeks out from the screen.*) Have you heard? They're taking the brigade away from us. The men are to be transferred somewhere far away.

OLGA. It's only a rumor.

IRINA. We'll be left alone. . . . Olga!

OLGA. What?

IRINA. Dear, kind Olga. I respect the baron, I think well of him, he's a good man. I'm going to marry him, I'm willing, only let's go to Moscow. Please, please! There's no better place than Moscow in the whole world! Let's go, Olga. Let's go. Please!

Curtain

ACT IV

The old garden of the PROZOROVS' *house. A long avenue lined with firs, a river visible at its end. A forest on the far side of the river. On the right, the terrace of the house, on it a table with bottles and glasses—they have been drinking champagne. Noon. Now and then people walk through the garden on their way from the street to the river. Five soldiers rapidly pass by.* CHEBUTYKIN, *in a good mood, which stays with him over the course of the act, is in an easy chair in the garden, waiting to be summoned. He is wearing his army cap and has a walking stick.* IRINA, KULYGIN—*with a medal around his neck and his mustache shaved—and* TUZENBACH *are standing on the terrace, seeing off* FEDOTIK *and* RODÉ, *who are coming down the steps. Both officers are in field uniform.*

TUZENBACH (*embracing* FEDOTIK). You're a fine fellow, we've always gotten along. (*Embracing* RODÉ.) Once more. . . . Goodbye, my friend!

IRINA. Till we meet again!

FEDOTIK. Oh no, it's "goodbye." We'll never meet again!

KULYGIN. Who knows! (*Wipes his eyes, smiling.*) Now I'm crying too.

IRINA. Some day our paths will cross.

FEDOTIK. You mean in ten or fifteen years? But we'll barely recognize one another, we'll exchange greetings as if we were strangers. . . . (*Snaps a photograph.*) Hold it. . . . For the last time.

RODÉ (*embracing* TUZENBACH). We'll never meet again. . . . (*Kisses* IRINA'S *hand.*) Thanks for everything, for everything!

FEDOTIK (*irritated*). Hold it, please!

TUZENBACH. With luck we'll run into each other. But write. Be sure to write.

RODÉ (*glancing over the garden*). Goodbye trees! (*Shouts.*) Yoo-hoo! (*Pause.*) Goodbye echo!

KULYGIN. Most likely you'll get married there, in Poland. . . . Your wife will throw her arms around you and call you "honeybunch" in Polish. (*Laughs.*)

FEDOTIK (*looking at his watch.*) Less than an hour left. Solyony's the only one from our battery going on the barge, we're marching with the troops. Three batteries are leaving today, tomorrow another three. Then the town will be peaceful and quiet.

TUZENBACH. And deadly boring.

RODÉ. Where's Masha?

KULYGIN. In the garden.

FEDOTIK. We ought to say goodbye to her.

RODÉ. Goodbye. I'd better go now, or I'll start crying. . . . (*Hastily embraces* TUZENBACH *and* KULYGIN, *and kisses* IRINA'S *hand.*) We had a marvelous time here. . . .

FEDOTIK (*to* KULYGIN). Here's something to remember me by . . . a notebook and pencil. . . . We'll take this way to the river. . . . (*As they go off, both look back.*)

RODÉ (*shouts*). Yoo-hoo!

KULYGIN (*shouts*). Goodbye!

At the rear of the stage FEDOTIK *and* RODÉ *run into* MASHA *and say goodbye to her; they go off together.*

IRINA. They've gone. . . . (*Sits down on the bottom of the porch.*)

CHEBUTYKIN. They forgot to say goodbye to me.

IRINA. And what about you?

CHEBUTYKIN. I forgot too. But I'll be seeing them soon. I'm leaving tomorrow. Yes. . . . One more day to go. In a year I retire. I'll come back and spend the time left me near you. . . . I've only a year till I get my pension. . . . (*Stuffs a newspaper into his pocket, pulls out another.*) I'll come back and turn over a new leaf. I'll be as quiet as a clam, eag—eager to please, a good little boy. . . .

IRINA. You really ought to mend your ways, my pet. Whatever it takes, you really must.

CHEBUTYKIN. Yes. That's the way I feel. (*Sings softly.*)

Tara-ra-boom-di-ay. . . .
I sit on my stool all day. . . .

KULYGIN. Our doctor is incorrigible! Incorrigible!

CHEBUTYKIN. I ought to have gone to you for instruction. That would have straightened me out.

IRINA. Fyodor has shaved his mustache. I can't bear to look at him.

KULYGIN. Why not?

CHEBUTYKIN. I could tell you what your mug looks like now, but I won't.

KULYGIN. Well, what of it? It's the fashion, the modus vivendi. The principal shaved off his mustache, so when I became his assistant, I shaved mine too. No one likes it, but I don't mind. I'm content. With or without a mustache, I'm content. . . . (*Sits.*)

At the rear of the stage ANDREY *wheels a baby carriage containing a sleeping child.*

IRINA. My dear Ivan Romanych, my kind friend, I'm terribly worried. You were in town yesterday. Tell me what happened.

CHEBUTYKIN. What happened? Nothing. Not a damn thing. (*Reads his newspaper.*) And what does it matter!

KULYGIN. They say Solyony and the baron ran into each other on the street near the theater. . . .

TUZENBACH. Oh, pipe down! Really! . . . (*With a wave of the hand walks into the house.*)

KULYGIN. Near the theater . . . Solyony began to pick a quarrel with the baron, and the baron lost his temper and said something insulting. . . .

CHEBUTYKIN. I don't know anything. Anyhow, it's all nonsense.

KULYGIN. In some seminary the teacher wrote "nonsense" on an essay and the pupil read it as "non compos mentis"—thought it was in Latin. (*Laughs.*) Now that's a howler for you! They say Solyony's in love with Irina and has got it in for the baron. . . . That makes sense. Irina's a very nice girl. She even resembles Masha, the way she's all wrapped up in her thoughts. Only you have a more gentle character, Irina. Though Masha has a good character too. I very much love my Masha.

Offstage from the garden someone calls: "Yoo-hoo! Yoo-hoo!"

IRINA (*shudders*). For some reason everything's making me jittery today. (*Pause.*) I'm all packed, after dinner I'll send my things off. Tomorrow I marry the baron, then we leave for the brickyard. The next day I'll be teaching school. A new way of life will open for me. I pray to God things turn out well! When I passed my teachers' exam I cried for joy, I was so moved. (*Pause.*) The cart will be here soon for my luggage. . . .

KULYGIN. That's all very well and good, only it doesn't seem quite serious. Ideas off the top of the head that don't amount to much. Still, I sincerely wish you good luck.

CHEBUTYKIN (*moved*). My dear child, my lovely, precious child . . . you've gone far, there's no catching up with you now. I've fallen behind, like a bird too old to fly. Fly away, my dears, fly away, and God bless you! (*Pause.*) You shouldn't have shaved off your mustache, Kulygin.

KULYGIN. That's enough from you! (*Sighs.*) The garrison is leaving today, and things will go on as before. No matter what people may say, Masha is a decent, honest woman. I love her very much and I'm grateful for my good fortune. Fate is fickle. . . . There's a fellow in the tax office here by name of Kozyrev. We went to school together, they flunked him out of the fifth year because he couldn't get the hang of *ut consecutivum.* Now he's as poor as a church mouse—sick too—and when I run into him, I'll say, "Hi, *ut consecutivum.*" He'll answer, "That was it, *ut consecutivum.*" . . . And the poor fellow is coughing away. But as for me, all my life I've been lucky. I'm happy. I even have a medal, the Order of Stanislav, Second Class. Now I teach others *ut consecutivum.* Of course, I'm an intelligent man, smarter than most, but that doesn't make for happiness. . . .

The "Maiden's Prayer" is being played on the piano in the house.

IRINA. By tomorrow evening I won't be hearing that tune, and I won't be running into Protopopov either. . . . (*Pause.*) He's installed himself in the living room. Even today he showed up.

KULYGIN. The headmistress hasn't come home yet?

MASHA *silently strolls across the back of the stage.*

IRINA. No. We sent for her. If you only knew how difficult it is for me here, all alone, without Olga. . . . She lives at the school. Being headmistress keeps her busy all day, and I'm alone, bored, without anything to do, and then there's that hateful room of mine. . . . I've made up my mind—if I'm not to live in Moscow, well, that's that. It's fate. Nothing to be done about it. . . . Everything's in God's hands—how true! The baron proposed to me. . . . Well, I thought it over and came to a decision. He's a good man, it's really astonishing how good he is. . . . It was as if I'd suddenly grown wings. I felt cheerful, carefree, and once again I had the urge to work. Work and work. . . . Only something happened yesterday. I could feel something mysterious hanging over me like a dark cloud. . . .

KULYGIN. "Nonsense." "Non compos mentis."

NATASHA (*through the window*). The headmistress!

KULYGIN. The headmistress has come home. Let's go. . . . (*Goes off with* IRINA *into the house.*)

CHEBUTYKIN (*reading his newspaper and softly singing*).

> *Tara-ra-boom-di-ay . . .*
> *I sit on my stool all day. . . .*

MASHA *approaches;* ANDREY *wheels the carriage in the background.*

MASHA. And there he sits, letting the grass grow under his feet. . . .

CHEBUTYKIN. What of it?

MASHA (*sits*). Nothing. . . . (*Pause.*) Did you love my mother?

CHEBUTYKIN. Very much.

MASHA. And did she love you?

CHEBUTYKIN (*after a pause*). That I can't remember.

MASHA. Is my man here? That's what our cook used to call her policeman—"my man." Is my man here?

CHEBUTYKIN. Not yet.

MASHA. When you pick up your crumbs of happiness in snatches, and then lose it all, as I have, you gradually turn hard and nasty. (*Pointing to her breast.*) I'm seething inside. (*Looking at her brother* ANDREY *wheeling the carriage.*) There goes Andrey, our brother. . . . All our dreams down the drain. . . . A thousand people hoist a huge bell, loads of money and work go into the effort, and suddenly it slips and smashes to pieces. Just like that and for no reason. That's Andrey's story. . . .

ANDREY. When are we going to have some peace and quiet around here? It's so noisy!

CHEBUTYKIN. It won't be long now. (*Looks at his watch, then winds it; it strikes.*) I have an old-fashioned watch, it strikes on the hour. . . . The first, second, and fifth batteries leave at one o'clock sharp. (*Pause.*) I go tomorrow.

ANDREY. For good?

CHEBUTYKIN. I don't know. Maybe I'll come back in a year or so. Who the hell knows. . . . It makes no difference. . . .

Somewhere in the distance a harp and violin play.

ANDREY. The town will be dead. As if it were under a bell jar. (*Pause.*) Yesterday something happened near the theater. Everybody's talking about it, but I've no idea what it was.

CHEBUTYKIN. It was nothing. Sheer idiocy. Solyony was pestering the baron, the baron blew up and insulted him, and the upshot was Solyony thought it his duty to challenge him to a duel. (*Looks at his watch.*) About now, I'd say. . . . They were to start at half past twelve, in the forest across the river, you can see it from here. . . . Bang, bang. (*Laughs.*) Solyony imagines he's Lermontov, he even writes poems. Joking aside, it's already his third duel.

MASHA. Whose?

CHEBUTYKIN. Solyony's.

MASHA. And the baron?

CHEBUTYKIN. What about the baron? (*Pause.*)

MASHA. I can't keep my thoughts straight. . . . Still, I say we shouldn't allow it. He might wound the baron, or even kill him.

CHEBUTYKIN. The baron's a nice fellow, but one baron more or less—what does it matter? Let them have their duel! It makes no difference! (*A cry from beyond the garden:* "Yoo-hoo! Yoo hoo!") We'll have to wait a while. That's Skvortsov yelling, one of the seconds. He's in a boat. (*Pause.*)

ANDREY. If you ask me, taking part in a duel, even as a doctor, is quite immoral.

CHEBUTYKIN. It merely seems so. . . . The world isn't real, neither are we. We don't exist, but only seem to exist. . . . And does anything really matter?

MASHA. Talk, talk, talk—all day long nothing but talk! (*Going.*) You have to put up with the lousy climate, out of the blue it can start snowing, and on top of it all this talk. . . . (*Stops.*) I won't go into the house, I just can't take it. . . . When Vershinin gets here, let me know. . . . (*Goes along the path.*) The birds are flying away. . . . (*Looks up.*) They're swans, or maybe geese. . . . My dear birds, my happy birds. . . . (*She goes out.*)

ANDREY. The house will be empty. The officers are leaving, you're leaving, my sister's getting married. I'll be left alone.

CHEBUTYKIN. What about your wife?

FERAPONT *enters with papers.*

ANDREY. My wife is . . . well, a wife. She's honest, decent—a good woman, as they say—yet there's something about her that lowers her to the level of a scruffy little animal, blind to the world. In any case, she's not human. I'm telling you this as a friend, there's no one else I can confide in. I love Natasha, that's so, but at times she strikes me as incredibly vulgar. Then I feel lost, I can't understand why I love her so much, or, at least, why I once loved her. . . .

CHEBUTYKIN (*stands*). I'm leaving tomorrow, my friend. Perhaps we'll never meet again. Here's my advice: put on your cap, pick up a walking stick, and get out of here. . . . Keep on going and don't look back. The farther, the better.

SOLYONY *walks along the rear of the stage with two officers. Seeing* CHEBUTYKIN, *he turns toward him. The officers continue on their way.*

SOLYONY. Doctor, it's time! Already half past twelve. (*Exchanges greetings with* ANDREY.)

CHEBUTYKIN. In a minute. I'm sick of the lot of you. (*To* ANDREY.)

Andrey, if anybody asks for me, tell them I'll be right back. . . . (*Sighs.*) Ugh!

SOLYONY.

> *And he no sooner made a sound,*
> *Than the bear knocked him to the ground.*

(*Walks along with* CHEBUTYKIN.) What are you groaning about, old man?

CHEBUTYKIN. Enough of that!

SOLYONY. How are you feeling?

CHEBUTYKIN (*angrily*). Fit as a fiddle.

SOLYONY. No reason to get hot under the collar, grandpa. I'll only toy with him, wing him as if he were a woodcock. (*Takes out cologne and sprinkles his hands.*) I used up a whole bottle today, and they still stink. They stink like the hands of a corpse. (*Pause.*) Yes, indeed. . . . Do you remember Lermontov's lines?

> *The rebel seeks the raging storm,*
> *As if the storm could bring him peace. . . .*

CHEBUTYKIN. Yes.

> *And he no sooner made a sound,*
> *Than the bear knocked him to the ground.*

(*Goes off with* SOLYONY.)

Cries of "Yoo-hoo! Yoo-hoo!" ANDREY *and* FERAPONT *enter.*

FERAPONT. Papers to sign, sir. . . .

ANDREY (*nervously*). Leave me alone, will you? Just leave me alone! (*Goes out wheeling the carriage.*)

FERAPONT. What are papers for if you don't sign 'em? (*Goes to the back of the stage.*)

IRINA *and* TUZENBACH, *who is wearing a straw hat, enter.*
KULYGIN *walks across the stage calling,* "Halloo, Masha, halloo!"

TUZENBACH. That must be the only man in town who's happy the army is leaving.

IRINA. It's understandable. (*Pause.*) The town will be empty now.

TUZENBACH. I'll be right back, my darling.

IRINA. Where are you going?

TUZENBACH. I have to go into town, then . . . see my friends off.

IRINA. That's not so. . . . Nikolay, you seem distracted today. What's wrong? (*Pause.*) What happened at the theater yesterday?

TUZENBACH (*making an impatient gesture*). I'll be back in an hour. We'll be together again. (*Kisses her hands.*) My love. (*Gazes into her eyes.*) I've loved you for five years now, and I still can't get used to it. You're more beautiful than ever. Such marvelous, lovely hair! Your eyes! Tomorrow I'll take you away from here, we'll work, we'll be rich, my dreams will come true. And you'll be happy. Only . . . only you don't love me!

IRINA. I can't help it! I'll be your wife, I'll honor and obey you, but I don't love you. What can I do? (*Weeps.*) In all my life I've never once been in love. Oh, I've dreamed of love. I've dreamed of it day and night, but my heart is like an expensive piano—it's locked and the key is lost. (*Pause.*) You look worried.

TUZENBACH. I didn't sleep a wink last night. There's nothing particularly dangerous about my life, nothing that might make me afraid. It's only that lost key that tears at me and won't let me sleep. Say something. (*Pause.*) Say something. . . .

IRINA. What shall I say? What? Everything is so mysterious, the way those old trees just stand there, their silence. . . . (*Lays her head on his chest.*)

TUZENBACH. Say something.

IRINA. What? What is there to say? What?

TUZENBACH. Anything.

IRINA. Don't! Please don't! (*Pause.*)

TUZENBACH. It's strange how silly trifles, the small change of life, sometimes loom large. And for no reason at all. You laugh them off as you've always done, still think of them as trifles, but you go right on with what you're doing and can't stop yourself. Oh, let's not talk about it! I'm feeling cheerful. It's as if for the first time in my life I really see those fir trees, those maples and birches. They seem to be watching me curiously, waiting. . . . They're such beautiful trees. When you think about it, how beautiful life should be around trees like these! (*Cries of* "Yoo-hoo! Yoo-hoo!") I have to go now, it's time. . . . That tree is dead, but it goes on swaying in the breeze with the others. It must be the same for me. If I die, I'll still be a part of life, one way or another. Goodbye, my love. . . . (*Kisses her hands.*) The papers you gave me are on my desk, under the calendar.

IRINA. I'm going with you.

TUZENBACH (*anxiously*). No, no! (*He walks quickly, stops on the path.*) Irina!

IRINA. What?

TUZENBACH (*not knowing what to say*). I haven't had my coffee this morning. Tell them to put up a pot for me. . . . (*Goes off quickly.*)

IRINA *stands wrapped up in her thoughts, then goes to the rear of the stage and sits on a porch swing.* ANDREY *enters, wheeling the carriage;* FERAPONT *appears.*

FERAPONT. They're not my papers, sir. They're official papers. I didn't make them up.

ANDREY. Oh, where has it all gone? The past when I was young, sensible, happy. When I dreamed beautiful thoughts, when my present and future were bright with hope? Why is it that no sooner do we begin to live than we become dull, drab, boring, lazy, indifferent, useless, and unhappy. . . . Our town is two hundred years old, a hundred thousand people live here, and they're all as alike as peas in a pod. No one has ever accomplished anything—not in the past and not now. We haven't had a single scientist, a single artist, anyone who might stand out a bit from the common run and inspire envy or the wish to be like him. All people do around here is eat, drink, sleep, and then die. . . . Then others are born to do the eating, drinking, and sleeping. To keep from dying of boredom, they spice up their lives with nasty gossip, vodka, cards, or by dragging their neighbors into court. Wives cheat on their husbands, husbands lie through their teeth, pretending they're deaf and blind to what's going on. All this cheap vulgarity has to have an impact—it crushes the children, snuffs out the divine spark in them, until they turn into pitiful corpses like their mothers and fathers, one indistinguishable from the other. . . . (*To* FERAPONT, *angrily*.) What do you want?

FERAPONT. How's that, sir? There's papers to sign.

ANDREY. I've had it with you.

FERAPONT (*handing him the papers*). Just now the porter at the Tax Office was saying how this winter it was three hundred below zero in Petersburg.

ANDREY. Life today is hateful, but when I think about the future, oh, how grand! I feel so free and easy. A light gleams in the distance, I have a vision of freedom. I can see how I and my children will be liberated from idleness, from a life of guzzling beer and gorging ourselves on goose and cabbage, snoozing in the middle of the day . . . this vile sponging off others. . . .

FERAPONT. He says two thousand people froze. Folks was in a panic, he says. Maybe it was Petersburg, but then again maybe it was Moscow—I don't rightly remember.

ANDREY (*in a rush of tenderness*). My dear sisters, my wonderful sisters! (*Through tears.*) Masha, my sister. . . .

NATASHA (*in the window*). Who is that making that racket out there? Is that you, Andrey? You'll wake up little Sofochka! *Il ne faut pas faire du bruit, la Sophie est dormée déjà. Vous êtes un ours.* (*Flaring up.*) If you must talk, let someone else wheel the carriage. Ferapont, take the carriage from the master!

FERAPONT. Yes, ma'am. (*Takes the carriage.*)

ANDREY (*shamefaced*). I wasn't talking loudly.

NATASHA (*from behind the window, cooing over her little boy*). Bobik! Naughty Bobik! Bad little Bobik!

ANDREY (*looking over the papers*). Very well, I'll look over the papers, sign what I have to, and you can take them back to the board. . . . (*Goes into the house, while perusing the papers.* FERAPONT *wheels the carriage.*)

NATASHA (*from behind the window*). Bobik, what's your mommy's name? Oh, you little cutie pie! And who's this? It's Auntie Olga. Now say, "Hello, Auntie Olga!"

Two street musicians, a man and a girl, play on a violin and a harp. VERSHININ, OLGA, *and* ANFISA *come out of the house and listen in silence for a moment.* IRINA *approaches them.*

OLGA. Our garden is like a city street. People just walk or drive through. Nanny, give the musicians something! . . .

ANFISA (*tipping the musicians*). Run along, my dears, and God be with you. (*The musicians bow and leave.*) Poor things. When your stomach's full, you don't play music on the street. (*To* IRINA.) How are you, Irina? (*Kisses her.*) Oh, my child, I'm having a lovely time of it! Living in clover! In a government apartment at the school, my precious, together with Olga. God has been kind to me in my old age. I've never had it so good, old sinner that I am. . . . It's a big apartment, a government apartment. I've got a room to myself, and my own bed. All rent-free. I'll wake up in the middle of the night and—Oh Lord, Oh Holy Mother of God! No one's happier than me!

VERSHININ (*glancing at his watch*). We'll be leaving soon, Olga. It's time I was on my way. (*Pause.*) I wish you the best . . . the best of. . . . Where's Masha?

IRINA. She's somewhere in the garden. I'll go find her.

VERSHININ. Please. I'm in a hurry.

ANFISA. I'll go look too. (*Yells.*) Masha! Oh, Masha! (*Goes with* IRINA *to the rear of the garden.*) Yoo-hoo! Yoo-hoo!

VERSHININ. Everything comes to an end. Now we too must part. (*Looks at his watch.*) The town treated us to a farewell lunch of sorts, there was champagne, the mayor made a speech. I ate and listened, but my thoughts were here, with you. . . . (*Looks around the garden.*) I've grown attached to you all.

OLGA. Will we ever meet again?

VERSHININ. I don't suppose so. (*Pause.*) My wife and the girls will stay another two months. If anything happens or should they need something, please . . .

OLGA. Yes, by all means. You needn't worry. (*Pause.*) By tomorrow there won't be a single soldier left in town. It will all be only a memory. Of course, we'll begin a new life. . . . (*Pause.*) Nothing turns out the way we plan. I never wanted to be a headmistress, and yet here I am. And we're not going to Moscow. . . .

VERSHININ. Well . . . Thank you for everything. If in any way

I acted improperly, do forgive me. . . . I've done an awful lot of talking—forgive me for that too. Don't think too badly of me.

OLGA (*wiping the tears from her eyes*). What can be keeping Masha? . . .

VERSHININ. What else can I say before I go? Are there any more speeches for me to make? . . . (*Laughs.*) Life is difficult. For many it's a hopeless dead end. Yet I'd say things are getting brighter and easier. It looks as if the time is not far off when the darkness will lift and everything will be clear. (*Looks at his watch.*) I really must be going! In the past men kept themselves busy fighting wars; they filled their lives with campaigns, raids, conquests. But that sort of thing has seen its day. We've been left with a vast empty space and, for now, nothing to fill it with. People are desperately seeking something and in the end they'll find it. Ah, it can't be too soon! (*Pause.*) You know, if we could join education to hard work, and hard work to education. . . . (*Looks at his watch.*) But I must be going. . . .

OLGA. Here she is. (MASHA *enters.*)

VERSHININ. I came to say goodbye. (OLGA *steps aside so as not to get in the way of their leavetaking.*)

MASHA (*looking into his eyes*). Goodbye. (*A prolonged kiss.*)

OLGA. That's enough now. . . . (MASHA *sobs convulsively.*)

VERSHININ. Write. . . . Don't forget! Let me go now . . . it's time. . . . Olga, you take her, I must . . . it's time . . . I'm late. . . . (*Deeply moved, he kisses* OLGA'S *hands, then embraces* MASHA *again and quickly walks out.*)

OLGA. There, there Masha! That's enough now, my dear. . . .

KULYGIN (*enters; embarrassed*). Never mind, let her cry, it's all right. . . . My dear Masha, my good, kind Masha. You're my wife, and I'm happy, no matter what went on . . . I'm not complaining, I'm not accusing you. . . . Olga here is my witness. . . . Let's go back to living as we used to. I won't say a word, I won't even hint about it. . . .

MASHA (*holding back her sobs*).

> *A green oak by a curving shore,*
> *Upon that oak a golden chain . . .*
> *Upon that oak a golden chain . . .*

I'm going out of my mind . . . "A curving shore . . . a green
oak. . . . "

OLGA. Calm down, Masha. . . . Pull yourself together. . . . Get her
some water.

MASHA. I'm not crying any more. . . .

KULYGIN. She's not crying any more. . . . She's a good girl. . . .

The muted sound of a shot in the distance.

MASHA.

> *A green oak by a curving shore,*
> *Upon that oak a golden chain . . .*

"Green cat . . . green oak. . . . " I'm getting it mixed up. (*Drinks
the water.*) My life's a mess. . . . There's nothing for me now. . . .
I'll be all right in a moment. . . . It makes no difference. . . . "A
curving shore." What does that mean? Why do those words keep
drumming in my head? My thoughts are all tangled.

IRINA *enters.*

OLGA. Calm down, Masha. That's it, now you're being sensible. . . .
Let's go inside.

MASHA (*angry*). I won't go in there. (*Sobs, but immediately stops.*)
I'm not going into that house, now or ever. . . .

IRINA. Let's sit a while, together. We don't have to talk. After all,
I'm leaving tomorrow. . . . (*Pause.*)

KULYGIN. Yesterday I took this mustache and beard from a boy in
the third year. . . . (*Puts on the mustache and beard.*) I look like
our German teacher. . . . (*Laughs.*) Don't I? Those boys are a
laugh a minute.

MASHA. You really do resemble that German of yours.

OLGA (*laughs*). Yes, he does. (MASHA *weeps.*)

IRINA. Enough, Masha!

KULYGIN. The very picture of the man. . . .

NATASHA (*enters; to the maid*). What was that? Oh, never mind. . . .
Protopopov will keep an eye on Sofochka, my husband can wheel
Bobik around. Children are such a bother. . . . (*To* IRINA.) So

you're leaving tomorrow, Irina—it's a shame. Stay at least another week. (*Catching sight of* KULYGIN, *she shrieks. He laughs and removes the mustache and beard.*) Oh, you dreadful man, you gave me such a scare! (*To* IRINA.) I've gotten used to having you around. Do you think it will be easy for me to see you go? I'll have them move Andrey into your room along with his fiddle. He can saw away in there for all he's worth! And we'll put little Sofochka in his room. She's a marvelous child, a divine child! What an adorable little girl! Today she looked up at me with those teeny-weeny eyes of hers and said—"Mommy!"

KULYGIN. A capital child, no doubt about it.

NATASHA. So tomorrow I'll be on my own here. (*Sighs.*) First I'll have that row of fir trees cut down, then that maple. At night it looks so scary, just hideous. (*To* IRINA.) My dear, that sash doesn't suit you at all . . . it's in rather poor taste. You should be wearing a bright color. And I'll plant flowers all over the place, little flowers everywhere, the smell will be delicious. . . . (*Sternly.*) What is a fork doing on this bench? (*As she walks into the house, to the maid.*) I asked, what is a fork doing on this bench? (*Screams.*) Keep your trap shut!

KULYGIN. She's at it again!

A march plays offstage; all listen.

OLGA. They're leaving.

CHEBUTYKIN *enters.*

MASHA. Our friends are leaving. Well . . . I wish them a happy journey. (*To her husband.*) We ought to go home. . . . Where are my hat and cape? . . .

KULYGIN. I left them in the house . . . I'll bring them right away. (*Goes into the house.*)

OLGA. Yes, now we can all go home. It's time.

CHEBUTYKIN. Olga.

OLGA. What? (*Pause.*) What is it?

CHEBUTYKIN. Nothing really . . . I don't know how to put it. . . . (*Whispers in her ear.*)

OLGA (*aghast*). It can't be true!

CHEBUTYKIN. Yes . . . a nasty business . . . I'm tired, sucked dry. I don't want to talk any more. . . . (*Annoyed.*) Besides, it doesn't matter!

MASHA. What happened?

OLGA (*embraces* IRINA). It's been a terrible day. . . . My darling, I don't know how to tell you. . . .

IRINA. What is it? Tell me at once—what is it? For God's sake! (*Bursts into tears.*)

CHEBUTYKIN. The baron was just killed in a duel.

IRINA. I knew it, I knew it. . . .

CHEBUTYKIN (*sits on a bench at the rear of the stage*). I'm all done in. . . . (*Takes a newspaper out of his pocket.*) Let them have their cry. . . . (*Sings softly.*)

> Tara-ra-boom-di-ay . . .
> I sit on my stool all day. . . .

What does anything matter!

The three sisters stand pressing against each other.

MASHA. Oh, how the music plays. They're leaving us. One is gone forever, and we shall be left alone to start our lives over. We must go on living. . . . We must go on. . . .

IRINA (*lays her head on* OLGA'S *breast*). Someday we'll know why we live, why we suffer so, nothing will be hidden from us. Till then we must go on living . . . we must work and work! Tomorrow I'll be leaving you. I'll teach school and devote my life to people who may need me. It's fall now, soon it will be winter, snow will blanket the ground, and I'll work, I'll work.

OLGA (*embraces both sisters*). The music is so cheerful and gay. Oh, I so much want to live! Dear God. Time will pass and we shall depart this place forever. We shall be forgotten, they'll forget our faces, our voices, how many of us there were. But our sufferings will turn into joy for those who come after us, happiness and peace will descend upon the earth, and we who are alive today shall be remembered kindly and with gratitude. Oh, my dear, dear sisters, our lives are not over yet. We shall live! The music is so gay, so joyous, it seems we'll soon know why we are alive and why we suffer. . . . If we only knew, if we only knew!

The music grows fainter and fainter. KULYGIN, *cheerful and smiling, brings the hat and cape.* ANDREY *wheels* BOBIK *in the baby carriage.*

CHEBUTYKIN (*sings softly*).

> *Tara-ra-boom-di-ay . . .*
> *I sit on my stool all day. . . .*

(*Reads his newspaper.*) It doesn't matter! Nothing matters!

OLGA. If we only knew, if we only knew!

Curtain

The Cherry Orchard

A Comedy in Four Acts

CAST OF CHARACTERS

Ranévskaya, Lyubóv Andréyevna (Lyúba)
a landowner

Ánya
her daughter, seventeen years old

Várya
her adopted daughter, twenty-four years old

Gáyev, Leoníd Andréyevich
Ranevskaya's brother

Lopákhin, Yermoláy Alekséyevich
a merchant

Trofímov, Pyótr Sergéyevich (Pétya)
a student

Simeónov-Píshchik, Borís Borísovich
a landowner

Charlótta Ivánovna
a governess

Yepikhódov, Semyón Pantéléyevich
a clerk

Dunyásha
a maid

Firs
the butler, eighty-seven years old

Yásha
a young servant

A Tramp

A Stationmaster

A Postman

Guests and Servants

The action takes place on Ranevskaya's estate.

ACT I   *A room still called the nursery. One of the*
doors leads to ANYA'S *room. Dawn, before*
sunrise. May. The cherry trees are in blossom,
though it is cold in the orchard—there is a
morning frost. The windows are closed.
DUNYASHA *enters with a candle,* LOPAKHIN
with a book in his hand.

LOPAKHIN. Thank God, the train is in. What time is it?

DUNYASHA. Almost two. (*Snuffs the candle.*) It's light already.

LOPAKHIN. How late was the train? Two hours at least. (*Yawns and
stretches.*) A fine one I am, playing the fool! I drove over with the
idea of meeting them at the station and then overslept. Dozed off
in my chair. Damn nuisance. . . . You should have waked me.

DUNYASHA. I thought you'd left. (*Listens.*) I think they're coming.

LOPAKHIN (*listens*). No . . . they have to get their luggage, tend to
things. . . . Lyubov Andreyevna has been abroad for five years. I
don't know what she's like now. . . . She's a good person. Easygoing,
unpretentious. I remember when I was a boy of fifteen, my
father—he had a store in the village then—he punched me in the
face with his fist, made my nose bleed. . . . We had come into the
yard together, and he was roaring drunk. Lyubov Andreyevna, I
remember it as if it were today, she was still young and slender,
she took me to the washbasin, in this room—it was the nursery
then. "Don't cry, little peasant," she said. "It'll heal in time for your
wedding. . . . " (*Pause.*) Little peasant. . . . My father was a peasant,
that's true, and here I am in a white vest and yellow shoes. A bull
in a china shop. Sure, I'm rich, I have piles of money, but if you
think about it, I'm a peasant to the bone. . . . (*Leafing through the
book.*) I was just reading this book and didn't understand a word.
Read and dozed off. (*Pause.*)

DUNYASHA. The dogs were up all night. They can sense the masters
are coming.

LOPAKHIN. What's wrong, Dunyasha, you're so. . . .

DUNYASHA. My hands are trembling. I'm about to faint.

LOPAKHIN. You're too soft, Dunyasha. You dress like a lady. And the
way you do your hair. It's not right. You ought to know your
place.

YEPIKHODOV *enters with a bouquet. He wears a jacket and highly polished boots which squeak loudly. As he comes in, he drops the bouquet.*

YEPIKHODOV (*lifting the bouquet*). The gardener sent these, said you're to put them in the dining room. (*Hands the bouquet to* DUNYASHA.)

LOPAKHIN. And bring me a glass of kvass.

DUNYASHA. Yes, sir. (*Goes out.*)

YEPIKHODOV. There's a frost this morning, it's twenty-seven degrees, and the cherry trees are in blossom. I can't approve of our climate. (*Sighs.*) I really can't. Our climate is not properly conducive. And, Yermolay Alexeyich, permit me to add, I bought myself a pair of boots the other day, and I may be so bold as to assure you, they squeak. It's simply intolerable. What should I polish them with?

LOPAKHIN. Get out. I'm fed up with you.

YEPIKHODOV. Every day I meet with some misfortune. But I don't complain, I'm used to it, I even smile. (DUNYASHA *returns and hands* LOPAKHIN *a glass of kvass.*) I'm leaving. (*Bumps into a chair, which falls over.*) There I go again. . . . (*As if in triumph.*) Pardon the expression, but accidents like these . . . they're simply phenomenal! (*Goes out.*)

DUNYASHA. I ought to tell you, Yermolay Alexeyich, Yepikhodov has proposed to me.

LOPAKHIN. Ah!

DUNYASHA. I really don't know. . . . He's a quiet man. But when he gets to rattling away, you can't make heads or tails of it. It's all very proper, full of feeling, only it doesn't make sense. I sort of like him, and he's crazy about me. He's an unlucky man . . . every day it's one thing or another. They tease him about it here. We call him Twenty-Two Disasters.

LOPAKHIN (*listening*). There, I think that's them.

DUNYASHA. It is them! What's wrong with me? I'm shivering all over.

LOPAKHIN. They're really coming. Let's go meet them. Will she recognize me? It's been five years.

DUNYASHA (*in a flutter*). I'm going to faint . . . Oh, I'm going to faint!

Two carriages are heard driving up to the house. LOPAKHIN *and* DUNYASHA *go out quickly. The stage is empty. Noise in the adjoining rooms.* FIRS, *who has gone to meet* RANEVSKAYA, *hurries across the stage, leaning on a cane. He is wearing old-fashioned livery and a tall hat. He mutters to himself inaudibly. The hubbub offstage mounts.* A Voice: "Come, let's go through here. . . . " RANEVSKAYA, ANYA, *and* CHARLOTTA *with a dog on a leash, are in traveling clothes.* VARYA *is wearing an overcoat and a kerchief.* GAYEV, SIMEONOV-PISHCHIK, LOPAKHIN, DUNYASHA *with a bundle and an umbrella, servants with luggage—all walk across the room.*

ANYA. Let's go through here. Do you remember this room, mama?

RANEVSKAYA (*joyfully, through tears*). It's the nursery!

VARYA. How cold it is, my hands are numb. (*To* RANEVSKAYA.) Your rooms, both the white and the violet, are just as you left them, mama.

RANEVSKAYA. The nursery, my dear, lovely nursery. . . . I slept here when I was a child. . . . (*Weeps.*) And now I'm like a child. . . . (*Kisses her brother,* VARYA, *then her brother again.*) Varya hasn't changed, she still looks like a nun. And I even recognized Dunyasha.

GAYEV. The train was two hours late. Can you believe it! What a way to run a railroad line!

CHARLOTTA (*to* PISHCHIK). My dog eats nuts.

PISCHIK (*amazed*). You don't say!

All go out, except ANYA *and* DUNYASHA.

DUNYASHA. We waited and waited. . . . (*Takes* ANYA'S *hat and coat.*)

ANYA. Four nights on the train and I didn't sleep a wink . . . now I'm frozen.

DUNYASHA. It was Lent when you left, there was snow, frost. And now. . . . Dear Anya! I waited so long, my angel, my joy. . . . I must tell you something, it won't hold another minute.

ANYA (*listlessly*). What now?

DUNYASHA. After Easter the clerk Yepikhodov proposed to me.

ANYA. You're at it again. . . . (*Arranges her hair.*) I've lost all my hairpins. . . . (*She is exhausted, even staggers.*)

DUNYASHA. I don't know what to make of it. He loves me—he loves me a lot!

ANYA (*looking toward the door of her room, tenderly*). My room, my windows, it's as if I never left. Home at last! Tomorrow morning I'll wake up, run to the orchard. . . . Oh, if I could only sleep! I didn't sleep the whole way, I was so anxious.

DUNYASHA. Pyotr Sergeyich came the day before yesterday.

ANYA (*joyfully*). Petya!

DUNYASHA. He's asleep in the bathhouse, he's settled in there. He says he's afraid of getting in the way. (*Checking her pocket watch.*) I really ought to wake him up, but your sister told me not to. "Don't you wake him," she says.

VARYA (*enters, a bunch of keys at her belt*). Dunyasha, coffee. On the double. . . . Mama is asking for coffee.

DUNYASHA. I won't be a minute. (*Goes out.*)

VARYA. Well, thank heavens, you've come. You're home again. (*Fondling her.*) My darling has come! My beautiful sister is home!

ANYA. I've been through so much.

VARYA. I can imagine!

ANYA. It was Easter week when we left, it was cold then. Charlotta chattered the whole way, she did her little magic tricks. Why did you saddle me with her?

VARYA. You couldn't very well travel alone, my darling—at seventeen!

ANYA. We came to Paris, it was cold there too, snowing. My French is awful. Mama was living on the fifth floor. I found her with some Frenchmen—who knows where she picked them up—there were ladies, an old priest reading a brochure. The room was thick with smoke, cramped. I felt sorry for Mama, so sorry I took her head in my hands, hugged her, and couldn't let go. Mama kept fondling me, crying all the time. . . .

VARYA (*tearfully*). Don't tell me about it, don't. . . .

ANYA. She had already sold her house at Menton. She has nothing left, nothing. I was also without a kopek, we barely managed to get home. But Mama doesn't understand! We would stop at a station, she'd order the most expensive items on the menu and then tip the waiters a ruble each. Charlotta also. And Yasha had to have his share too. It was just dreadful. Mama has a footman now—Yasha. We brought him along. . . .

VARYA. Yes, I've seen the scamp.

ANYA. Well, what's happening? Have you made the mortgage payments?

VARYA. How could we?

ANYA. Oh my God! My God! . . .

VARYA. In August the estate will be up for sale.

ANYA. My God. . . .

LOPAKHIN (*peeps in at the door and moos like a cow*). Moo. . . . (*Disappears.*)

VARYA (*tearfully*). Oh, how I'd like to give it to him. . . . (*Threatens him with her fist.*)

ANYA (*embracing* VARYA, *softly*). Has he proposed, Varya? (VARYA *shakes her head.*) But he loves you. . . . Why don't you have it out with him? What are you waiting for?

VARYA. I don't believe anything will ever come of it. He's very busy, he has no time . . . he doesn't even notice me. I've washed my hands of him. It pains me to see him. . . . Everybody talks about our getting married, they congratulate me, and actually there's nothing to it. It's all a dream. . . . (*Altering her tone of voice.*) You have a new brooch—a bee, isn't it?

ANYA (*dejectedly*). Mama bought it. (*She goes off to her room, speaks cheerfully, like a child.*) In Paris I flew in a balloon!

VARYA. My darling has come! My beautiful sister is home! (DUNYASHA *has returned with a coffeepot and is preparing coffee.* VARYA *stops at the door.*) Dearest, I spend my days looking after the house, dreaming all the while. If we could marry you to a rich man, I would be at peace. I would go to a convent, then to Kiev . . . to Moscow, visit all the holy places. . . . Just wander on and on. What a blessing that would be!

ANYA. The birds are singing in the orchard. What time is it?

VARYA. It must be after two. Time you were in bed, my sweet. (*Goes into* ANYA'S *room.*) A blessing! . . .

YASHA (*comes in with a plaid blanket and a traveling bag, crosses the stage mincingly*). May I pass through here, miss?

DUNYASHA. No one would recognize you, Yasha. Life abroad has done wonders for you.

YASHA. Hmm. . . . And who might you be?

DUNYASHA. When you went away I was this high. . . . (*Indicating with her hand.*) I'm Dunyasha, Fyodor Kozoyedov's daughter. Don't you remember?

YASHA. Hmm. . . . A peach! (*Looks about and embraces her; she cries out and drops a saucer.* YASHA *goes out quickly.*)

VARYA (*at the door, in an annoyed tone*). What now?

DUNYASHA (*tearfully*). I broke a saucer.

VARYA. That means good luck.

ANYA (*coming out of her room*). We ought to tell Mama Petya's here. . . .

VARYA. I gave orders not to wake him.

ANYA (*musing*). Six years ago Father died, a month later our brother Grisha drowned in the river, a beautiful boy, he was only seven years old. It was more than Mama could bear, she ran off without as much as looking back. . . . (*Trembles.*) How well I understand her. If she only knew! (*Pause.*) Petya was Grisha's tutor, he may remind her. . . .

FIRS (*enters, in a jacket and white vest; goes up to the coffeepot. Preoccupied*). Madam will have her coffee here. . . . (*Puts on white gloves.*) Is the coffee ready? (*Severely, to* DUNYASHA.) Say, you! Where's the cream?

DUNYASHA. Oh Lord! . . . (*Runs off in haste.*)

FIRS (*fussing over the coffeepot*). Ugh, you nincompoop. . . . (*Mumbling to himself.*) They've come from Paris. . . . And the old master used to go to Paris . . . by carriage. . . . (*Laughs.*)

VARYA. What is it, Firs?

FIRS. Yes, ma'am? (*Joyfully.*) My mistress has come home! Home at last! Now I can die. . . . (*Weeps with joy.*)

RANEVSKAYA, GAYEV, LOPAKHIN, *and* SIMEONOV-PISHCHIK *enter.* SIMEONOV-PISHCHIK *is wearing a peasant's tight-waisted pleated coat of fine cloth and wide trousers.* GAYEV, *upon entering, makes a gesture with his arms and body as if he were playing billiards.*

RANEVSKAYA. How does it go? Let's see if I remember. . . . Yellow
ball in the corner pocket! Bank shot into the side!

GAYEV. Cut it into the corner! Once you and I slept in this very
room, my dear sister, and now I'm fifty-one, strange as that
seems. . . .

LOPAKHIN. Yes, time passes.

GAYEV. Who?

LOPAKHIN. I said, time passes.

GAYEV. It reeks of cheap scent here.

ANYA. I'm going to bed. Good night, Mama. (*(Kisses her mother.)*)

RANEVSKAYA. My precious child. (*Kisses her hands.*) Are you happy
to be home? It's as if I'm dreaming.

GAYEV (*kisses her face, hands*). God bless you. How like your mother
you are! (*To his sister.*) At her age, Lyuba, you were just like her.

ANYA *shakes hands with* LOPAKHIN *and* PISHCHIK, *and goes out,
closing the door behind her.*

RANEVSKAYA. She's very tired.

PISHCHIK. It must have been a long trip.

VARYA (*to* LOPAKHIN *and* PISHCHIK). Well, gentlemen? It's well past
two, high time you were going.

RANEVSKAYA (*laughing*). You haven't changed, Varya. (*Draws her
close and kisses her.*) I'll just finish my coffee, then we'll all go.
(FIRS *places a cushion under her feet.*) Thank you, my friend.
Coffee has become a habit. I drink it day and night. Thank you,
you dear old man. (*Kisses* FIRS.)

VARYA. I'd better check if all your things have been brought in.
(*Goes out.*)

RANEVSKAYA. Can this really be me sitting here? (*Laughs.*) I feel
like dancing, waving my arms about. (*Covers her face with her
hands.*) And what if it is a dream! I love my country, I love it with
such tenderness, God only knows. I couldn't bear to look out the
train window, I cried all the way. (*Tearfully.*) But I must have my
coffee. Thank you, Firs, thank you, you dear old man. I'm so glad
you're still alive.

FIRS. Day before yesterday.

GAYEV. He's hard of hearing.

LOPAKHIN. I have to go now. I'm leaving for Kharkov at five. Damn nuisance! I'd love to just stare at you a while, talk. . . . You're magnificent, as always.

PISHCHIK (*breathing heavily*). She's gotten even prettier. . . . Decked out like some lady from Paris. . . . Knock me over with a feather if she isn't something!

LOPAKHIN. Your brother Gayev says I'm a boor, a money-grubbing peasant, but I really don't care. Let him talk. Trust me the way you once did, look at me again with those marvelously touching eyes of yours—that's all I want. Dear God! My father was your grandfather's serf, your father's serf. But you did so much for me that I've put all that out of mind. I love you like my own sister . . . even more than a sister.

RANEVSKAYA. I can't sit still, I just can't. . . . (*Jumps up and paces in extreme excitement.*) My happiness is too much for me. . . . Go ahead and laugh at me, I'm a silly fool. . . . My dear little bookcase. . . . (*Kisses the bookcase.*) My dear table.

GAYEV. While you were away, Nanny died.

RANEVSKAYA (*sits and drinks her coffee*). Yes, may she rest in peace. They wrote me about it.

GAYEV. And Anastasy died. Petrushka Kosoy walked out on me and is working for the police chief in town. (*Takes a box of sugar candies from his pocket and sucks on one.*)

PISHCHIK. My daughter Dashenka . . . sends her regards. . . .

LOPAKHIN. I'd like to inform you of something very pleasant—even cheerful. (*Looks at his watch.*) I'm off in a moment, there's no time to talk. . . . Well, I'll be brief. As you're aware, your cherry orchard is to be sold to pay your debts. The auction is scheduled for the twenty-second of August. But there's no need to worry, my dear lady, you can sleep peacefully—there's a way out. . . . Here's my plan. Attention please! Your estate is only fifteen miles from town, the railway runs nearby. Now if you parceled out the cherry orchard plus the land along the river and leased the lots for summer cottages, you would realize a profit of at least twenty-five thousand rubles a year.

GAYEV. I beg your pardon, but that's ridiculous!

RANEVSKAYA. I don't quite understand you, Yermolay Alexeyich.

LOPAKHIN. You'll take in at least ten rubles a year per acre. If you advertise immediately, I guarantee you by autumn you won't have a square foot left. They'll snap it all up. To cut it short, congratulations! You're saved. It's a wonderful location, the river is deep here. Of course, we'll have to do some clearing up . . . for example, tear down the old outbuildings, this house too—it isn't of any use now. We'll cut down the cherry orchard. . . .

RANEVSKAYA. The cherry orchard? My dear friend, forgive me, but you don't know what you're talking about. If there's one thing in the entire province that's of interest, even remarkable, then it's our cherry orchard.

LOPAKHIN. The only remarkable thing about it is that it's big. It gives cherries once every two years, and you can't even get rid of them—no one buys them.

GAYEV. Our orchard is mentioned in the Encyclopedia.

LOPAKHIN (*glancing at his watch*). If we don't come up with something, then on the twenty-second of August the cherry orchard and the entire estate will be sold at auction. Make up your minds! There's no other way out, you can take my word for it. None, none.

FIRS. In the old days, about forty or fifty years ago, we dried the cherries, soaked and marinated them, made jam, and we would . . .

GAYEV. Shut up, Firs.

FIRS. And we would ship the dried cherries by the cartload to Moscow and Kharkov. . . . They'd bring in piles of money! In those days the dried cherries were soft and juicy and sweet, they smelled nice. . . . They knew the way to do things then. . . .

RANEVSKAYA. And where are those ways now?

FIRS. They've forgotten. No one remembers.

PISHCHIK (*to* RANEVSKAYA). What's doing in Paris? Eh? Did you eat frogs?

RANEVSKAYA. We ate crocodiles.

PISHCHIK. Imagine that!

LOPAKHIN. Until recently only the gentry and peasants lived in the country, but now these summer people have showed up. Summer cottages circle all the cities, even the smaller ones. It's safe to say that in another twenty years the summer population will have grown beyond your wildest dreams. Today your summer resident only sits on his porch and sips tea, but he may take to farming his little acre, and then your cherry orchard will turn into a rich, prosperous, and happy place.

GAYEV (*indignant*). Poppycock!

VARYA *and* YASHA *enter.*

VARYA. There are two telegrams for you, Mama. (*Chooses a key from the bunch at her belt and with a clang opens the antique bookcase.*) Here they are.

RANEVSKAYA. From Paris. (*Tears them up without reading them.*) Paris is over and done with.

GAYEV. Lyuba, do you know how old this bookcase is? Last week I pulled out the bottom drawer and saw the date burned into it. It was built exactly a hundred years ago. What do you think of that! We could celebrate its centenary. True, it's an inanimate object, but all the same, no matter how you look at it, it is a bookcase.

PISHCHIK (*amazed*). A hundred years. . . . Imagine that!

GAYEV. Yes. . . . It's a thing. . . . (*Tapping it.*) My dear, honorable bookcase! Hail to thee. Over a hundred years you have served the luminous ideals of goodness and justice. Your silent summons to fruitful toil has not slackened over the course of a century, sustaining (*tearfully*) the generations of our lineage with courage and faith in a better future, fostering ideals of virtue and social responsibility. (*Pause.*)

LOPAKHIN. Hmm. . . .

RANEVSKAYA. You haven't changed a bit, Leonid.

GAYEV (*somewhat embarrassed*). Off the red into the righthand corner! Cut into the side pocket!

LOPAKHIN (*looking at his watch*). It's time I was going.

YASHA (*handing* RANEVSKAYA *her medicine*). Will you be taking your pills now, madam?

PISHCHIK. You shouldn't be taking medicines, my precious. . . . They're harmless enough, but they're of no use. . . . Give them to me, dearest lady. (*Takes the pills, dumps them onto his palm, blows on them, puts them in his mouth, and washes them down with kvass.*) There you go!

RANEVSKAYA (*alarmed*). You must be mad!

PISHCHIK. Swallowed the lot of them.

LOPAKHIN. The man's a glutton. (*All laugh.*)

FIRS. When the gentleman was here at Easter, he gulped down half a barrel of pickles. . . . (*Mutters.*)

RANEVSKAYA. What is he saying?

VARYA. He's been mumbling like that for three years now. We've gotten used to it.

YASHA. A case of advanced senility.

CHARLOTTA *crosses the stage in a white dress. She is very thin, tightly laced, has a lorgnette attached to her belt.*

LOPAKHIN. I'm sorry, but I haven't yet had a chance to say hello to you, Charlotta. (*Tries to kiss her hand.*)

CHARLOTTA (*pulling her hand away*). If I let you kiss my hand, it'll be my elbow next, then my shoulder. . . .

LOPAKHIN. No luck for me today. (*All laugh.*) Show us a trick, Charlotta!

RANEVSKAYA. Do show us a trick, Charlotta.

CHARLOTTA. No. I want to go to bed. (*Goes out.*)

LOPAKHIN. I'll see you in three weeks. (*Kisses* RANEVSKAYA'S *hand.*) Goodbye for now. I must be going. (*To* GAYEV.) Goodbye. (*Embraces* PISHCHIK.) Until we meet again. (*Shakes hands with* VARYA, *then* FIRS *and* YASHA.) I don't feel like going. (*To* RANEVSKAYA.) If you come to a decision about the summer cottages, let me know and I'll arrange a loan of fifty thousand or so. Give it some serious thought.

VARYA (*angrily*). For heaven's sake, go already!

LOPAKHIN. I'm going, I'm going. . . . (*Goes out.*)

GAYEV. The man's a boor! Oh, *pardon.* Varya is going to marry him. He's Varya's fiancé.

VARYA. Uncle, don't start in.

RANEVSKAYA. Why not, Varya? It would make me happy. He's a fine man.

PISHCHIK. He's . . . take my word for it, he's . . . an admirable man. . . . My Dashenka . . . she also says . . . well, she says all sorts of things. (*Drops off and snores, but immediately wakes up.*) By the way, my dear lady, would you lend me . . . two

hundred and forty rubles . . . my mortgage payment is due
tomorrow.

VARYA (*alarmed*). No, no!

RANEVSKAYA. I really don't have it.

PISHCHIK. It'll turn up. (*Laughs.*) Never say die. I'll be thinking
everything's gone down the drain, I'm sunk, and wham!—they've
run a railroad through my land and . . . paid me for it. You'll see,
something will turn up, if not today then tomorrow. . . . My
Dashenka is liable to win two hundred thousand . . . she has a
lottery ticket.

RANEVSKAYA. Coffee's done, now to bed.

FIRS (*brushing* GAYEV'S *clothes, reprovingly*). You've put on the
wrong trousers again, sir. What am I to do with you?

VARYA (*softly*). Anya's asleep. (*Noiselessly opens a window.*) The sun
is up, it's not cold now. Look mama, how lovely the trees are! The
air—my heavens, the air! And the starlings are singing!

GAYEV (*opens another window*). The orchard is all white. You
haven't forgotten, Lyuba? There, that long lane runs so very
straight, like a ribbon stretched taut. The way it gleams on
moonlit nights. You remember, don't you? You haven't forgotten?

RANEVSKAYA (*gazing through the window at the orchard*). Oh, my
childhood, my innocent childhood! I slept in this nursery, from
here I looked out at the orchard. Every morning I awoke to
happiness. It was just like this, nothing has changed. (*Laughs
from joy.*) All, all white. Oh, my orchard! After the dark, dismal
autumn and the cold, cold winter you're young again, full of
happiness. God's angels haven't forsaken you. . . . If only I could
cast off the stone that weighs on my breast and shoulders, if only
I could forget my past!

GAYEV. Yes. And the orchard will be sold to pay our debts, as
strange as that seems. . . .

RANEVSKAYA. Look, mother is walking through the orchard . . . in a
white dress! (*Laughs.*) It's Mother!

GAYEV. Where?

VARYA. God save you, Mama.

RANEVSKAYA. There's no one there. I imagined it. To the right, at
the turn to the summer house, that small white tree leaning to

the side, it looks like a woman. . . . (TROFIMOV *enters, wearing a worn student's uniform and eyeglasses.*) It's such a wonderful orchard! A sea of white blossoms, the blue sky. . . .

TROFIMOV. Lyubov Andreyevna! (*She turns to look at him.*) I'll just pay my respects and leave. (*Warmly kisses her hand.*) I was told to wait till morning but I ran out of patience. . . . (RANEVSKAYA, *puzzled, looks at him.*)

VARYA (*tearfully*). It's Petya Trofimov. . . .

TROFIMOV. Petya Trofimov. I taught your Grisha. Have I really changed so much? (RANEVSKAYA *embraces him and weeps softly.*)

GAYEV (*embarrassed*). There, there, Lyuba. That's enough.

VARYA (*weeps*). I did tell you to wait till later, Petya.

RANEVSKAYA. My Grisha . . . my poor boy . . . Grisha . . . my son. . . .

VARYA. It can't be helped, Mama. It was God's will.

TROFIMOV (*softly and tearfully.*) Don't cry, don't cry.

RANEVSKAYA (*weeping softly*). My boy is gone, drowned. . . . Why? Why, my dear friend? (*Softer yet.*) Anya's sleeping, and here I am, speaking in a loud voice . . . raising a racket. . . . So, Petya? Why have you grown so ugly? Why have you aged?

TROFIMOV. Some peasant woman on a train called me a "mangy-looking gentleman."

RANEVSKAYA. You were only a boy then, an adorable young student, and now your hair has thinned out, you're wearing glasses. You can't be still a student, can you? (*Walks toward the door.*)

TROFIMOV. It looks like I'll always be a student.

RANEVSKAYA (*kisses her brother, then* VARYA). Go to bed. . . . You've aged too, Leonid.

PISHCHIK (*following her*). So, we're off to bed now. . . . Oh, my gout. I'm staying over. And tomorrow morning, Lyubov, my darling . . . that two hundred and forty rubles.

GAYEV. He never gives up.

PISHCHIK. Two hundred and forty . . . my mortgage payment.

RANEVSKAYA. I have no money, my dear.

PISHCHIK. I'll pay it back. . . . It's not that much.

RANEVSKAYA. Well, all right. Leonid will give it to you. . . . Give him the money, Leonid.

GAYEV. Give him money? Not on your life.

RANEVSKAYA. What else can we do? . . . He needs it. . . . He'll pay it back.

RANEVSKAYA, TROFIMOV, PISHCHIK, *and* FIRS *go out.* GAYEV, VARYA, *and* YASHA *remain.*

GAYEV. My sister hasn't lost her habit of tossing money around. (*To* YASHA.) Step back, my good man. You reek of chicken.

YASHA (*grinning*). You haven't changed, sir.

GAYEV. What's that? (*To* VARYA.) What did he say?

VARYA (*to* YASHA). Your mother's come from her village. She's been waiting in the servants' quarters since yesterday. She wants to see you. . . .

YASHA. To hell with her!

VARYA. You ought to be ashamed of yourself!

YASHA. That's all I need. She could just as well have come tomorrow. (*Goes out.*)

VARYA. Mama is the same, she hasn't changed a bit. If she had her way, she'd give everything away.

GAYEV. Yes. . . . (*Pause.*) When many remedies are proposed for an illness, it's a sure sign that it's incurable. I think about it all the time, I really rack my brains. I've come up with many remedies, hundreds of them, and that means that in fact I have none. It would be a good turn if someone left us some money, it would be good to marry off Anya to some millionaire, it would be good to skip down to Yaroslavl and try my luck with that aunt of ours . . . the countess. Our aunt is very, very rich.

VARYA (*cries*). If only God would help us!

GAYEV. Don't bawl. Auntie is very rich, but she doesn't like us. For one, my sister married a lawyer, not someone from the nobility. . . . (ANYA *appears in the doorway.*) She married beneath her and she hasn't led what you'd call a blameless life. She's a good woman, a kind, splendid woman, I love her very much. But however you varnish the facts, you still have to admit she's promiscuous. It shows in her every move.

VARYA (*in a whisper*). Anya is at the door.

GAYEV. Who? (*Pause.*) How odd—something's gotten into my right eye . . . I can't see straight. And on Thursday when I was at the district court. . . .

ANYA *enters.*

VARYA. Why aren't you asleep, Anya?

ANYA. I can't sleep. I just can't.

GAYEV. My little kitten. (*Kisses* ANYA'S *face, hands.*) My child. . . . (*Tearfully.*) You're not my niece, you're my angel, you're the whole world for me. Believe me. . . .

ANYA. I believe you, uncle. We all love you, and respect you. . . . But, dearest uncle, you must learn to keep your mouth shut. What were you saying just now about my mother, about your own sister? Why did you say those things?

GAYEV. Yes, yes. . . . (*Covers his face with her hand.*) Really, that was despicable! God forgive me! And a while ago I made a speech to the bookcase . . . so stupid of me. Only when I finished did I realize that it was stupid.

VARYA. That's so, uncle, you have to hold your tongue, keep it to yourself, that's all.

ANYA. If you stay silent, you'll be calmer.

GAYEV. I'm silent. (*Kisses their hands.*) I'm silent. Only a word about business. Thursday I was at the district court. Well, some of us got together, we struck up a conversation about one thing and another, and it seems we can arrange a loan to make our mortgage payment.

VARYA. I hope to God!

GAYEV. I'll go on Tuesday, and talk it over with them again. (*To* VARYA.) Don't cry. (*To* ANYA.) Your mother will speak to Lopakhin. I'm sure he won't refuse her. . . . And as soon as you've rested up, you can drive down to the countess in Yaroslavl, you know, your great aunt. So, we'll attack it from three fronts—and the cat's in the bag. We'll make the mortgage payment—I'm convinced of it. . . . (*Sticks a candy drop in his mouth.*) By my word of honor, by anything you wish, I swear—the estate will not be sold! (*Excited.*) I'll stake my chances of happiness on it! Here's my hand. Call me a vile, dishonorable wretch if I let it come to an auction! Body and soul, I swear it!

ANYA (*in a calm mood again, happy*). What a good man you are, uncle, and so smart! I'm calm now! I'm calm! And happy!

FIRS (*enters. Reproachfully*). Have you no fear of God, sir? When are you going to bed?

GAYEV. Right away, right away. You can go, Firs. I'll . . . don't worry, I'll undress myself. Well, children, nightie-night. . . . The details will hold till tomorrow, now go to bed. (*Kisses* ANYA *and* VARYA.) I'm a man of the eighties. Nowadays they don't have a good word for those years, but I can honestly say that I've suffered much for my convictions. It's not without reason that the peasants love me. You have to know your peasant. You have to know from what angle . . .

ANYA. You're at it again, uncle!

VARYA. Uncle, keep quiet.

FIRS (*angry*). Sir!

GAYEV. I'm coming, I'm coming. . . . Go to bed. Double bank into the side! Clean as a whistle. . . . (*Goes out,* FIRS *trotting after him.*)

ANYA. I'm calm now. I don't feel like going to Yaroslavl, I don't much care for my great aunt, but all the same I'm calm. Thanks to uncle. (*Sits.*)

VARYA. We must get some sleep. I'm going now. Something unpleasant happened while you were away. The old servant quarters, you're aware that only the old-timers live there now—Yefimyushka, Polya, Yevstigney, oh yes, and Karp. Well, they got to letting all sorts of riffraff spend the night there . . . I didn't say a word. Then I heard they were spreading a rumor that I wouldn't let them have anything but dried peas. Out of stinginess, you see. . . . It was all Yevstigney's doing. . . . Very well, I think to myself. If that's your game, just you wait. So I sent for Yevstigney. . . . (*Yawns.*) I told him, "How could you, Yevstigney? . . . you're an old fool. . . . " (*Glancing at* ANYA.) Anya! (*Pause.*) She's asleep. (*Takes* ANYA *by the arm.*) Come to bed. . . . Come! (*Leads her.*) My darling has fallen asleep! Come. (*They go.*)

Far beyond the orchard a shepherd is playing on a reed. TROFIMOV *crosses the stage and, seeing* VARYA *and* ANYA, *stands still.*

VARYA. Shh. . . . She's asleep . . . asleep. . . . Come, my precious.

ANYA (*softly, half asleep*). I'm so tired . . . bells, bells . . . Uncle . . . dear Uncle . . . Mama and Uncle.

VARYA. Come, my sweet, come. . . . (*They go off to* ANYA'S *room.*)

TROFIMOV (*moved*). My sun! My springtime!

Curtain

ACT II

A meadow. An old lopsided, long-abandoned chapel. Nearby, a well, an old bench, large stone slabs apparently once tombstones. The road to the GAYEV *estate may be seen. To one side poplars loom darkly; the cherry orchard begins there. Telegraph poles in the distance, and far away on the horizon the faint outline of a large city, visible only in very clear weather. The sun is about to set.* CHARLOTTA, YASHA, *and* DUNYASHA *are sitting on the bench;* YEPIKHODOV *stands nearby and plays a guitar. All are wrapped in thought.* CHARLOTTA *is wearing an old peaked cap. She has taken a gun from her shoulder and is adjusting the buckle on the strap.*

CHARLOTTA (*musing*). I haven't a real passport. I don't know how old I am, and I always suppose I'm very young. When I was a little girl, Mama and Papa toured the fairs and put on shows, very good shows too. I performed somersaults and other tricks. When Mama and Papa died, a German lady took me in and began my education. Very good. I grew up and became a governess. But who I am or where I come from—I don't know. . . . Who were my parents? Maybe they weren't even married . . . I don't know. (*Takes a cucumber out of her pocket and eats.*) I don't know anything. (*Pause.*) I so much long to talk, but there's no one to talk to . . . I have nobody.

YEPIKHODOV (*strums a guitar and sings*).

> *What do I care for the world's bustle,*
> *What's friend or foe to me . . . ?*

How nice it is to play the mandolin!

DUNYASHA: That's a guitar, not a mandolin. (*Looks in a hand mirror and powders her face.*)

YEPIKHODOV. For a man madly in love it's a mandolin . . . (*Sings.*)

> *If only the heart were afire,*
> *With flames of requited love. . . .*

(YASHA *joins in.*)

CHARLOTTA. Horrible the way these people sing. . . . Pfew! They howl like jackals.

DUNYASHA (*to* YASHA). Still, how wonderful to have been abroad.

YASHA. Yes, of course. My sentiments exactly. (*Yawns and lights a cigar.*)

YEPIKHODOV. It stands to reason. Everything abroad has long since reached its full constitution.

YASHA. That goes without saying.

YEPIKHODOV. I'm an educated man, I read all sorts of important books. But I don't get the drift, I mean what it is I want. Do I go on living, so to speak, or do I shoot myself? Just in case, I always carry a revolver on me. See . . . ? (*Takes out a revolver.*)

CHARLOTTA. Done. I'm off. (*Slings the gun over her shoulder.*) You're a very clever man, Yepikhodov, a real daredevil. Women must be crazy about you. Brr! (*Starts to go.*) All these brainy men are plain fools. There's no one for me to talk to. I'm alone, always alone. I have no one. . . . Who I am, why I'm alive—it's beyond me. . . . (*Goes out slowly.*)

YEPIKHODOV. Other considerations aside, so to speak, I have to say that, as for myself, fate treats me mercilessly. Like a storm tossing a rowboat. Let's say I'm mistaken. Then why do I, just to take one example, wake up this morning and find on my chest a spider of terrifying dimensions. . . . I mean, this big. (*Indicates size using both hands.*) Or I'll pour myself a glass of beer and what do you know!—there's something quite indecent floating about in it—in the nature of a cockroach. (*Pause.*) Have you read Buckle? (*Pause; to* DUNYASHA.) If it's no trouble, I should like to have a few words with you.

DUNYASHA. Well, go ahead.

YEPIKHODOV. I should prefer it to be in private. . . . (*Sighs.*)

DUNYASHA (*embarrassed*). Very well . . . only first bring me my cape. . . . You'll find it by the cupboard. . . . It's a bit damp out.

YEPIKHODOV. Certainly. . . . At your service. . . . Now I know what to do with my revolver. . . . (*Goes out, strumming on his guitar.*)

YASHA. Twenty-two Disasters! Between you and me, the man's an idiot. (*Yawns.*)

DUNYASHA. I hope to God he doesn't shoot himself. (*Pause.*) I've become so nervous, I worry all the time. The mistress took me into the house when I was still a little girl. I've lost touch with the way ordinary people live. Look, my hands are white as snow, like a lady's. I've turned soft, so delicate and genteel, everything scares me. . . . It's just awful, being like this. If you deceive me, Yasha, I don't know what that would do to my nerves.

YASHA (*kisses her*). Mm, you're a peach. Of course, a young lady should never forget herself. There's nothing I dislike so much in a girl as loose behavior.

DUNYASHA. I've fallen head over heels in love with you. You're educated, you have an opinion about everything. (*Pause.*)

YASHA (*yawns*). Quite true. . . . Now the way I see it, if a girl loves a man, that means she's immoral. (*Pause.*) It's pleasant to smoke a cigar in the open air. . . . (*Listens.*) Someone's coming. . . . It's my missus and the others. . . . (DUNYASHA *impulsively embraces him.*) Go on home. Pretend you've been to the river for a swim. Take that path. Otherwise they'll run into you and think I arranged a rendezvous. I can't stand that sort of thing.

DUNYASHA (*coughs quietly*). Your cigar's given me a headache. . . . (*Goes out.*)

YASHA *remains, sitting near the chapel. Enter* RANEVSKAYA, GAYEV, *and* LOPAKHIN.

LOPAKHIN. Make up your minds once and for all—time's running out. Look, it's a very simple question. Do you agree to lease your land for summer cottages, or don't you? Answer in one word—yes or no? Just one word!

RANEVSKAYA. Who's been smoking such foul cigars here? . . . (*Sits.*)

GAYEV. Now that they've put in a railroad line, life is convenient. (*Sits.*) We ran into town for some lunch. Yellow in the side pocket! I ought to pop into the house for a game.

RANEVSKAYA. There's time.

LOPAKHIN. Just one word! (*Imploring.*) Give me your answer!

GAYEV (*yawning*). Who?

RANEVSKAYA (*looks into her purse*). Yesterday there was a wad of money in here and today it's almost empty. My poor Varya scrimps by feeding everyone milk soup, the old servants get nothing but dried peas, and I throw away money. . . . (*Drops her purse, scattering gold coins*). There they go. . . . (*Shows annoyance.*)

YASHA. Allow me, I'll pick them up. (*Gathers up the coins.*)

RANEVSKAYA. Please, Yasha. And why did I go out for lunch? . . . That nasty restaurant of yours with its music and the tablecloths smelling of soap. . . . Why do you drink so much, Leonid? Why do you eat so much? Why do you talk so much? Today in the restaurant you went on and on and it was all so out of place. About the seventies, about the Decadents. And to whom? Talking to waiters about the Decadents!

LOPAKHIN. That's so.

GAYEV (*with a wave of the hand*). Its obvious, I'm a hopeless case. . . . (*Irritably, to* YASHA.) What is this? Why do you keep dancing in front of me? . . .

YASHA (*laughs*). I can't hear your voice without laughing.

GAYEV (*to his sister*). It's either him or me.

RANEVSKAYA. You may leave, Yasha. Run along now. . . .

YASHA (*hands* RANEVSKAYA *her purse*). In a minute. (*Barely containing his laughter.*) In a minute. (*Goes out.*)

LOPAKHIN. Deriganov is prepared to buy your estate. He's very rich. They say he's coming to the auction in person.

RANEVSKAYA. Where did you hear that?

LOPAKHIN. They're buzzing about it in town.

GAYEV. Our aunt from Yaroslavl promised to send something, but when and how much, nobody knows. . . .

LOPAKHIN. How much will she send? A hundred thousand? Two hundred?

RANEVSKAYA. Hmm. . . . Ten, maybe fifteen, if we're lucky.

LOPAKHIN. Forgive me, ladies and gentlemen, but I've never met such a frivolous, unbusinesslike, and odd bunch. I'm telling you in plain Russian, your estate is to be sold, and you don't understand a word.

RANEVSKAYA. What are we to do? Tell us, what?

LOPAKHIN. I tell you every day. Every day I repeat the same things. You have to rent out the cherry orchard and your land for summer cottages, and right away, as soon as possible—the ax is about to fall! Try to understand! Once you finally decide on summer cottages, you'll have as much money as you like. You'll be saved.

RANEVSKAYA. Cottages, summer people—excuse me, but it's all so vulgar.

GAYEV. I agree completely.

LOPAKHIN. I'm going to cry or scream. Or faint. I can't take it any more! You've exhausted me! (*To* GAYEV.) You're an old woman!

GAYEV. What?

LOPAKHIN. An old woman! (*Makes to leave.*)

RANEVSKAYA (*frightened*). Don't go, don't go, stay, my dear. Please. We may think of something!

LOPAKHIN. What is there to think about?

RANEVSKAYA. Don't go please. It's more cheerful when you're here. . . . (*Pause.*) I keep expecting something to happen. As if the house were about to come crashing down on our heads.

GAYEV (*wrapped up in his thoughts*). Bank shot into the corner. . . . Three cushions into the side. . . .

RANEVSKAYA. We've sinned much. . . .

LOPAKHIN. What sort of sins could you have . . . ?

GAYEV (*putting a candy in his mouth*). They say I've eaten up my fortune in candy. . . . (*Laughs.*)

RANEVSKAYA. Yes, I've sinned. I've squandered money carelessly, like a lunatic. I married a man good only at getting into debt. Champagne did my husband in—he was a terrible drunkard. It was my misfortune to fall in love again, we lived together, and just then—that was my first punishment, a blow to the head—here, in the river . . . my little boy drowned. I went abroad, forever, never to return, never to see this river again. . . . I shut my eyes and just ran, out of my mind, but *he* pursued me . . . pitiless, brutal. I bought a villa near Menton because *he* fell ill there. For three years I didn't know a moment's peace, day or night. That sick man wore me out, sucked my heart dry. And just last year we sold the villa to pay our debts. I ran off to Paris where he robbed me blind, abandoned me, took up with another woman. I tried to poison myself. . . . So stupid, so shameful. . . . And suddenly I felt drawn back to Russia, to my own country, to my little girl. . . . (*Wipes her tears.*) Oh, Lord, Lord, be merciful, forgive my sins! Don't punish me any more! (*Takes a telegram out of her pocket.*) This came from Paris today. . . . He asks me to forgive him, begs me to go back to him. . . . (*Tears up the telegram.*) Is that music? (*Listens.*)

GAYEV. It's our famous Jewish orchestra. Four violins, a flute, and a bass fiddle. Remember?

RANEVSKAYA. Are they still around? We should invite them sometime, have a party.

LOPAKHIN (*listening*). I can't hear a thing. . . . (*Sings softly.*) "For a ruble or two, a German will make a Frenchie of you." I saw a play yesterday—very funny.

RANEVSKAYA. There was probably nothing funny about it. You shouldn't be looking at plays; you should spend more time looking at yourselves. How drab your lives are, and what rubbish you speak.

LOPAKHIN. That's so. I have to say it outright, it's a life for fools. . . . (*Pause.*) My father was a peasant, an idiot. He knew nothing, taught me nothing, only got drunk and beat me—with a stick too. When you come right down to it, I'm just like him—a numbskull and an idiot. I was never taught anything, my handwriting is bad, I'm ashamed to let people see the way I write—like a pig.

RANEVSKAYA. You ought to get married, my dear.

LOPAKHIN. Yes . . . that's so.

RANEVSKAYA. To our Varya. She's a nice girl.

LOPAKHIN. Yes.

RANEVSKAYA. She came to us from simple people, she works hard, and most of all she loves you. And you've been fond of her for a long time now.

LOPAKHIN. Well, I've nothing against it. . . . She's a nice girl. (*Pause.*)

GAYEV. They've offered me a position in the bank. Six thousand a year. Have you heard?

RANEVSKAYA (*to* GAYEV). You in a bank! Better stay where you are. . . .

FIRS (*enters carrying a coat; to* GAYEV). Please, put this on, sir. It's damp here.

GAYEV (*putting on the coat*). You're a bore, my friend.

FIRS. Enough of that. . . . Going off in the morning without saying a word. (*Looks him over.*)

RANEVSKAYA. How you've aged, Firs!

FIRS. How's that, ma'am?

LOPAKHIN. The lady says you've aged!

FIRS. I've lived a long time. They were arranging my wedding and your papa wasn't born yet. . . . (*Laughs.*) And when the freedom came I was already the head butler. I wouldn't have any of their freedom, so I stayed with the masters. . . . (*Pause.*) I remember, they were all happy, but why they were happy—they themselves didn't know.

LOPAKHIN. Things were just dandy in the old days. At least you could do some flogging.

FIRS (*not hearing*). Yes. The peasants kept to the masters, the masters kept to the peasants. Now everybody's gone their own way. You can't tell fish from fowl.

GAYEV. Shut up, Firs. I have to go into town tomorrow. They promised to introduce me to some general who might be good for a loan.

LOPAKHIN. Nothing will come of it. And you won't make your mortgage payment, that's for certain.

RANEVSKAYA. He's raving. There is no general.

TROFIMOV, ANYA, *and* VARYA *enter.*

GAYEV. Here come our young people.

ANYA. There's Mama on the bench.

RANEVSKAYA (*tenderly*). Come here, come here. . . . My dear children. . . . (*Embracing* ANYA *and* VARYA.) If you only knew how much I love you. Sit beside me. There, like that. (*All sit.*)

LOPAKHIN. Our eternal student is eternally with the young ladies.

TROFIMOV. That's none of your business.

LOPAKHIN. He's going on fifty and he's still a student.

TROFIMOV. Enough of your stupid cracks.

LOPAKHIN. You're not angry, are you? You're a queer one.

TROFIMOV. And you're a pest.

LOPAKHIN (*laughs*). I'd like to know what you think of me.

TROFIMOV. What do I think of you, Yermolay Alexeyich? I think you're a rich man, soon you'll be a millionaire. Beasts of prey that devour whatever gets in their way are a necessary part of the natural process. So you're necessary too. (*All laugh.*)

VARYA. Petya, tell us about the planets.

RANEVSKAYA. No, let's continue yesterday's conversation.

TROFIMOV. What was it about?

GAYEV. The proud man.

TROFIMOV. We spoke for a long time yesterday but didn't come to any conclusions. According to you, the proud man has something mystical about him. Maybe you're right in your own way. But if you think about it plainly, without any fancy trimmings, what's so proud about him? Does pride make sense if a human being is such a poor physical specimen, if in the overwhelming majority of cases he's crude, stupid, and profoundly unhappy? We must stop admiring ourselves. We must work, that's the long and short of it.

GAYEV. All the same, you'll die.

TROFIMOV. Who knows? And what does "dying" mean? Perhaps a human being has a hundred senses and when he dies only the five known to us perish, and the remaining ninety-five survive.

RANEVSKAYA. How clever you are, Petya! . . .

LOPAKHIN (*ironically*). A genius!

TROFIMOV. Humanity is on the march, the human race is perfecting its powers. Everything that is now unattainable will someday be within our reach. It will all be as clear as day. We only have to work, and help with all our might those who seek the truth. In Russia very few of us work. Most of the intellectuals I know seek nothing, do nothing, and are incapable of work. They call themselves "the intelligentsia" and yet are rude to their servants and treat the peasants as if they were animals. They make poor students, read trash, and do absolutely nothing except talk about science. About art they know next to nothing. They're all self-important, have solemn faces, talk only about weighty matters, and argue for the sake of argument. Meanwhile, everybody knows working people are fed slop, sleep on straw—thirty and forty to a room, bedbugs for company—the stench is sickening, there's dampness, moral degradation. . . . Obviously the only point of all our high-minded discussions is to pull the wool over our eyes. Show me the public nurseries we've heard so much about, the libraries. They write about them in novels, in reality they don't exist. There's only filth, coarseness, Asiatic backwardness. . . . I don't like solemn faces, I'm afraid of them, I'm afraid of serious talk. We'd do better to keep our mouths shut!

LOPAKHIN. You know, I get up before five. I work from the crack of dawn until late at night. Money is always passing through my hands—some of it mine, some belongs to others. I can see what people around me are really like. You only have to get into a job to see how few honest and decent people there are. Sometimes, when I can't sleep, I get to thinking: "Lord, You gave us immense forests, boundless fields, wide horizons. Living among them, we ought to be giants."

RANEVSKAYA. It's giants you want, is it? They're good only in fairy tales, otherwise they're frightening.

YEPIKHODOV *passes backstage, playing a guitar.*

RANEVSKAYA (*pensively*). There goes Yepikhodov. . . .

ANYA (*pensively*). There goes Yepikhodov. . . .

GAYEV. Ladies and gentlemen, the sun has set.

TROFIMOV. Yes.

GAYEV (*in a low voice, as if making a speech*). O nature, wondrous nature, you sparkle, eternally radiant, beautiful and indifferent. You, whom we call Mother, encompass both life and death! You create and destroy.

VARYA (*pleading*). Uncle!

ANYA. Uncle, you're at it again!

TROFIMOV. You'd better bank the yellow in the side pocket.

GAYEV. I'm silent, I'm silent.

They sit wrapped in thought. Silence. Only FIRS'S *low mumbling is audible. Suddenly a distant sound is heard, as if coming from the sky, the mournful dying sound of a breaking string.*

RANEVSKAYA. What was that?

LOPAKHIN. I don't know. Somewhere far away in the mines a bucket fell. But very far away.

GAYEV. It might be a bird . . . a heron perhaps.

TROFIMOV. Or an owl. . . .

RANEVSKAYA (*shudders*). I don't know why but it makes me nervous. (*Pause.*)

FIRS. Before the disaster the same thing happened. The owl screeched and the samovar whistled all the time.

GAYEV. What disaster?

FIRS. The freedom, sir. (*Pause.*)

RANEVSKAYA. What do you say we go, my friends? It's getting dark. (*To* ANYA.) There are tears in your eyes. What is it, my child? (*Embraces her.*)

ANYA. It's nothing, Mama. I'm all right.

TROFIMOV. Someone's coming.

A TRAMP *appears; he is wearing a shabby white cap and an overcoat and is slightly drunk.*

TRAMP. Begging your pardon, but will this take me to the station?

GAYEV. It will. Just follow that path.

TRAMP. My heartfelt thanks, sir. (*Coughing.*) Glorious weather. (*Declaims.*) "My brother, my brother in pain. . . . Go to the Volga, hear it groan. . . . " (*To* VARYA.) Mademoiselle, can you spare thirty kopeks for a starving Russian . . . ?

VARYA, *frightened, cries out.*

LOPAKHIN (*angrily*). Even drunks ought to know their limits!

RANEVSKAYA (*flustered*). Here, take this. . . . (*Fumbles in her purse.*) I don't have any change. . . . Never mind, here's a gold piece. . . .

TRAMP. My heartfelt thanks. (*Goes out.*)

Laughter

VARYA (*frightened*). I'm going . . . I'm going . . . Oh, Mama, at home the servants have nothing to eat and you give away a gold coin.

RANEVSKAYA. It's hopeless, I'm such a fool. When we get home, I'll give you every kopek I have. Yermolay Alexeyich, lend me some more money! . . .

LOPAKHIN. At your service.

RANEVSKAYA. Let's go, my friends, it's time. By the way, Varya, we finally have a husband for you. Congratulations.

VARYA (*in tears*). Mama, that's no way to joke.

LOPAKHIN. "Auriphilia, get thee to a nunnery. . . . "

GAYEV. My hands are trembling. I haven't played billiards for ages now.

LOPAKHIN. "O Auriphilia, o nymph, in thy orisons be all my sins remembered."

RANEVSKAYA. Come, my friends. It's almost supper time.

VARYA. He frightened me. My heart's pounding so.

LOPAKHIN. Let me remind you, my friends—on the twenty-second of August the cherry orchard will be up for sale. Think about that! . . . Think! . . .

All leave except TROFIMOV *and* ANYA.

ANYA (*laughing*). Thank you, tramp. You gave Varya a scare, and now we're alone.

TROFIMOV. Varya's afraid we'll fall in love. For days on end she tags after us. She's too narrow-minded to grasp that you and I are above love. We are going to bypass all the petty illusions that keep people from being happy and free—that's the goal of our life, its meaning. Forward then! We are advancing toward that bright star glowing in the distance. Nothing can hold us back! Forward march! Don't lag behind, my countrymen!

ANYA (*clapping her hands*). How eloquently you speak! (*Pause.*) It's a lovely day.

TROFIMOV. Yes, remarkable weather.

ANYA. What have you done to me, Petya? Why don't I love the cherry orchard the way I once did? I loved it so tenderly. I thought there was no spot more beautiful in the whole world than our cherry orchard.

TROFIMOV. All Russia is our orchard. Our land is vast and glorious, it has many wonderful places. (*Pause.*) Think about it, Anya. Your grandfather, your great-grandfather, all your ancestors were serf-owners, they owned living men and women. Human faces peer at you from every cherry, every leaf, every tree trunk. Can't you hear their voices? . . . Power over men of flesh and blood has corrupted you, in the past and now too. Your mother and uncle, you too, you're not even aware that you're living on credit, on other people, men and women whom you won't even let through the front door. . . . Russia is at least two hundred years behind, we have nothing, we haven't come to terms with our past. All we do is prattle about grand ideas, complain about boredom, and guzzle vodka. It's clear as day—to live in the present we first have to make up for our past, to have done with it once and for all. And we can make up for it only by suffering, by tremendous, unceasing work. You must understand that, Anya.

ANYA. For a long time now the house where we live hasn't been a home. I'm leaving, I give you my word.

TROFIMOV. If you have the keys, fling them into the well and fly away. Be as free as the wind.

ANYA (*ecstatic*). How beautifully you speak!

TROFIMOV. Believe in me, Anya, believe in me! I'm not yet thirty, I'm young, still a student, but I've suffered so much! My life has been one long winter. I've been hungry, sick, troubled. I'm as poor as a church mouse. Where hasn't fate driven me! Where haven't I been! And yet at every moment, day and night, my mind is teeming with marvelous visions of the future. I have a vision of happiness, Anya. I can already see it. . . .

ANYA (*pensively*). The moon is rising.

YEPIKHODOV *can be heard playing the same sad tune on the guitar. The moon rises. Somewhere near the poplars* VARYA, *looking for* ANYA, *calls,* "Anya! Where are you?"

TROFIMOV. Yes, the moon is rising. (*Pause.*) There it is—happiness. There. It's on its way, it's coming closer and closer. I can already hear its footsteps. And if we are not meant to see it, if we are not to know it, what does that matter? Others will!

VARYA (*from offstage*). Anya! Where are you?

TROFIMOV. Varya again! (*Angrily.*) What a pain in the neck!

ANYA. Never mind. Let's go down to the river. It's pretty there.

TROFIMOV. Let's. (*They go.*)

VARYA (*from offstage*). Anya! Anya!

Curtain

ACT III   *The living room, separated by an arch from the ballroom. A chandelier is lit. The Jewish band mentioned in Act II is playing in the anteroom. Evening. The party is dancing the Grand Rond in the ballroom.* PISHCHIK *calls:* "Promenade à une paire!" *They come into the living room in couples:* PISHCHIK *and* CHARLOTTA, *then* TROFIMOV *and* RANEVSKAYA, *then* ANYA *and the* POSTMAN, *then* VARYA *and the* STATIONMASTER, *and so on.* VARYA *weeps silently and wipes her tears away while dancing.* DUNYASHA *is in the couple bringing up the rear. They promenade around the living room.* PISHCHIK *calls:* "Grand Rond, balancez!" *and* "Les cavaliers à genoux et remerciez vos dames." FIRS, *wearing a dress coat, brings in a tray with seltzer.* PISHCHIK *and* TROFIMOV *come into the living room.*

[handwritten margin note: Speaking French]

PISHCHIK. High blood pressure, that's what it is. I've already had two strokes. Dancing doesn't come easy, but, as they say, "If you run with the pack, you don't have to bark, but at least wag your tail." I'm as strong as a horse. My father—may he rest in peace—he liked his little jokes. Ask him about our genealogy and he'd say that the ancient line of Simeon-Pishchik descends from the horse Caligula seated in the Roman senate. . . . (*Sits.*) But the trouble is, I'm broke! A hungry dog believes in only one thing—meat. . . . (*Snores and immediately wakes up.*) The same with me . . . all I think about is money.

TROFIMOV. You *are* built a bit like a horse.

PISHCHIK. So what? . . . A horse is a fine animal. . . . You can always sell a horse. . . .

The sound of clicking billiards from the adjoining room. VARYA *appears in the archway.*

TROFIMOV (*teasing*). Madam Lopakhin! Madam Lopakhin!

VARYA (*angrily*). You mangy gentleman!

TROFIMOV. Yes, that's what I am and I'm proud of it.

VARYA (*reflecting bitterly*). Hiring musicians! And how do we pay them! (*Goes out.*)

TROFIMOV (*to* PISHCHIK). The energy you've spent over the course of your life scrounging money to pay off your mortgage—had you used it for something else, you might have turned the world upside down.

PISHCHIK. Nietzsche . . . the philosopher . . . the greatest, the most famous philosopher in the whole world . . . a man of colossal intellect . . . in his books he says it's all right to print counterfeit money.

TROFIMOV. You've read Nietzsche?

PISHCHIK. Well, not exactly . . . Dashenka told me about him. Right now I'm in such a fix that forging money is about the only. . . . The day after tomorrow I have to come up with three hundred and ten rubles. . . . I've already got a hundred and thirty. (*Alarmed, rummages in his pockets.*) My money's gone! I've lost my money! (*In tears.*) Where's my money? (*Joyfully.*) Ah, here it is, in the lining. . . . Whew, I even broke into a sweat. . . .

RANEVSKAYA *and* CHARLOTTA *enter.*

RANEVSKAYA (*hums a Caucasian dance tune, the* Lezginka). Why isn't Leonid back from town? What can he be up to? (*To* DUNYASHA.) Dunyasha, offer the musicians tea. . . .

TROFIMOV. Most likely the auction hasn't come off.

RANEVSKAYA. It's the wrong time for musicians and the wrong time for a party. . . . Oh, what does it matter. . . . (*Sits and hums quietly.*)

CHARLOTTA (*hands* PISHCHIK *a deck of cards*). Take this deck of cards. Think of a card.

PISHCHIK. I've got one.

CHARLOTTA. Now shuffle the pack. Very good. Give them to me, my dear Herr Pishchik. *Ein, zwei, drei!* Now your card. You'll find it in your side pocket.

PISHCHIK (*taking the card out of his pocket*). The eight of spades! Right on the button! (*Amazed.*) Who would believe it!

CHARLOTTA (*holding out the deck in the palm of her hand, to* TROFIMOV). Quick, what's the top card?

TROFIMOV. What? Oh, all right. The queen of spades.

CHARLOTTA. The queen of spades it is! (*To* PISHCHIK.) And what's the top card now?

PISHCHIK. The ace of hearts.

CHARLOTTA. And here's your ace of hearts! (*Claps her hands and the deck disappears.*) Lovely weather we're having today!

A VOICE (*feminine and mysterious, as if from beneath the floor*). Oh yes, miss, the weather is splendid.

CHARLOTTA. You are the dream of my life.

THE VOICE. I like you too, miss.

STATIONMASTER (*applauding*). Madam the ventriloquist! Bravo!

PISHCHIK (*amazed*). Who would believe it! Charlotta, you're enchanting . . . I'm head over heels in love with you. . . .

CHARLOTTA. In love? (*Shrugging her shoulders.*) Are you capable of love? *Guter Mensch, aber schlechter Musikant.*

TROFIMOV (*slapping* PISHCHIK *on the shoulder*). You old stallion. . . .

CHARLOTTA. Attention, please. One more trick. (*Takes a plaid lap blanket from a chair.*) Here's a good blanket. I want to sell it. . . . (*Shakes it out.*) Do I have any buyers?

PISHCHIK (*still amazed*). Who would believe it!

CHARLOTTA. *Ein, zwei, drei!* (*Quickly raises the blanket.* ANYA *appears behind it. She curtsies, runs to her mother, embraces her, and runs back to the ballroom amid general rapture.*)

RANEVSKAYA (*applauding*). Bravo, bravo!

CHARLOTTA. And again! *Ein, zwei, drei!* (*Raises the blanket;* VARYA *appears behind it and bows.*)

PISHCHIK (*amazed*). Who would believe it!

CHARLOTTA. Finis! (*Throws the blanket over* PISHCHIK, *curtsies, and runs into the ballroom.*)

PISHCHIK (*pursuing her*). You sly witch. . . . What a woman you are! What a woman! (*Runs out.*)

RANEVSKAYA. Leonid's still not here. What has he been up to in town all this time? I don't understand. It must be all over by now. Either the estate's been sold or the auction has been called off. Why keep us in the dark for so long?

VARYA (*trying to console her*). Uncle bought it, I'm certain of it.

TROFIMOV (*mockingly*). Sure.

VARYA. Auntie gave him permission to acquire it in her name and transfer the mortgage. She's doing it for Anya. I'm sure God will help us and Uncle will buy it.

RANEVSKAYA. Our aunt from Yaroslavl sent fifteen thousand to purchase the estate in her name—she doesn't trust us. It won't even cover the interest. (*Covers her face with her hands.*) Today my fate will be decided, my future. . . .

TROFIMOV (*teasing* VARYA). Madam Lopakhin!

VARYA (*angrily*). The student who never graduates! Twice thrown out of the university.

RANEVSKAYA. Why get upset, Varya? He's teasing you about Lopakhin, well, what of it? If you want to—go ahead and marry Lopakhin. He's a good man, an interesting man. If you don't, then don't. Nobody's forcing you, my dear. . . .

VARYA. I regard this matter seriously, Mama. I must be direct. He's a decent man and I'm fond of him.

RANEVSKAYA. Then marry him. Why wait? It's beyond me.

VARYA. Mama, I can't very well propose to him myself. For two years now everyone's been chattering about him. People gossip and he either keeps silent or cracks jokes. I understand. He's busy getting rich and has no time for me. If I had some money, just a little, even a hundred rubles, I'd wash my hands of it all and go off somewhere. I'd go into a nunnery.

TROFIMOV. Glory be to heaven!

VARYA (*to* TROFIMOV). A student ought to have some brains! (*Gently, in tears.*) Petya, how ugly you've become, how you've aged! (*No longer crying; to* RANEVSKAYA.) I can't live without working, Mama. I have to be busy every minute.

YASHA (*enters, barely holding back a laugh*). Yepikhodov has broken a cue! . . . (*Goes out.*)

VARYA. What's Yepikhodov doing here? Who gave him permission to play billiards? I don't understand these people. . . . (*Goes out.*)

RANEVSKAYA. You shouldn't tease her, Petya. She has troubles enough.

TROFIMOV. She's a busybody, always sticking her nose into other people's business. All summer she's been after me and Anya. Afraid we'll have an affair. How does it concern her? Besides, I've given no signs, such vulgarity is beneath me. We're above love!

RANEVSKAYA. In that case I suppose I'm beneath it. (*Very anxious.*) What can be keeping Leonid? If I only knew whether the estate has been sold. A calamity like that seems so incredible. I don't know what to think, I'm at my wit's end. . . . I could scream . . . do something crazy. Save me, Petya. Say something, talk to me. . . .

TROFIMOV. The estate may be sold today and then again it may not—does it make any difference? It's been finished for a long time now. There's no turning back, the road is overgrown with weeds. Calm down, my dear. Don't deceive yourself. For once in your life, look truth in the eye.

RANEVSKAYA. What truth? You can see the truth but I seem to have lost my eyesight. I don't see a thing. How boldly you settle all the difficult questions, but tell me, my dear boy, isn't that because you're young and haven't suffered yet? You look fearlessly ahead, but isn't that because you don't expect anything fearful, because life is still hidden from your innocent eyes? You're more daring, honest, deeper than the rest of us, but put yourself in my place, show a drop of generosity, pity me. After all, I was born on this estate, my father and mother lived out their lives here, my grandfather. . . . I love this house, without the cherry orchard my life has no meaning. If it has to be sold, then sell me with it. . . . (*Embraces* TROFIMOV *and kisses him on the forehead.*) My son drowned here. You're a kind and good person. Pity me.

TROFIMOV. You have my warmest sympathy, you know that.

RANEVSKAYA. But that's not how you ought to have put it. . . . (*Takes out a handkerchief, a telegram falls to the floor.*) You can't imagine how depressed I feel today. It's so noisy here, my heart trembles at every sound, I'm shaking all over, and I can't go off to my room. The silence terrifies me. Don't blame me, Petya . . . I love you as if you were my own. I would gladly let you marry Anya, only, my dear boy, you must do some studying, you have to get your degree. You don't do anything, fate tosses you about like a matchstick. It's so strange. . . . That's so, isn't it? And you must

do something about that beard of yours, let it grow out. . . .
(*Laughs.*) You look ridiculous!

TROFIMOV (*picks up the telegram*). I have no wish to be an Adonis.

RANEVSKAYA. That's a telegram from Paris. I get one every day.
Yesterday and today again. That preposterous man is ill again,
he's in a bad way. . . . He asks my forgiveness, begs me to come,
and I really ought to go to Paris and be near him. Petya, you look
so stern, but what am I to do, my dear boy? He's sick, he's all
alone, he's unhappy. Who is there to care for him, keep him out
of trouble, give him his medicine on time? And what's the point of
hiding it or keeping silent—I love him! That's only too clear. I
love him, I love him. . . . He's a millstone around my neck, he'll
drag me to the bottom, but I love that stone and can't live without
it. (*Presses* TROFIMOV'S *hand.*) Don't think badly of me, Petya, and
don't say anything, not a word. . . .

TROFIMOV (*tearfully*). Excuse my frankness, but for God's sake, he
robbed you!

RANEVSKAYA. No, no, no, you mustn't say such things. . . . (*Covers
her ears.*)

TROFIMOV. He's a snake. You're the only one who doesn't know it!
A petty thief, a nobody.

RANEVSKAYA (*holding in her anger*). You're twenty-six or twenty-
seven, but you're still a schoolboy.

TROFIMOV. That may be so.

RANEVSKAYA. Be a man. At your age you should understand people
who love. You should love someone yourself . . . for once in your
life fall in love! (*Angrily.*) Yes, Yes! It's not purity with you, it's
just prudishness. You're a crank, a comical freak.

TROFIMOV (*aghast*). What's that?

RANEVSKAYA. "I'm above love!" You're not above love, you're
what our Firs calls a nincompoop. Not to have a mistress at
your age!

TROFIMOV (*horrified*). This is shocking! What can she be saying?
(*Runs into the ballroom clutching his head.*) Awful . . . I can't stand
it, I'm leaving. . . . (*Goes out but immediately returns.*) It's all over
between us! (*Goes out to the anteroom.*)

RANEVSKAYA (*shouts after him*). Petya, wait! You're being silly, I
was just joking! Petya!

Sound from the anteroom of somebody running quickly downstairs and falling with a crash. ANYA *and* VARYA *cry out, but a moment later the sound of laughter.*

RANEVSKAYA. What's happened?

ANYA (*runs in, laughing*). Petya fell down the stairs. (*Runs out.*)

RANEVSKAYA. What a queer bird our Petya is!

The STATIONMASTER *stands in the middle of the ballroom and recites Alexey Tolstoy's "Magdalene." They listen, but after a few lines the reading breaks off, as the sounds of a waltz are heard from the anteroom. All dance.* TROFIMOV, ANYA, VARYA, *and* RANEVSKAYA *enter from the anteroom.*

RANEVSKAYA. Good, pure Petya . . . forgive me. . . . Let's dance.

RANEVSKAYA *and* PETYA *dance together.* ANYA *and* VARYA *dance.* FIRS *comes in and places his cane by the side door.* YASHA *also enters from the living room and watches the dancers.*

YASHA. Well, Grandpa?

FIRS. I'm feeling poorly. In the old days there was generals, barons, admirals dancing at the balls here. Now we send for the postman and the stationmaster. And they're not too keen about coming, either. I've got one foot in the grave. The old master that's dead, he gave everyone a dose of sealing wax, no matter what ailed 'em. I've been taking sealing wax every day for twenty years now, it could be more. Maybe that's what's kept me alive.

YASHA. I'm fed up with you, Grandpa. (*Yawns.*) It's time you croaked.

FIRS. Nincompoop! (*Mumbles.*)

TROFIMOV *and* RANEVSKAYA *dance from the ballroom into the living room.*

RANEVSKAYA. *Merci!* I'll sit for a while. . . . (*Sits down.*) I'm tired.

ANYA (*enters; agitated*). Just now in the kitchen a man said the cherry orchard was sold today.

RANEVSKAYA. To whom?

ANYA. He didn't say. He left. (*Dances off into the ballroom with* TROFIMOV.)

YASHA. It was some old geezer talking rubbish. A stranger.

FIRS. And Leonid Andreyich isn't back yet. He's wearing his light coat. Likely he'll catch cold. Eh, these young ones.

RANEVSKAYA. This will be the death of me. Yasha, go find out who bought it.

YASHA. But he's long gone, the old fool. (*Laughs.*)

RANEVSKAYA (*annoyed*). Why are you laughing? What's there to be happy about?

YASHA. That Yepikhodov's funny. A scatterbrain. Twenty-two Disasters!

RANEVSKAYA. Firs, if the estate is sold where will you go?

FIRS. Where you order me, that's where I'll go.

RANEVSKAYA. Why do you look like that? Are you ill? You ought to go to bed.

FIRS. That's right. . . . (*With a smirk.*) I'll go to bed. And without me who's going to bring out the coffeepot? Who will see to things? I've got the whole house on my shoulders.

YASHA (*to* RANEVSKAYA). Lyubov Andreyevna, allow me to make a request! If you go back to Paris, take me with you, do me that favor. It's absolutely impossible for me to remain here. (*Looking around, in a low voice.*) What's the point of saying it, you can see for yourself. The country's uncivilized, the people have no morals, and besides, it's boring. The food is lousy, and there's Firs hobbling about, mumbling all sorts of nonsense. Take me with you, please!

PISHCHIK (*enters*). May I have the pleasure of a waltz with you, lovely lady? . . . (RANEVSKAYA *accepts.*) All the same, my charmer, I'll have that loan of a hundred and eighty rubles from you . . . I will have it. . . . (*They dance.*) A hundred and eighty rubles. . . . (*They dance off into the ballroom.*)

YASHA (*sings softly*). "If you but knew the passions of my heart. . . . "

In the ballroom a figure in a gray top hat and checked trousers leaps and waves its hands. Shouts of: "Bravo, Charlotta!"

DUNYASHA (*stops to powder her face; to* FIRS). The mistress told me to dance. There are lots of young gentlemen and we're short on ladies. But dancing makes me dizzy. My heart thumps. And just now the postman told me something that took my breath away. (*The music dies down.*)

FIRS. What did he say?

DUNYASHA. "You're like a flower."

YASHA (*yawning*). How boorish. . . . (*Goes off.*)

DUNYASHA. "A flower." I'm so delicate. I just adore pretty speeches.

FIRS. You'll come to a bad end.

YEPIKHODOV (*enters*). Dunyasha, you avoid me as if I were an insect. (*Sighs.*) Ah, life!

DUNYASHA. What do you want?

YEPIKHODOV. No doubt you may be right. (*Sighs.*) But, of course, if you look at it from a perspective, then, if I may say so—forgive me for being so frank—you have completely reduced me to a state of mind. I know the kind of luck I have, every day brings some new disaster, but I'm used to it. I face fate with a smile. You gave me your word, and though I . . .

DUNYASHA. Excuse me, we'll talk about it later. Now leave me alone. I'm living in a dream. (*Plays with her fan.*)

YEPIKHODOV. Every day a new disaster. And if I may say so, I merely smile, I even laugh.

VARYA (*comes out of the ballroom; to* YEPIKHODOV). Are you still here? What an ill-mannered fellow you are. (*To* DUNYASHA.) Run along, Dunyasha. (*To* YEPIKHODOV.) Either you're smashing the billiard cues, or strutting about as if you were a guest.

YEPIKHODOV. If I may so express myself, you can't make me pay.

VARYA. I'm not asking you to pay, I'm just telling you. All you do is mope about, you don't work at your job. We keep you as a clerk, God only knows what for.

YEPIKHODOV (*offended*). Whether I work or go for a walk, whether I eat or play billiards—only reasonable and mature individuals may discuss such matters.

VARYA (*flaring up*). You dare speak to me like that? You dare? Are you saying I'm not reasonable? Get out of here! This minute!

YEPIKHODOV (*frightened*). May I ask you to express yourself in a more delicate manner?

VARYA (*beside herself*). This minute! Out of here! Go! (*He makes for the door; she in pursuit.*) Twenty-Two Disasters! Never set foot in here again! Never let me catch sight of you!

YEPIKHODOV (*goes out. His voice is heard from beyond the door*). I shall enter a complaint.

VARYA. Oh, you're coming back, are you? (*She grabs the cane left near the door by* FIRS.) Come on, come on. . . . Just come, I'll show you. . . . So you're coming, are you? Take that. . . . (*Swings the cane just as* LOPAKHIN *enters.*)

LOPAKHIN. Thank you very much.

VARYA (*angry and derisive*). I beg your pardon!

LOPAKHIN. It's nothing. Thanks for the charming reception.

VARYA. Don't mention it. (*Walks away, then looks back and asks softly.*) I didn't hurt you, did I?

LOPAKHIN. No, it's nothing. There'll be a whale of a bump though.

VOICES (*from the ballroom*). Lopakhin has come! Yermolay Alexeyich is here!

PISHCHIK. A sight for sore eyes. (*Kisses* LOPAKHIN.) You smell of cognac, my dear friend. And we've been kicking up our heels too.

RANEVSKAYA (*entering*). Is that you, Yermolay Alexeyich? What kept you? Where's Leonid?

LOPAKHIN. He came with me. He's on his way. . . .

RANEVSKAYA (*agitated*). Well, what happened? Did the sale take place? Tell me everything!

LOPAKHIN (*embarrassed, fearful of showing his joy*). The auction was over at four o'clock. We missed the train and had to wait till half past nine. (*Sighing heavily.*) Whew! I'm a bit dizzy. . . .

GAYEV *enters, holding parcels in his right hand while wiping away tears with his left.*

RANEVSKAYA. Leonid, what happened? Leonid! (*Impatiently, tearfully.*) Out with it, for God's sake.

GAYEV (*doesn't answer; merely waves his arm. Weeping, to* FIRS). Here, take these. . . . Anchovies, herrings. . . . I haven't eaten all day. . . . What I've been through! (*The door to the billiard room is open. The sound of* YASHA'S *voice:* "Seven and eighteen!" GAYEV'S *expression changes; he no longer weeps.*) I'm dead tired. Firs, help me change my clothes. (*Goes out, followed by* FIRS.)

PISHCHIK. What about the auction? Tell us!

RANEVSKAYA. Has the cherry orchard been sold?

LOPAKHIN. <u>Yes</u>.

RANEVSKAYA. Who bought it?

LOPAKHIN. I <u>bought</u> it. (*Pause.* RANEVSKAYA *is crushed. She would collapse if not for the chair and table near her.* VARYA *takes the keys from her belt, flings them to the floor in the middle of the drawing room, and stalks out.*) I bought it! Hold it a minute, my friends, please, my head's swimming, I can't talk straight. . . . (*Laughs.*) We came to the auction, Deriganov was already there. Leonid Andreyich had only fifteen thousand, and right off Deriganov bid thirty thousand over the mortgage. I saw how the land lay, took him on, and bid forty thousand. He ups me by five. I go to fifty-five. He keeps on raising by fives, I by tens. . . . Well, we wrapped it up. I bid ninety thousand and that was it. The cherry orchard is mine now! Mine! (*Laughs uproariously.*) God Almighty, the cherry orchard is mine! Tell me I'm drunk, out of my mind, that it's all a dream. . . . (*Stamps his feet.*) Don't laugh at me! If my father and grandfather could rise from their graves and see their Yermolay now—a boy who was whipped, who could barely read or write, who ran barefoot in winter—if they could see how their Yermolay has bought the most magnificent estate in the world. I bought the estate where my father and grandfather were slaves, where they weren't even allowed into the kitchen. I'm asleep, I'm dreaming, it's only make-believe. . . . The fruit of my imagination. It's all so mysterious. (*Picks up the keys, smiling amiably.*) She threw the keys away, wants to show she's no longer mistress here. . . . (*Jingles the keys.*) Well, it doesn't matter. (*The band tunes up.*) Hey, musicians! Play! Let's hear it! Everybody come and see Yermolay Lopakhin put the ax to the cherry orchard, see the trees tumble to the ground. We'll build summer cottages here, our children and grandchildren will have a different life. . . . Music! Play!

The band plays. RANEVSKAYA *sinks into a chair and weeps bitterly.*

LOPAKHIN (*reproachfully*). Why didn't you listen to me? Why? My poor woman, my dear friend, there's no bringing it back now. (*In tears.*) Oh, if only we could get through this quickly! If only the unhappy, confused way we live would somehow change.

PISHCHIK (*takes him by the arm, in a low voice*). She's crying. Let's go into the ballroom, she needs to be alone. . . . Come. . . . (*Leads him by the arm into the ballroom.*)

LOPAKHIN. What happened? Hey, musicians, play so I can hear you! Things better be the way I want them! (*Ironically.*) Here comes the new master, the owner of the cherry orchard. (*Accidentally bumps into a small table, almost upsetting the candelabra.*) I can pay for everything, everything! (*Goes out with* PISHCHIK.)

No one remains in the ballroom and drawing room except RANEVSKAYA. *She sits huddled and weeping bitterly. Music plays softly.* ANYA *and* TROFIMOV *rush in.* ANYA *goes up to her mother and falls to her knees.* TROFIMOV *stands in the doorway to the ballroom.*

ANYA. Mama! . . . Mama, you're crying. Dear, kind Mama . . . my beautiful, precious Mama, I love you. Bless you, Mama. The cherry orchard is sold, it's gone. That's so, but don't cry, Mama. You have your whole life ahead of you. You're still a pure, good person. Come with me, let's go away from here, my darling, come! . . . We'll plant a new orchard, more splendid than this one. You'll see it and then you'll understand. And like the sun at evening, joy will descend into your heart. You'll know a profound and calm happiness, and you'll smile, Mama! Come, my darling! Come!

Curtain

ACT IV   *Same as in Act I. No curtains on the windows,
no pictures on the walls. Only a few pieces of
furniture piled in a corner, as if for sale. A
sense of emptiness. Suitcases, traveling bags,
etc. around the outer door and at the rear of
the stage. The door on the left is open; the
voices of* VARYA *and* ANYA *may be heard.*
LOPAKHIN *stands waiting.* YASHA *with a tray
of glasses filled with champagne. In the
anteroom* YEPIKHODOV *is tying up a box.
Offstage, from the rear, a hum of voices;
peasants have come to say goodbye.*

GAYEV (*from offstage*). Thank you, my friends, thank you.

YASHA. The peasants have come to say goodbye. As I see it,
Yermolay Alexeyich, the peasants are a good-natured but ignorant
lot.

The hum dies down. RANEVSKAYA *and* GAYEV *enter. She is no
longer crying but is pale, her face twitches and she cannot speak.*

GAYEV. You gave them your purse, Lyuba. You shouldn't! You know
you shouldn't!

RANEVSKAYA. I couldn't help myself! I just couldn't! (*They go out.*)

LOPAKHIN (*calling after them*). Please, I beg you, a glass of
champagne to say goodbye! I didn't think of it in town and found
only one bottle at the station. Please! (*Pause.*) What is it, my
friends? Don't you want any? (*Moves away from the door.*) Had I
known, I wouldn't have bought it. In that case I'm not drinking
either. (YASHA *carefully sets the tray down on a chair.*) At least
you have a glass, Yasha.

YASHA. To those who are going away! And to those who are staying!
(*Drinks.*) This champagne isn't the genuine article, you can lay
money on that.

LOPAKHIN. Eight rubles a bottle. (*Pause.*) Damn, it's cold in here.

YASHA. They didn't light the stoves today. It wasn't worth it, since
we're leaving. (*Laughs.*)

LOPAKHIN. What's so funny?

YASHA. I'm just in a good mood.

LOPAKHIN. October's here but it's as sunny and peaceful as summer. Good weather for building. (*Looking at his watch, calls through the door.*) Remember, folks, only forty-six minutes till train time! That means we ought to start for the station in twenty minutes. Better hurry up.

TROFIMOV (*enters wearing an overcoat*). It must be time to go. The carriages are at the door. Where are my damn galoshes? They've disappeared. (*Calls through the door.*) Anya, my galoshes aren't here! I can't find them.

LOPAKHIN. I have to go to Kharkov. We're on the same train. I'll spend the winter there. I've had enough of shooting the breeze with you people. Loafing has done me in. I just can't live without working. I don't know what to do with my hands. They hang from my shoulders as if they didn't belong to me.

TROFIMOV. We'll soon be gone and you can return to your useful labors.

LOPAKHIN. Have a glass of champagne.

TROFIMOV. No, thanks.

LOPAKHIN. So it's Moscow?

TROFIMOV. Yes. I'll see them into town and tomorrow I'm off for Moscow.

LOPAKHIN. Well, I bet the professors have canceled their lectures. They're all waiting for you to show up!

TROFIMOV. That's none of your business.

LOPAKHIN. How many years have you been in the university?

TROFIMOV. Can't you think of a new line? That's old and stale. (*Looks for his galoshes.*) We'll probably never see each other again. Let me give you a last bit of advice. Don't wave your arms about! Get out of the habit. And building summer cottages, figuring that in time the summer residents will own their own land—that's waving your arms about too. . . . All the same, I like you. You have slender and delicate fingers, like an artist. At heart you must be gentle and delicate. . . .

LOPAKHIN (*embracing him*). Goodbye, my friend. Thanks for everything. Let me give you some money for the trip, in case you run short.

TROFIMOV. What for? I don't need it.

LOPAKHIN. But you don't have a ruble to your name!

TROFIMOV. Yes, I do. Thank you. I got something for a translation. It's here in my pocket. (*Anxiously.*) Where are my galoshes?

VARYA (*from another room*). Take your nasty things! (*Throws a pair of galoshes on stage.*)

TROFIMOV. What are you so angry about, Varya? Hmm . . . and these aren't even my galoshes!

LOPAKHIN. I planted three thousand acres of poppy in the spring and now I've cleared forty thousand. The poppies in bloom—what a sight that was! I'm offering you a loan because I can afford it. Why turn up your nose at it? I'm a peasant. I call a spade a spade.

TROFIMOV. Your father was a peasant; mine was a druggist. That means absolutely nothing. (LOPAKHIN *takes out his wallet.*) Don't . . . put it away. . . . If you were to offer me two hundred thousand, I wouldn't take it. I'm a free man. All of you, rich and poor alike, what you value so highly hasn't the slightest power over me. It's so much fluff floating in the air. I can manage without you, I can pass by you. I'm strong and proud. Humanity is moving toward a revelation of the highest truth, to the most sublime happiness possible on earth, and I'm in the front ranks!

LOPAKHIN. Will you get there?

TROFIMOV. Yes. (*Pause.*) I'll get there, or I'll show others the way.

In the distance the sound of axes chopping down the cherry trees.

LOPAKHIN. Well, so long, my friend. It's time to go. You and I, we turn up our noses at each other, but life goes on. When I'm working hard, without letup, my mind's at ease, and I think I know why I'm alive. But how many people in Russia just exist and nobody knows why. Well, it doesn't matter. That's not what makes the wheels go round. They say Leonid Andreyich has taken a job in the bank at six thousand a year. . . . Only he won't stick it out, too lazy. . . .

ANYA (*in the doorway*). Mama begs you not to chop down the cherry trees until she's gone.

TROFIMOV. Really, you should have more tact. (*Goes out through the anteroom.*)

LOPAKHIN. I'll take care of it. Right away. Ekh, what people. (*Goes out after him.*)

ANYA. Has Firs been taken to the hospital?

YASHA. I told them this morning. I guess they took him.

ANYA (*to* YEPIKHODOV *who is crossing the room*). Yepikhodov, please find out whether Firs has been taken to the hospital.

YASHA (*insulted*). I told Yegor this morning. Are you going to ask a dozen times?

YEPIKHODOV. The venerable Firs, in my definitive opinion, is beyond repair. He's ready to join his ancestors. And I can only envy him. (*Puts his suitcase down on a hat box and crushes it.*) There I go again. I just knew it. (*Goes out.*)

YASHA (*mockingly*). Twenty-Two Disasters! . . .

VARYA (*from behind the door*). Has Firs been taken to the hospital?

ANYA. Yes.

VARYA. Then why didn't they take the note for the doctor?

ANYA. We'll have to send it after him. . . . (*Goes out.*)

VARYA (*from the neighboring room*). Where's Yasha? Tell him his mother's come. She wants to say goodbye.

YASHA (*with a wave of his hand*). These people just try my patience.

DUNYASHA (*has been fussing with the luggage. Seeing* YASHA *alone, she goes up to him*). If you'd only look at me, Yasha. You're going away . . . you're leaving me. . . . (*Weeps and throws her arms around his neck.*)

YASHA. What's there to cry about? (*Sips champagne.*) In six days I'll be in Paris again. Tomorrow we board the express and away we go. That's the last you'll see of us. Somehow I can't believe it. *Vive la France!* This place is not for me, I just can't live here. . . . There's nothing to be done about it. I've had my fill of ignorance. . . . (*Sips champagne.*) What are you crying about? Behave proper, then you won't cry.

DUNYASHA (*powdering her face while looking in a pocket mirror*). Write me from Paris. I loved you, Yasha, I loved you so much! I'm a sensitive person, Yasha!

YASHA. Somebody's coming. (*Fusses with the luggage, singing softly.*)

RANEVSKAYA, GAYEV, ANYA, *and* CHARLOTTA *enter.*

GAYEV. We should be on our way. There's not much time. (*Looking at* YASHA.) Someone here smells of herring!

RANEVSKAYA. Just ten minutes and then to the carriages. . . . (*Looks about the room.*) Goodbye dear house, goodbye ancestral home. Winter will pass, spring will come, and you'll no longer be here. They'll tear you down. How much these walls have seen! (*Kisses* ANYA *warmly.*) My precious child, you're radiant, your eyes are sparkling like diamonds. Are you happy?

ANYA. Very happy! We're starting a new life, Mama!

GAYEV (*cheerfully*). Yes, everything's fine now. Before selling the orchard we worried, it was painful. But when the question was settled once and for all, we calmed down, even felt cheerful. I'm a bank employee now, a financier . . . yellow ball in the side pocket. And you're looking better, Lyuba, no doubt about it.

RANEVSKAYA. Yes, my nerves have quieted down, that's so. (*She is handed her hat and coat.*) I'm sleeping well. Take my things, Yasha. It's time. (*To* ANYA.) We'll see each other soon, my dear girl . . . I'm off to Paris. I'll live on the money your aunt sent to buy the estate. Long live Auntie! Though it won't last long.

ANYA. You'll come back soon, Mama . . . won't you? I'll study hard and pass my high school exams. Then I'll go to work and help you. We'll read together, won't we Mama? (*Kisses her mother's hands.*) On autumn evenings we'll read many books, and a new and wonderful world will open up for us. . . . (*Dreamily.*) Mama, come back. . . .

RANEVSKAYA. I'll come, my angel. (*Embraces her daughter.*)

LOPAKHIN *enters.* CHARLOTTA *hums softly.*

GAYEV. Happy Charlotta. She's singing!

CHARLOTTA (*picks up a bundle that looks like a baby in swaddling clothes*). Bye, bye, little baby. . . . (*Sound of a baby crying;* "Wah! Wah!") Hush, hush, sweet baby, good baby. ("Wah! Wah!") I feel so sorry for you! (*Throws the bundle down.*) . . . Please find me a job. I can't go on like this.

LOPAKHIN. We'll find you something, Charlotta. Don't worry.

GAYEV. Everybody's deserting us. Varya's leaving. . . . No one needs us now.

CHARLOTTA. There's no place for me in town. I have to move on. (*Hums.*) It makes no difference.

PISHCHIK *enters.*

LOPAKHIN. Behold! One of nature's wonders!

PISHCHIK (*gasping*). Oh, let me catch my breath . . . I'm pooped. . . . My most esteemed friends. . . . Give me some water. . . .

GAYEV. He must want money. Here's where I head for the hills. . . . (*Goes out.*)

PISHCHIK. It's been ages, most charming lady. (*To* LOPAKHIN.) You're here too. . . . Glad to see you . . . you're a man of colossal intelligence. . . . Here you are. (*Hands* LOPAKHIN *money.*) Four hundred rubles . . . I still owe you eight hundred and forty. . . .

LOPAKHIN (*shrugs his shoulders in astonishment*). I must be dreaming. . . . Where did you get four hundred rubles?

PISHCHIK. One moment. . . . It's broiling. . . . Most extraordinary. Some Englishmen came to my place and discovered a white clay in the ground. . . . (*To* RANEVSKAYA.) And here's four hundred for you . . . most lovely . . . most charming lady. . . . (*Hands over the money.*) The rest, later. (*Drinks water.*) A young man in the train was saying some great philosopher recommends jumping off roofs. "To jump or not to jump," he says. "That's the question." (*In astonishment.*) Would you believe it? Water, please! . . .

LOPAKHIN. Who are these Englishmen?

PISHCHIK. I leased them the tract with the clay for twenty-four years. . . . But excuse me, there's no time . . . must dash on. . . . First to Znoykov, then to Kardamonov. . . . I owe everybody. . . . (*Drinks.*) Have a good day. I'll drop by on Thursday. . . .

RANEVSKAYA. We're about to drive into town. Tomorrow I'm going abroad.

PISHCHIK. What's that? (*Upset.*) Why into town? So that's why the furniture . . . the suitcases. . . . Well, never mind. . . . (*Tearfully.*) Never mind. . . . Men of most colossal intelligence . . . those Englishmen. . . . It's nothing. . . . Be happy . . . God help you. . . . It's nothing, nothing at all. . . . Everything comes to an end. . . .

(*Kisses* RANEVSKAYA'S *hand.*) If news reaches you that I've kicked the bucket, remember . . . this old horse. Tell people there once lived a man called Simeon-Pishchik . . . may he rest in peace. . . . Marvelous weather we're having. . . . Yes. . . . (*Goes out very much disturbed, but at once turns back and says from the doorway.*) Dashenka sends her best! (*Goes out.*)

RANEVSKAYA. Now we can go. I'm leaving with two things troubling me. First, there's old Firs—he's not well. (*Glancing at her watch.*) We still have about five minutes.

ANYA. Mama, Firs is in the hospital. Yasha sent him there this morning.

RANEVSKAYA. Then there's my other worry—Varya. She's used to getting up early and working. Now without something to do, she's like a fish out of water. The poor girl's grown thin and pale, she cries all the time. . . . (*Pause.*) You're well aware of this, Yermolay Alexeyich. It was my dream . . . to see you married, all signs pointed to it. (*Whispers to* ANYA; ANYA *nods to* CHARLOTTA *and both go out.*) She loves you, you find her attractive. I don't know why you avoid each other. I just don't understand!

LOPAKHIN. I don't either. It's very strange. . . . I'm ready now, if there's time. . . . Settle it at a stroke. Done! But without your help, I'm afraid I'll never propose.

RANEVSKAYA. Splendid. After all, it only takes a minute. I'll call her right now. . . .

LOPAKHIN. We're in luck—there's a bottle of champagne. (*Looks at the empty glasses.*) Empty! Someone's drunk it. (YASHA *coughs.*) Now that's what I'd call licking your glass clean.

RANEVSKAYA (*animated*). Simply splendid. We'll leave you alone. . . . Yasha, *allez!* I'll call her. . . . (*Calls through the door.*) Varya, drop what you're doing and come here. Hurry! (*Goes out with* YASHA.)

LOPAKHIN (*Looking at his watch.*) Yes. . . . (*Pause.*)

Restrained laughter and whispering from behind the door. Finally, VARYA *enters.*

VARYA (*looking over the baggage for some time*). How odd, I can't find it anywhere. . . .

LOPAKHIN. What are you looking for?

VARYA. Packed it myself and can't remember. (*Pause.*)

LOPAKHIN. Where will you go now, Varya?

VARYA. What? . . . To the Ragulins. . . . I've agreed to look after their place . . . as a housekeeper.

LOPAKHIN. That's in Yashnevo, isn't it? About fifty miles from here. (*Pause.*) So life in this house has come to an end.

VARYA (*looking over the baggage*). Where can it be? . . . Maybe I put it in the trunk. . . . Yes, life here is over and done with. . . . And there's no bringing it back. . . .

LOPAKHIN. I'm going to Kharkov . . . on the next train. Business. I'll leave Yepikhodov here. . . . I've hired him.

VARYA. What!

LOPAKHIN. Last year at this time it was snowing. Remember? And now it's sunny and calm. But cold. . . . Three degrees below freezing.

VARYA. I haven't noticed. (*Pause.*) Our thermometer is broken. . . . (*Pause.*)

A VOICE (*from the yard*). Yermolay Alexeyich!

LOPAKHIN (*as if he had long awaited this call.*) This minute! (*Goes out in a hurry.*)

VARYA *sits on the floor, her head on a bundle of clothes, and sobs softly. The door opens and* RANEVSKAYA *enters cautiously.*

RANEVSKAYA. Well? (*Pause.*) We must be going.

VARYA (*no longer crying, wipes away her tears*). Yes, it's time, Mama. If we don't miss the train I'll make it to the Ragulins' today. . . .

RANEVSKAYA (*through the door*). Anya, get dressed!

ANYA *enters, then* GAYEV *and* CHARLOTTA. GAYEV *is wearing a heavy overcoat with a hood. Servants and coachmen enter.* YEPIKHODOV *fusses near the luggage.*

RANEVSKAYA. Now we can be on our way.

ANYA (*joyfully*). On our way!

GAYEV. My friends, my dear, dear friends! As we leave this house forever, can I remain silent? Can I refrain from expressing the emotions that at this moment of parting suffuse my very being? . . .

ANYA (*imploring*). Uncle!

VARYA. Uncle dear, don't.

GAYEV (*crestfallen*). Bank the yellow into the side pocket. . . . I'm silent.

TROFIMOV *enters, followed by* LOPAKHIN.

TROFIMOV. What about it! It's time to go!

LOPAKHIN. Yepikhodov, my coat.

RANEVSKAYA. I'll sit for a moment. It's as if I've never really noticed these walls, these ceilings, and now I gaze at them greedily, with tenderness.

GAYEV. I remember when I was six years old. It was Pentecost, I was sitting on this windowsill watching my father going to church. . . .

RANEVSKAYA. Have they taken out all our things?

LOPAKHIN. Yes, I think so. (*Puts on his overcoat; to* YEPIKHODOV.) Yepikhodov, see to it that everything's in order.

YEPIKHODOV (*in a hoarse voice*). Don't worry, Yermolay Alexeyich!

LOPAKHIN. What's wrong with your voice?

YEPIKHODOV. I just had a drink of water, I must have swallowed something.

YASHA (*contemptuously*). How ignorant. . . .

RANEVSKAYA. When we're gone there won't be a soul left here.

LOPAKHIN. Until spring.

VARYA (*pulls an umbrella out of a bundle as if she were about to strike someone.* LOPAKHIN *pretends to be frightened*). Oh, what's the matter with you! I hadn't the slightest intention. . . .

TROFIMOV. Ladies and gentlemen, to the carriages. . . . It's high time! The train will be in soon!

VARYA. Petya, here are your galoshes, near this suitcase. (*In tears.*) My God! they're filthy. . . .

TROFIMOV (*putting on the galoshes*). Let's go, folks!

GAYEV (*very upset, afraid of bursting into tears*). Train . . . station. . . . Three cushions into the side . . . bank the white into the corner. . . .

RANEVSKAYA. Let's go!

LOPAKHIN. Are we all here? No one left in there? (*Locks the door on the left.*) Valuables are stored in there. I'd better lock up. Let's go! . . .

ANYA. Goodbye, house! Goodbye to our old life!

TROFIMOV. And welcome to our new life! . . . (*Goes out with* ANYA.)

VARYA *looks around the room and slowly goes out.* YASHA *and* CHARLOTTA, *with her dog, go out.*

LOPAKHIN. And so, until spring. Come along, my friends. . . . Goodbye! . . .

LOPAKHIN *goes out.* RANEVSKAYA *and* GAYEV *remain alone. As if they had been waiting for this moment, they throw themselves on each other's necks and, afraid that they may be overheard, break into subdued, restrained sobs.*

GAYEV (*in despair*). My sister, my sister. . . .

RANEVSKAYA. Oh, my dear orchard, my dear beautiful orchard! My life, my youth, my happiness—farewell! . . . Farewell!

ANYA (*from offstage, cheerfully calling*). Mama!

TROFIMOV (*from offstage, cheerful and excited*). Yoo-hoo!

RANEVSKAYA. One last look at these walls, these windows. . . . My mother loved this room. . . .

GAYEV. My sister, my sister! . . .

ANYA (*from offstage*). Mama!

TROFIMOV (*from offstage*). Yoo-hoo!

RANEVSKAYA. We're coming! (*They go out.*)

The stage is empty. A key can be heard locking all the doors, then the sounds of the carriages driving away. Silence. In the stillness the dull thud of an ax against a tree, mournful and lonely. Footsteps. FIRS *appears in the door at the right. Dressed, as always, in a jacket and white vest and wearing slippers. He is ill.*

FIRS (*goes to the door and tries the doorknob*). Locked! They've gone. . . . (*Sits on the sofa.*) Forgot all about me. . . . Never mind.

. . . I'll sit here a while. . . . Leonid Andreyevich probably didn't put on his fur. Drove off in that light coat of his. . . . (*Worried, he sighs.*) Should have kept an eye on him. . . . Ah, these young ones. (*Mumbles something incomprehensible.*) Life has slipped by, it's as if I've never lived. . . . (*Lies down.*) I'll lie down for a while. . . . No strength left, nothing's left, nothing. . . . Oh, you old nincompoop! . . . (*Lies motionless.*)

As if from the sky, the distant sound of a breaking string mournfully dying away. Silence descends. The thud of an ax striking a tree deep in the garden.

Curtain